Contents

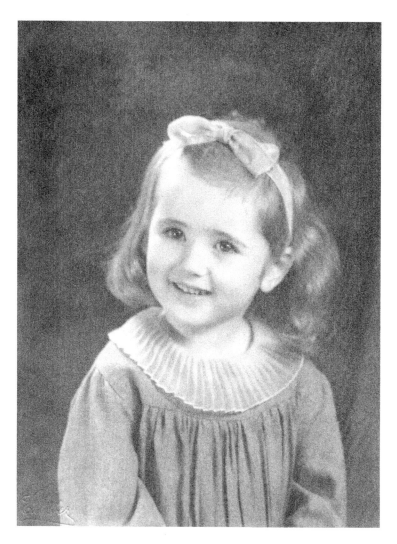

Selina aged 3.

To Jeff + Catrin
Love Selina

LETTERS FROM AN INTREPID BALLET DANCER

Letters from an Intrepid Ballet Dancer

Selina Molteno

Edited by Jason Cohen

Oxford Publishing Services

Oxford Publishing Services
34 Warnborough Road, Oxford OX2 6JA

First edition published in 2015
Second edition 2022

Copyright © Selina Cohen, née Molteno 2015, 2022

The right of the Selina Cohen, née Molteno, to be identified as the author
of this work has been asserted by the editor in accordance with the
Copyright, Design and Patents Act 1988.

All rights reserved. Except for brief quotations in a review, this book,
or any part thereof, may not be reproduced, stored in or introduced
into a retrieval system, or transmitted, in any form or by any means,
electronic, mechanical, photocopying, recording or otherwise, without
the prior written permission of the publisher.

ISBN 978-0-9955278-9-8

Copy-edited and typeset in Berkeley Oldstyle by
Oxford Publishing Services, Oxford

Cover by Jason Cohen
Back cover portrait by Susanne du Toit

Illustrations

Addressees

Anna	Selina's younger sister, Annabel.
Anthony	Selina's older brother.
Apa	English corruption of the Afrikaans word *oupa*, meaning grandfather. Selina's maternal grandfather, B. C. Judd, who served 48 years in the Cape Mounted Rifles and signed himself 'Colonel B. C. Judd'.
Frankie	Selina's youngest brother.
Georgie	Selina's cousin.
Kulu or Makulu	Selina's maternal grandmother. [Zulu for wife/ grandparent with an implication of 'great'].
Margie	Selina's mother, Margaret Molteno, née Judd.
Martin	Selina's younger brother.
Miss Howes	Dulcie Howes, the most notable promoter of ballet in South Africa and Selina's patron.
Miss Robinson	Cecily Robinson, a Cape Town ballet teacher.
Peter	Selina's father Christopher Jarvis Molteno, who was always known as 'Peter'.
Vicky	Selina's youngest sister, Victoria.

Introduction

These letters were written over a four-year period 1959 to 1963, by Selina Molteno, now Selina Cohen, to her family, mainly to her mother.[1] Her family bore a name that carried weight in her birthplace, Cape Town. More than sixty years have passed since these letters were completed. A new black elite has inherited political power in South Africa and the pre-eminence of the old Cape families has eroded. However, Selina's parents strongly identified with their genealogy. Her father's grandfather was prime minister of the Cape Colony and distinguished politicians, eminent lawyers, and wealthy apple farmers adorn the family tree.[2] Unlike a number of their illustrious forebears, Selina's parents never held public office and were careful with their money, sometimes because they needed to be. As these letters show, Selina inherited the resultant combination – a confidence born of gentility and the need to take inventive measures to make ends meet.

Selina was raised in Cape Town and, like many young girls, dreamed of nothing else but being a ballet dancer. She poured over news clippings and kept scrapbooks and photos of her favourite dancers. She was something of a prodigy as a young girl and trained at the University of Cape Town ballet school, where she was taken under the wing of the doyenne of South African ballet, Dulcie Howes. South Africa had no national ballet company at that time and it was clear that if she was to advance professionally it had to be abroad or, as the South Africans said, 'overseas'. 'Overseas' was Europe – nothing else counted

1. Occasionally Jason has included letters from third parties about Selina, which are marked with a grey background.
2. See the family website compiled by Robert Molteno https://www.molteno family.net/

Family photo, c.1953.

Back row (left to right): May Judd 'Kulu' (maternal grandmother), Vicky (youngest sister), Selina, B. C. Judd 'Apa' (maternal grandfather), Celeste (aunt), Margie (mother). *Front row:* Martin (brother), Anthony (brother), Sue Judd (cousin), Alexandra Judd (cousin), Annabel (sister).

at the time. So Selina, aged just 18, steamed to the UK on the Union Castle line. Thereafter, the letters tell their own tale – a frantic whirl of training, classes, auditions, contracts, arrivals and departures. London, Malmö, Stockholm, Copenhagen and Paris feature large in her peregrinations. Being taken on by the prestigious Grand Ballet du Marquis de Cuevas, also led to tours in many other cities in Europe (and Israel). All the hard work had paid off. Among some aficionados this was the company that counted. As Clement Crisp observed:

> Le Grand Ballet du Marquis de Cuevas was a delight to ballet-goers. It possessed that most precious of attributes, theatrical glamour. Its performances seemed always to have a frisson of

excitement to them. It was rich in star dancers, artists who thrilled by their bravura as by their emotional command over their roles, and their audience, which made even the most dubious creations seem oddly exhilarating ... from 1947 until its last gasp in 1962, was always exhilarating: you breathed a theatrical ozone more heady, more intoxicating, than the quieter airs inhaled during the usual run of dutiful performance on home ground.[3]

Selina's letters provide acute and often brilliant observations of places, performances and people. She wrote prolifically about her family, friends, teachers and fellow dancers, provided critiques of plays, ballets and movies and interjected comments about social life and the politics of the moment (like the cold war and the Algerian war of independence). Not all her sentiments were worthy but, in general, they were progressive and socially tolerant (she was relaxed about people being gay, but she didn't get on with many Swedes). It is perhaps important to bear in mind that the first letters were written when she was only eighteen.

She danced mainly with the troupers in the corps de ballet but, now and again, solo parts arrived and stardom beckoned. Excitingly, she rubbed shoulders with some of the paramount dancers of the twentieth century – Rudolf Nureyev, Nina Vyroubova, Marilyn Jones, Serge Golovine, Marcia Haydée, Léonide Massine and Rosella Hightower, to name just a few described in these letters. How good was she? Independent testimony suggests she was a remarkable jumper: she and Nureyev used to delight in friendly competition during classes. She was technically proficient and had enormous vivacity. She was pert, energetic and nimble. Whether she could have been a great dancer will forever be unknown.

As her letters make clear, Selina realized that ultimately it was not going to work. She had endless problems with her South African passport (visas and work permits were required at every turn), while even a modicum of emotional and financial support from home was not

3. Clement Crisp, 'The Grand Ballet du Marquis de Cuevas', *Dance Research: The Journal of the Society for Dance Research*, 23 (1) 2005, p. 1.

Rudolf Nureyev, 1963.

forthcoming. In partial defence of her mother, Margaret (Margie), it would have been difficult to respond to Selina's torrent of correspondence in equal measure. Above all, Selina wanted some conventional things in her life – a home, a family and, especially, a higher education. When the Marquis de Cuevas company collapsed in 1962 amidst tears, bankruptcy and other goings on (the letters provide some detail), the die was cast.

Selina returned to Cape Town with the full intention of resuming a normal life. Of course she did not. How could anyone that spirited fall back into a predictable routine? I'm not sure we can match Selina's breathless pace, but we need to give a quick précis of her post-ballet days, so here goes: she studied anthropology at the University of Cape Town, had an affair with a revolutionary, was arrested for her subversive activities (twice), had the brake cable cut on her car, left South Africa, worked for the Anti-Apartheid Movement in London, was awarded a first-class degree from the Open University, lived in Nigeria during a civil war, spent two years in Trinidad, worked for a UN agency, ran a small publishing business, returned to a post-apartheid Cape Town for three years and finally washed up in North Oxford. There she lives a moderately contented life with her husband (Robin) and rejoices in the love of her two children (Miranda and Jason) and grandchildren (Amelia and Louis).

Jason has compiled this collection of letters and photos as a birthday tribute and family record. However, we hope that Selina's letters from 1959 to 1963 will interest others too. She was a true ingénue, a colonial innocent abroad gazing at everything she saw with wide-eyed wonderment. For those who love dance and want to find out what it was like to work in a ballet company, Selina's views from the dressing room and barre will provide a rich source of enlightenment.

Robin Cohen, 2022

Chapter 1

En Route

30 January 1959 (from Pendennis Castle, Union Castle Line)[1]

Well, I'm on my way now and believe it or not I'm really rather enjoying myself. Peter's zoologist friend and his wife were very kind to me and gave me a drink and talked to me for ages about all sorts of weird things. Then at supper I met a group of people at table and from then on I was well on the right path. After supper I was invited by a crowd of boys to have a drink – they're hardly any girls on board – and then we chatted until the small hours of the morning. They were all very nice to me and told me that I was the liveliest girl on board.

Gosh, but it's lovely on deck in the evening. I haven't got seasick yet but my head keeps on floating away from my body – anyway it's quite a nice feeling as long as it doesn't travel down below.

Saturday 31 January

Today was fairly quiet. I was woken up with a nice cup of coffee and then a bath was run for me, which I enjoyed thoroughly. After breakfast I tried my hand at deck quoits and Ping-Pong. After lunch I watched a children's film matinée and then, as I was absolutely clapped, went down to my cabin for a nap. I slept solidly from 3.30 till 7.00. After supper there was a film show, which was not very good except for a wonderful short on the Lake District, but I was missing you all terribly and so wasn't really in the mood for enjoying anything.

1. Unless otherwise stated, the letters are to Selina's mother, Margie.

Selina's mother, Margie.

I find the people on board rather boring on the whole and also find them difficult to shake off. You know, I had no idea that I could be so bored with people so quickly. What I love doing most is standing on the deck at night and looking into the sea. All you can see is blackness with white waves and it's so peaceful to feel the ship just going on and on with its slow slight roll. But then, just as I'm beginning to absorb the atmosphere of it all, some corny drip comes up and asks an equally corny question and then before I know where I am I'm surrounded by a whole lot of people with nothing much to say for themselves but with a lot to say (if you know what I mean). Never mind. Perhaps it's just because I feel like being on my own that I find their company irritating. I'll probably feel different tomorrow.

Sunday and Monday

Oh well, I suppose they aren't so bad after all – at least they stand me to a lot of cool drinks and the voyage has begun to liven up. Tonight the captain is having a cocktail party and then after dinner we are going to dance. Gosh, how I miss home though. I never realized before how much one really leans on other people! At 12 o'clock this afternoon we were opposite St Helena Island and so far every day has been fine and calm.

This afternoon I'm going to have my hair cut, washed and set at the hairdresser and I'm dreading to see the result. I'm hopeless at deck games and never once have I ever even approached winning one. The other girls, which I don't really see much of because of the abundance of men, all seem to be much older than me.

Tuesday and Wednesday

The hairstyle must have done something for me because ever since I've had my hair cut I've enjoyed every moment of the trip. We've had two terrific dances on deck and the band is marvellous. Tonight we had a tombola game, but of course I didn't win a bean. Other people are just beginning to emerge from their cabins now and I've met some very interesting people among them. I'm afraid I haven't a hope as far as deck tennis is concerned – I'm hopeless. But still I enjoy playing it and I have won one game out of about 20 or 30. We've just crossed the line now and tomorrow we are going to celebrate. I met Mrs Troughton's[2] friend at our dance tonight and he said that 'the first class is as dead as mutton – you see it's just full of old crocks.' So far, the sea has been calm and still and guess what? I hit a Ping-Pong ball overboard!

2. The Troughtons were a wealthy Norwegian couple who had bought a house in St James in Cape Town and had a daughter called Tula. Mr Troughton was in the whaling trade, had a fabulous flat in Mayfair, in London, and used to spend a few months in Cape Town each summer.

Everybody is madly friendly and the waiter even puts my napkin onto my lap for me now, calls me 'Madame' and treats me like a queen. Yesterday a ship went past very close to us and at the time I would have given anything to jump onto it and sail back home.

Thursday, Friday, Saturday

On Thursday we had a crossing the line ceremony, but I made quite sure that I wasn't thrown in. That evening we had a film, *Separate Tables*. I believe it was quite good, but unfortunately I feel asleep after it had only been going for about five minutes.

On Friday we had a fancy dress dance and a chap called J.J. and I went together as 'Departed Spirits'. He dressed as a devil and I as an angel and we draped empty liquor bottles all over us. My costume was a ship's sheet and a deck quoit for a halo. I had such fun making the devil's tail. It had a red bow on the end. The horns were silver and also had a red bow. J.J. carried a fork and whisky bottle and I carried a candle and gin bottle – most angelic. We won second prize. Another chap went as a ballerina and I taught him a dance to do for the judge. Unfortunately, during the execution of his jetés, he landed the wrong way up. He won a prize too. I slept the whole of today and woke up at about five o'clock this evening. This evening we had a derby and I went as 'Holy Smoke' by 'Bishop out of Breath'.

We are reaching Las Palmas in the morning. Must post now.

7 February 1959 (to Dulcie Howes)[3]

I'm not really writing to you for any reason, but somehow it's just what I feel like doing now.

The voyage so far has been great fun and up until now we've had lovely, calm weather. At the moment the ship's pitching and rolling like mad and it's making me feel extremely odd. Every now and again the ship lurches forward and the whole boat vibrates as the propellers come out of the sea.

3. Dulcie Howes (1908–1993) was Selina's ballet teacher. She opened a ballet school attached to the College of Music at the University of Cape Town. She was also founder of the UCT Ballet Company and is generally regarded as a key figure in the evolution of South African ballet.

From the security of home, good jobs and wonderful friends the world looks so easy to cope with, but somehow when that's taken away it feels like a slightly different story. Anyway Miss Howes, it will toughen me up if nothing else and even already I feel I'm finding it a bit easier to cope with awkward situations.

Every night there has been organized entertainment and last night we had a fancy-dress parade. … As soon as we started dancing though, my sheet started to come adrift so I had to go and change. My deck games are unmentionable. I'm too appalling for words. However well they have the deck netted in, I always somehow manage to throw or hit what I'm hitting overboard. No one is amused for they are all such 'jolly good sports' and think that a Ping-Pong ball should be treated with a certain amount of respect. Oh well!

This evening we had a derby. I was a horse and was owned by a difficult lad who almost cried when I came last. 'What's the good,' he said, 'you've lost me ten bob.' Well, anyone who is silly enough to put 10/- on me affords to lose it. I was 'Holy Smoke' by 'Bishop out of Breath'.

There are more men than women on the ship and I got myself into trouble the other day by promising to go to the same film with two different men. After all, if they were so enthusiastic one could sit on each side, but somehow they didn't feel that way about it at all. After five minutes I was sound asleep anyway, so I would have been better off if I hadn't gone at all.

We arrive in Las Palmas on Monday, so I will send this letter from there. Thank you so much Miss Howes for the stockings, and for all that you've done for me and for all your support in the past. I hope all is going well at the ballet school.

Sunday 8 February 1959 (from Pendennis Castle*)*

Well, I wonder if you've got my last letter yet. I had to have it posted by six o'clock this evening; that's why it ended off so abruptly. You will probably get this one before it but don't panic – it will come in time, for Las Palmas is a sleepy hollow, I'm sure.

It's nearly 11.30 on Sunday night and as soon as I wake up tomorrow morning I will be in Las Palmas. I'm so excited; I just don't know how I'm going to sleep. Four of us have decided that we don't want to go on

An early experience of the limelight. Selina taking part in a documentary film aged around 14. Margie standing next to the cameraman.

a conducted tour because then we'll be told all about Sir Francis Drake and I won't remember it in any case; so J.J., a 26 year-old chap going to Europe on holiday; John, a doctor from Johannesburg going to England on business; Edith, a very nice woman of about 33, but unattached so is considered my contemporary and I are going into Las Palmas on our own and we will drink in all we can in our own way without looking at stones with letters engraved on them.

Monday 9 February

Oh gosh, but I certainly did have a wonderful time in Las Palmas. The ship docked at five o'clock this morning and at about 6.45 I had my bath and got dressed. Breakfast was at 7.30 and it was through the dining-room portholes that I first saw Las Palmas. The sky was a brilliant, almost unreal, blue and so was the sea, and in between the two were fairly low hills and a long flat town underneath.

In the early morning light the colouring looked just like a picture postcard. We left the ship at eight o'clock with two additions, Bob and Chris, and managed to get a cheap taxi driver to take the six of us into town, all around and back again for only 3/4d each.

Mr and Mrs Molinaro got off at Las Palmas and Mr Molinaro asked me to give my 'diddy his luv' when I wrote – so Peter I hope you've taken that in. He also invited me to visit his mansion in Mouille Point when I returned to South Africa.

The taxi driver was an absolute scream and when we drew in our breath as he whizzed around the corner on the wrong side of the road, missing the cyclists and pedestrians by a fraction of an inch, he would let go the wheel, clap his hands and let out the most fantastic noise. It was meant to be a laugh but it sounded very much more like a horse without a voice box trying to neigh. Gosh, but he really gave us our money's worth. First of all he took us, via the beach, to a funny little shop where I bought four postcards. It cost me 11/- to buy and send those cards to South Africa, 2/3d airmail to South Africa – quite a price.

After that we went to the cathedral, which was teeming with priests, choir boys and women in black. It was very still and as I walked around looking at the various paintings, I kept on coming across people kneeling in dark corners. A little boy of about Martin's age dressed in a red gown with a white lace collar came up to me and firmly told me, in Spanish of course, to kindly stop talking. I was shaken out of my wits, but soon after that the whole church broke into song – the noise seemed to come from underground and eventually I saw a group of priests singing in a semi-underground black velvet enclosure.

After the cathedral we went to a museum, but were in a hurry so had to race through that. It included models of Columbus's ships, many rather lovely biblical paintings, a couple of brightly coloured parakeets and spans of other historical things. It would have taken me a whole day to observe it properly though. We then flew around to some other shops and really got into the atmosphere of the town. One shopkeeper got out his guitar and started singing to us, which he did very well and another shopkeeper gave Chris a drink 'on the house' literally translated from Spanish to English – FIREWATER.

We had to be back on board at 11.30 and so after seeing the Hotel Santa Catalina, we returned to the ship. I missed the Spanish dancers who came on board to dance, but saw them just as they were leaving. As we left we were seen off with a farewell unknown to me. Planes flew over, speed boats whizzed all over the show and the local talent was showing off their water skiing.

When I got back to my cabin I found a postcard with a lovely picture of Las Palmas on it, together with a pink carnation. It was from the Union Castle people in Las Palmas and was issued in honour of the maiden voyage – I really enjoyed my morning in Las Palmas.

Tuesday, 10 February

The weather is now getting steadily colder. I spent the morning doing the laundry for a couple of lazy men and in the afternoon I slept – I have now got a very painful neck. It must be fibrositis from the cold. This evening we were shown a very good film starring Cary Grant[4] and Ingrid Bergman;[5] it was called *Indiscreet*. Tomorrow we enter the Bay of Biscay, but already we have hit some pretty rough weather. I was given a voucher for 7/6d for the fancy dress prize and bought a lipstick and some nail polish. I miss you very much.

Wednesday 11 February

We are now in the Bay of Biscay but as yet it's as calm as anything. Tomorrow is my last day on board and I'm getting more and more excited all the time at the thought of arriving in England. I've been bothered with fibrositis all day and this afternoon Mr Detwiler – Tula's [Troughton] husband's sister's husband massaged it for me. He is the third person to try their hand as a masseur on me and I can assure you the most successful. Although he is in first class he has been very nice to me. He has a charming wife and three lovely children. I quite often go to the first class and nobody has objected at all. This morning I went along to listen to the auction and to have a cup of coffee. It is so luxurious and the Detwilers' cabins are really beautifully done out. I've

---

4. Cary Grant (1904–1986), Hollywood film actor.
5. Ingrid Bergman (1915–1982), Swedish actress and Hollywood star.

UNION-CASTLE LINE TO SOUTH AND EAST AFRICA

THE UNION-CASTLE ROYAL MAIL STEAMER "PENDENNIS CASTLE" 28,582 TONS

Postcard to brothers Martin and Frankie, 1959.

bought myself a pack of cards with a picture of the *Pendennis* on the back and those cards have been a wonderful time passer on the voyage. A very popular game among the tourist-class passengers is rummy and we play it for hours on end.

Guess what? I won some money with the tombola. I was the only one who hadn't got any numbers marked off at a certain stage in the game, so it was a booby prize more than anything – but still it was 5/- and appreciated. There's one man in the first class who spends £30 a day on auction tickets and today a man won £200, but of course you can't play with money unless you can afford to lose it.

Thursday, 12 February

Oh I'm so excited I can hardly write. I'm running round in circles getting my baggage ready and this letter has to be posted within half an hour. It's cold and chilly and, boy, am I excited! We are having a farewell dance tonight and tomorrow morning I will be in England. Oh Margie, will you be thinking of me then 'cos I'll certainly be thinking about you all? Gosh, I wish you were all here to share the

Selina on a ballet tour in Rhodesia (now Zimbabwe), c.1956.

excitement with me because besides the three-year-olds I seem to be the only one who can't sit still.

I must end off now because the bathroom steward is champing at the bit – I always want my baths at awkward times. In the mornings he attempts to wake me up by throwing a towel at me, but seldom succeeds. Oh Margie, I don't know what to say except that I feel as if I'm going to burst. Anyway, I'll tell you all about England in my next letter. Give my love to everybody. I'm even more excited than I was when we went to Las Palmas.

Chapter 2
London

Friday 13 February 1959 (from 2 Townshend Road, Richmond, Surrey)

How can I possibly explain to you the wonder of all that has happened to me today? I don't see how I can possibly convey all that I've felt, but anyway I'll try.

When I ended off my last letter from the ship there was a buzz in the air and everyone was madly rushing around getting their luggage ready. Afterwards there was a dance and we all went rip-roaring raving mad. We sang every South African song under the sun and then when we sang *Auld Lang Syne* I had such a lump in my throat. Anyway, the trip is over now and that is something that I'll always look back on with pleasure.

I got through the customs with the greatest of ease and all the officials were kind, sympathetic and most obliging. The journey from Southampton to Waterloo was fairly quick but I couldn't see a thing because of the mist. When we arrived in Waterloo I was so excited and Brigitte [Knight], Rose [Taylor] and Cornell [Senekal][1] rushed to meet me straight away. We dumped my luggage at the station and then walked to the Royal Festival Hall and from there I saw the beautiful Thames. We then went over Hungerford Bridge to a café where we talked for ages. Brigitte and Cornell left us there and then Rose and I went back to Waterloo from Charing Cross by underground. We

1. Cornell Senekal became a successful fashion model and now lives in Barrydale in South Africa.

got my luggage and the porter was so excited when he saw my fruit that the Taylors gave me and asked me if the avocado pear was a passion fruit. We took a surface train to Richmond and then a taxi to the flat.

The flat is tiny but very cosy. From the outside it looks like every other old flat in England, but the inside is nicely wall-papered and although the table is made out of suitcases and my dressing table is the top shelf of a tiny display cabinet, it is a home and I am very happy to be there. The thing that has struck me most about England is that everything is all the same colour and is covered by a haze of mist, but there is a nip in the air and I'm sure I'll be very happy here. I spent the afternoon unpacking and settling in and in the evening Niña [Horne] came back with a friend and the four of us had supper around the gas heater and then we talked for hours and hours.

Saturday 14 February 1959

This morning I did my washing and washed my hair. Then, at lunch-time, we walked downtown to Richmond. We had lunch at a lovely little café and then spent the afternoon walking along the banks of the Thames. It was terribly, terribly cold, but as yet I haven't seen a drop of rain. Oh, but the Thames is beautiful. Along the edge are the most lovely trees, which are as bare as bare can be, but so beautifully shaped and everything is just a different shade of grey. There were students training for rowing and men and small boys fishing for trout. Richmond Bridge is beautiful. It's made of huge big, soft looking grey stones and the whole atmosphere of the place is of quiet contentment. I miss you all terribly and at the moment am waiting for Niña, Rose and Gwen [Harris][2] to get ready so that we can go to the Royal Opera House to see Fonteyn[3] dance *Ondine*. It seems too wonderful to be true – I haven't woken up yet. I'm sure it's all just a dream. Brigitte is looking really beautiful and is so well groomed. She's really grown into a lady of refinement. Anyway bye now, I'm off to see Fonteyn! Gallery mind you, but still – yipee I'm so excited.

2. Gwen Harris was a friend of Dulcie Howes, who used to help backstage during UCT Ballet performances.
3. Margot Fonteyn (1919–1991) was a famous English ballerina.

Later

Oh Margie, she's wonderful. I can't explain her to you for she's too beautiful and wonderful to explain. All I can say is that she's an artist and her dancing is exquisite. We were sitting in the gallery slips, which are the worst seats in the house, but still every movement and every meaning came right across the footlights. I want to see *Ondine* lots and lots of times so that I can absorb everything.

You know what? When I walked up the miles and miles of back stairs to the gods, guess who I saw? Lindsey Williams.[4] She was ushering at Covent Garden and said that I could phone and visit her any time I liked, and I certainly will as soon as I can. In the interval I had my first bottle of cider and I felt mighty queer afterwards – don't worry I don't think I was drunk!

On the way to Covent Garden we went over Hammersmith Bridge in the bus and it's too lovely for words. Well, it's past five to two, so I'm going to bed now and I just hope that I won't be as cold as I was last night. It's two vests now for this lady.

Sunday 15 February 1959

I've just woken up now and boy am I cold. Tell Anna[5] to hurry up with the bed socks. By the way, do you think you could send my ballet pictures to England? We've only got Xmas cards and tinsel on the walls, so would love to have the pictures. This afternoon Pat Power, Cornell and two English girls are coming to a tea party in my honour. Mr Loughran, my steward, says that if ever you want to send anything to me, you should contact him when the *Pendennis* first goes through Cape Town and then on the way back to the UK he will collect the thing and see that I get it. It's nice to know anyway. It's on with the housework now, so goodbye and give my love to everyone I know.

16 February 1959

Today's epistle is going to be short and sweet as it's a quarter to twelve.

4. Lindsey Williams was the daughter of a close friend of Selina's mother's in Cape Town, Betty Williams. She married and had a small family, but sadly died young from a brain tumour.
5. Selina's sister Annabel (1942–2013).

I'm dog tired and unless I go to bed now I'll never get through class tomorrow morning.

This morning I went to my first class at Anna's.[6] She was absolutely super to me, but I felt a terrible cad as I was terrible and couldn't do a thing, but anyway that's a challenge and now I know that when I can master her classes I will have improved.

Cornell was there too and after class he took me to Leicester Square and Trafalgar Square – then I went to the bank to draw out some money and I got my cheque book. By the way Margie, I wonder if you would be kind enough to put that money that I gave to you on the docks into my account. There's no hurry as yet, but knowing how scatty you are I thought that you might like to be reminded.

We then had a cheap lunch at the self-service and afterwards went to a film at the Ritz. It was an excellent film called *The Reluctant Debutante*, starring Kay Kendall.[7] I enjoyed it immensely. After that Rose and I went back to Anna's to watch a class and there I saw [Svetlana] Beriosova[8] and Peter Cazalet.[9]

I cooked my first dinner tonight and it was a great success – nothing burnt thank goodness.

Tuesday 17 February 1959

Oh, lor di dor di dor, I'm so very sore, I am a crock, I've had a shock, lor di dor di dor. Boy am I stiff and weak. I'm dead before I've begun. I did class again this morning and did a little better, not quite as bad as before and thought that I could easily do another this afternoon, but little did I know the consequences. My legs buckled underneath me, my brain went into a wuzz and every muscle either turned to lead or

6. Anna Northcote (1907–1988), ballet teacher who had formerly danced under the name Anna Severskaya. Her studio was in West Street, Covent Garden, London WC2.
7. Kay Kendall (1927–1959) English actress who married Rex Harrison and died of leukaemia at the age of 32.
8. Svetlana Beriosova (1932–1998), Lithuanian-born English ballerina with the Royal Ballet and daughter of Nicolas Beriosoff (1906–1996).
9. Peter Cazalet (1934–). Born in Zimbabwe, he trained as an architect at UCT, danced with Scottish Ballet and finally became a superb designer of stage sets and costumes. Selina knew him from the UCT ballet school.

to jelly. I just couldn't finish it so I stopped and I won't try to do so much again. I was a silly fool but I've learnt my lesson.

Between the two classes I went to a café for lunch with Sylvia Edwards, who used to be a contemporary of Annabel's at ballet school, made a desperate attempt to phone Georgie[10] and, in the process, lost 2/3d and got a shilling stuck in the slot, I had to ask the man in the post office to find the right directory and how to use the phone – anyway Georgie was out, but I phoned her this evening and we have made arrangements to contact each other so that we can '*gaan besoek*' [visit] all the relations.

After the second class I met Rose and went with her to watch a Brunelleschi[11] Spanish class, which I found priceless, and after that Niña, Rose and I went to supper with Jennifer Nicholson[12] in their lovely flat in Lancaster Gate – a free meal – what a treat to sit down and be served with a three-course meal without having to cook it, lay the table, wash up or cough up; what a lovely meal it was too – chops, oxtail soup, tomatoes, peas, carrots, pudding and fresh fruit followed by coffee – I felt a different person after it. Food in London is very expensive. You know it cost me 3/9d to have a boiled egg, lettuce, tomato, half a potato and a cup of coffee. That's rather trying when one can't spend more than 6/- a day on food. Anyway, although we have to be careful we're managing fine and I'm still as big and buxom as ever.

I'm finding life killing at the moment because I haven't got used to this high-pressure living after my long holiday. My day usually goes as follows, or at least today did. Get up at 7. Read mail. By the way thanks for the letter, it makes such a difference; without letters from you I'd go mad, make my bed, tidy the flat, wash up the dishes, get dressed, go to class, which takes about an hour, have lunch, odd chores, go to the art gallery, go back to class, go to Bayswater to watch Spanish, go to dinner 15 minutes' walk away, catch three tubes home, have a bath,

---

10. Georgina Jaques, now Georgina Stuttaford, a close cousin born on 8 January 1940 living in South Africa.
11. Elsa Brunelleschi, Spanish dance teacher in London.
12. Jennifer Nicholson, Selina's contemporary who too had studied ballet in Cape Town.

write letters, wash up and so on and so on. Oh dear, I'm going to collapse any minute. After that it's twenty past twelve and Rose is yelling at me to come and dry up so I must run, so *totsiens* and give my love to the little Indian papoose and tell that wretched family to write. I've had six letters so far and, besides your one letter and one from Apa,[13] I haven't heard a peep. I had three letters waiting for me when I arrived and since then have got something every day. How long it will last for though – I just can't tell you. Goodnight, sleep tight, thank goodness there are no fleas in England.

Wednesday 18 February

Today was quite an eventful day. This morning when I woke up I was so stiff that I couldn't even walk, so I stayed in bed until about 11. Then Rose and I went into London and I saw Piccadilly [Circus] and the statue of Eros for the first time. I bought a pair of gloves at Swan and Edgars and then Rose and I wandered around Regent Street a bit and bought ourselves some lunch, which we ate in the Barclays Bank restroom. When we were leaving the bank I happened to see Dr John Cecil who was on the ship with me. On the voyage John was very nice to me and used to tell me who I should and who I shouldn't associate with. He is a doctor from Johannesburg who has come over to England for a few weeks in order to do some business and pass a specializing exam. When I saw him he invited me out to dinner that night.

Anyway, after the bank we went along to the Coliseum and got the cheapest tickets for *Cinderella*. It was terrible. Tommy Steele[14] made me sick; he's such a drip and a shocking actor. Jean Cragg[15] was in it and after the first act we went backstage to see her. She's as thin as a rake and looks very happy. She says she doesn't want to go back into ballet as she much prefers pantomime and musicals. I then tore home to change and tore back again to meet John in Piccadilly Circus. Dr and Mrs John Pryor were with him and were absolutely charming. We

13. Colonel B. C. Judd (1874–1963), Selina's maternal grandfather.
14. Tommy Steele (1936–), English singer and teen idol.
15. Jean Cragg, a former ballet student in Cape Town who then worked in musicals.

went to a very swish place. First of all Betty Pryor and I were shown into a room to hang our coats and were then ushered into another room where we had sherry and snacks. Then we went into the dining room cum ballroom for dinner. I had a huge juicy medium steak with beautifully cooked vegetables and delicious wine. Of course the crystallized grapes followed. The band was terrific and I really enjoyed the evening thoroughly as they were intelligent people with stimulating conversation. Anyway, after the wonderful free meal I had to run as the last tube left Hammersmith at 12.15 and I had to still get from Piccadilly Circus to Hammersmith. I waited on Piccadilly station for 20 minutes and on Hammersmith station for about an hour. The trains had got held up by the fog and I could hardly see beyond a foot in front of me. During that time I discussed various subjects with an Englishman from Lancashire and when I finally got to Richmond he went the other way and I was then left to battle my way through the fog for about a quarter of a mile home, but before I'd started to go a terrible looking smoothie with a walrus moustache came up to me, breathed his liquor fumes over my face and said, 'DOAH GIVE MY LOAVE TO JOHANNESBURG'. He'd overheard me talking to the respectable man and thought that that was a good opportunity to pounce. I couldn't get rid of him so I waited at the station for a taxi and buzzed off as quickly as I could. It's now two o'clock so I'd better go to bed.

Sunday 22 February 1959

I'm spending the day in the flat with Rose as she's in bed with flu and a septic corn. I'm shocking as I haven't written a thing for three days but I think I can remember more or less what has happened.

Well, on Thursday morning I stayed at home in the flat and did housework. Then in the afternoon I went into London to do class. Margit Muller, an ex-Festival Ballet dancer took the class and I couldn't do a thing. I was very depressed afterwards, but when I got home Rose and Niña talked sense into me and told me that I couldn't hope to be first class straight away.

On Friday morning I did class again with Margit Muller. I coped much better then and was much more cheerful afterwards. After class

I met an actress called Jennifer Schooling who told me that I should go to de Vos[16] as she went to her as well as Northcote. She felt that her classes were more beneficial as she got right to the base of one's faults and tackled the causes of the fault rather than battling at something the wrong way.

Well, after lunch I went to the telephone booth at Piccadilly Circus tube station and phoned her up. I spoke to the secretary and she told me to come along right away to speak to Miss de Vos. She told me how to catch the bus to Notting Hill Gate and I did exactly that.

When I got there de Vos was really sweet to me and we chatted for a long time. She said that I had a weak back and that would be the first thing that I must try to strengthen. She said that I built up muscle on my legs because of the weakness in my back and therefore was taking extra strain in my legs. She said that there are no jobs going now as the auditions are all over till next year and suggested I took a part-time job in the meantime. I don't really mind though because I realize now that I'm not ready for the job I want and perhaps in a year's time I will have conquered the faults that are holding me back. De Vos says that she would accept me as her pupil, as she felt that, like all South Africans, I have an open mind. She trained Nerina[17] and Beryl Grey.[18] Richard Glasstone[19] went to her while he was in London and she said she liked him very much because he was intelligent and eager to learn. I think she is the best person for me because she is kind and encouraging and anyway I'll give her a try.

16. Audrey de Vos (1900–1983) was considered to have been an outstanding teacher who was ahead of her time.
17. Nadia Nerina (1927–2008), born in Bloemfontein, South Africa, as Nadine Judd. Joined Sadler's Wells Theatre Ballet in 1946 and became a prima ballerina in 1952.
18. Beryl Grey, born in London in 1927, joined the Sadler's Wells Company in 1941 aged 14. Was artistic director of London Festival Ballet between 1968 and 1979.
19. Richard Glasstone, MBE (b.1935 Congo), came to the UCT Ballet School while Selina was there and went on to have a highly successful career as a character dancer, choreographer and teacher in the Netherlands, Turkey and Britain. He is also the author of several ballet books, the most recent being My Lifetime of Dance. He married an artist called Heather Magoon and they now live in London.

Selina and Georgie in
Trafalgar Square.

From Notting Hill Gate I caught a tube to Oxford Circus and from there took a taxi to Rhoda's[20] sister-in-law, Stella [Firth][21] and there saw Georgie for the first time. Stella is about 50, unmarried and really nice. She has a flat in Marylebone High Street and Georgie and I spent an enjoyable evening with her. After supper, which Georgie and I cooked, we went for a walk around that part of London. We walked up Harley Street, past the Royal Academy of Music, Madame Tussaud's and the Planetarium. We had Coca-Cola in a little café and then went back to the flat. Then Georgie and Stella put me on a bus to Victoria from where I caught a tube home.

The next morning I went to Piccadilly to meet Georgie, but I was late, as I didn't realize her hairdresser was so far from the station, and she had gone. We had a mad chase round London trying to contact each other and finally I got hold of her at Stella's flat. When I eventually made my way to Highbourne House in Marylebone High Street, it was almost 12, so we tore down to Baker Street tube station as we had an important engagement. We were going to Hampstead to visit Aunt Virginia,[22] Dr Moody and their delightful children.

When we left Georgie and I had hysterics because really it had been a most amusing visit. They have a very nice house but no idea of discipline at all. Virginia and Dr Moody are very nice but the children are terrible.

---

20. Rhoda Firth was the daughter of Iris Holcroft, the sister of Selina's maternal grandmother May Judd. Iris was also Georgina's grandmother.
21. Stella Firth was Rhoda's sister-in-law who had a career in the British Civil Service.
22. Virginia Moody was Selina's father's youngest sister, who died in Oxford in 2002. Her marriage to Dr Moody, a psychiatrist, ended in divorce.

Carol was at school, but Celia and Olivia were both there. Celia is 14, is a beautiful child, but is so terribly spoilt and bad mannered. And the funniest thing about it is that Virginia and her husband don't seem to notice their appalling behaviour. Olivia who is five is the prettiest and yet most unattractive child I have as yet met. She's terribly rude and badly behaved and gets away with it without any effort whatsoever. To start off with, she spilt the wine on the tablecloth, then spilt the orange juice into the macaroni. To end off the meal she spat at Georgie and me through a straw.[23] Surely, if Frankie[24] did that you would put a stop to it. If you said anything to Olivia she either didn't answer or said 'shut up'. I think you are a terribly good mother and all your children are angels compared with them. I'm surprised, given that Virginia is a psychologist. They have a German maid but never cease to complain about England. She seems envious of the family in South Africa. I can't understand why because there is so much in England, but they just harp on about its dis-advantages. After all, no country is perfect and England has a lot more to offer than most countries. She's got a lovely home and without spending much money could make it even lovelier but somehow has lost interest. Robert and Virginia are both very nice, except that Georgie and I felt as if we were rather a nuisance, but the children need some discipline.

I've spent the whole of today at home and have been doing house-work, cooking and writing letters. Tomorrow at 11.00 I'm going to my first class with de Vos but I won't get an outside job just yet. Rose can get me an afternoon job in a shop in Mayfair any time I should need it and I think that I'd rather have an outside job and wait until I can get a decent ballet one.

Margie, have you given my bike to Mr Taylor?[25] If not, please do so some time. I'm finding living here very expensive and I will need every

23. Selina became very fond of Celia (a near neighbour in Oxford) who sadly died during the 2021 Covid pandemic; she is somewhat embarrassed by these first impressions, but knows that Celia understood and hopes that Olivia will appreciate that South African child-rearing practices were rather strict at the time.
24. Frankie (Francis Oliver Molteno), Selina's youngest brother, born in 1955.
25. Rosemary Taylor's father. Rosemary, Brigitte Knight and Selina each had a scooter before leaving Cape Town, so presumably Mr Taylor had agreed to sell them on their behalf.

penny I can lay my hands on, but I don't want you to give me any. I'd rather earn my own. I'm happy here, but sometimes I miss you all so terribly that I can hardly bear it. Richmond is nice and quiet, but it's near the airport so jets and planes whizz over all the time.

Tomorrow night I'm going to see Brigitte and on Tuesday night I will deliver Juliette's[26] biltong to her. She's at the Sadler's Wells School now and seems very happy. Look after yourself Margie and give my love to Peter and the brood.

22 February 1959 (to brother Martin)

How's school and your friend dear Mrs Fort? Do write and tell me everything about it because I'd so love to hear from you. It's very cold here but London is so big and exciting that I don't really mind.

The *Pendennis Castle* was a super ship and didn't roll too much.

In England we go everywhere by underground trains called 'tubes'. The doors on the tubes shut automatically so if you don't get on quickly you are liable to be caught in the doors. I jolly nearly was once. One night when I was coming home the fog was so thick that I couldn't see in front of me, so I had to take a taxi from the station to our flat.

There's a long river that runs through London called the Thames and last Saturday Rose and Niña took me for a walk along its banks. All along the edge we saw little boys of your age fishing for trout, but I didn't see them catch anything though.

Today I'm staying at home in the flat because Rose is sick in bed and I must look after her.

24 February 1959 (to sister Annabel)

I don't know what could have happened to my letters because I have written lots and lots but perhaps they got held up in the post. Well, anyway, I am writing another so here goes.

Rose is in bed with flu so I am having to be the general dog's body, which is killing me. I'm also taking classes with Audrey de Vos in

26. Juliette Serrurier, who had been a friend and contemporary of Selina's at the ballet school, eventually became a professional pilot and is director of African Tours in Namibia.

Notting Hill Gate, which is where the riots took place.[27] I went to her class this morning but have spent the whole afternoon washing and preparing the evening meal. I'm giving them grilled chops, broccoli, carrots, onions and for Rose parsnips and swedes. For pudding I have made a divine fruit salad out of leftover pineapples, oranges and nuts. I tried desperately to beat up some milk for cream, but as soon as I stopped the bubbles popped and the milk was still milk. Never mind, I'm getting on famously.

Last night I had dinner with Brigitte [Knight] in London and we talked for hours. She's having a marvellous time and has prospects of travelling more or less everywhere. She gave me the name of a very good hairdresser and I'm going to look really chic. All the London girls have gorgeous hairstyles.

The weather is getting warmer now although it is still pretty cold. Most girls in London now are wearing bright coloured thick stockings in red, blue, black, green, yellow and every other colour under the sun. Now that I've got used to them they don't look bad at all. When I saw Georgie she gave me a gorgeous green cardigan, which she said was too small for her. I am of course thrilled to bits. I wear only one vest now, but still have six blankets.

I haven't joined the Richmond library yet but will as soon as I get a moment. Do write to me often Anna because I can't tell you how much a letter means to me. The family has been shocking about writing, so please chivvy them on. Send Vicky my love. I'm glad your music lessons are going so well. How's Vicky faring with hers?

Sunday 1 March 1959

I am so happy I could burst. Life's wonderful. London's wonderful, everybody is super and to crown it all we've had three beautiful days. So beautiful that they were almost like South Africa and when I hear the birds sing, see the sunshine pouring through my window and see flowers sprouting I just want to charge down the road and throw my arms around the milkman's neck. It's quite an effort stopping myself,

27. In late August and early September 1958 there had been an outbreak of serious racially-motivated riots in Notting Hill directed at the mounting influx of Caribbean migrants.

Outside Kew Gardens with
Georgie, 1959.

but, with the English so reserved perhaps it would offend the milkman.

On Friday morning I got up early and skipped off to de Vos. When walking down Linden Gardens a powder blue car stopped quite near me and from it jumped a man who ran into the studio and ran out again dragging de Vos behind him, they both jumped into the car, all smiles, and joined – guess who – Beryl Grey. She was laughing her head off and when they were all settled, the man, presumably her husband, drove off. Surely seeing that was a gift from heaven?

De Vos's assistant, Janet, took class and afterwards I went to Gamba to get some pointe shoes. Gamba shoes suit my feet beautifully and never before have I found such flattering ballet shoes. The shop assistant came right downstairs into the street with me to show me the way to Anna's studio and I went in that direction. I found my way to Lyons Corner House for lunch and there I met Dr John Cecil, my Johannesburg friend who stood me to a free lunch. He leaves for Jo'burg by plane on Tuesday.

From there I went to class and Rostoff[28] gave another divine class. I worked very hard and enjoyed every minute of it. Afterwards Margit Muller, an ex-Festival Ballet soloist, who fled from Hungary during the recent uprising, took me to a little street in Soho and showed me where I could buy fruit and veg for very little. I was so excited as the street, which was off Shaftesbury Avenue, was so full of life and atmosphere

28. Presumably this is Dimitri Rostoff, a former member of the Ballet Russes.

and I found some real bargains. From there I caught a tube home to show off my loot to the others; and guess who Rose had bumped into? Believe it or not Julian Bolt.[29] She says he's just the same as ever and hasn't gone to the dogs at all.

On Saturday the weather was the nicest it had been. I got two letters in the morning and went to class at 11.30. It was during class that my happiness reached its peak. Rose and Niña came to watch and sat next to Anna, and while I was doing a step round the room on my own, Rostoff went up to Anna and said, 'that girl's good, yes very good!' Rose and Niña told me afterwards and I'm still feeling the glow. After class we went to Regent's Park and ate our lunch on the grass. My feet were sore so we didn't go up the Mall as far as Buckingham Palace, but instead sat on the grass and drank in the sunshine. From there we went to Brunelleschi's studio where Rose and Niña had a Spanish rehearsal. I spent the afternoon there writing letters and watching them rehearse. They had a wonderful guitarist and there's no doubt that Brunelleschi is both crazy and gifted.

We spent this morning generally cleaning up. I cleaned the windows and now you can see through them.

We had lunch at about two and afterwards went for a walk in Richmond. Oh it's so beautiful – the river, the view from the top of the hill and everything in general. We came home past Richmond Green, which is surrounded by lovely Georgian or Edwardian (not quite sure which) houses. Shakespeare's house was there too and, round various corners, we would unexpectedly fall on quaint little antique shops, and then our walk would be interrupted while we would stand with our noses pressed against the windows trying to decide what would and what wouldn't look right in our flat. Cornell visited us this evening and he and I talked while Rose and Niña went to church.

3 March 1959 (to brother Martin)

Thank you so much for your letter. I was really very pleased to get it. When it arrived I danced all over the flat and Rose and Niña got quite a fright when I let out such a scream of joy. Today is cold and pouring

---

29. Julian Bolt (1936–1993) had been a student at the UCT Ballet School.

with rain. I wish I was back in South Africa in my nice comfortable bed with Constance to cook my meals and you to run errands for me.

You can hardly believe it but I'm a jolly good cook now. I don't make puddings that don't set any more. All my puddings set and I haven't burnt the milk for over a week.

I am sorry that school is so awful and that Mrs Fort is always shouting at people. Does that mean that she shouts a lot at you too? Don't worry about it though because when you come to join me in England you'll be able to speak Afrikaans and then we can say exactly what we want and nobody will understand. Sometimes when Rose, Niña or I want to say something in front of someone we just say it in Afrikaans and they look around and think 'Oh how clever', but little do they know that we are probably talking about them.

I wish you could see the underground trains we have here. I can just imagine you and Jannie[30] going quite mad on them. What with all the arrows and automatic doors, lifts with loudspeakers, escalators going all sorts of different ways and these funny little trains that go roaring through underground tunnels. If you catch one of these tubes at about half past five there is such a squash that when they open the doors fat men sometimes fall out. Sometime soon I will send you a postcard with a picture of London on it so that you can see exactly what it's like.

Just think Martin, the children here only get out of school at half past four, so you are quite lucky really, and no children of your age here can swim as well as you do because it's always too cold to get into the water. Please write again Martin.

Tuesday 3 March 1959

Thank you so much for your letter. I received it this morning and so enjoyed reading all the family news. I can't tell you how much I miss you all. I miss you especially today, probably because I've been on my own and am also very tired. When I have finished writing to you I will then wash my togs, wash the dishes, have a bath and climb into bed. I'm tired for a reason though, because last night I went to Covent Garden. I went with Cornell and saw Beryl Grey, in *Swan Lake*. It was

---

30. Jannie was the Hofmeyer's youngest son and a bit older than Martin.

so super seeing it from the front, especially as it is almost identical to our version. Their third act was beautifully designed and the czarda and mazurka costumes were gorgeous. The whole of Covent Garden went absolutely mad and never in my life have I seen or heard such a terrific ovation at a ballet performance.

After the show Cornell took me to Soho to show me the tarts. I was quite shocked to see such pathetic, over made-up women trying so hard to solicit customers, but when you think of it, it's terribly sad to think there are people who have to lower themselves to such an extent to earn a living. Anyway, it was an education and gives one a clear idea of what one doesn't want to be.

This evening Rose and Niña have gone to a Spanish rehearsal. I wish they would come home though because it's now 9.30. Just hang on a minute while I go and run my bath water. There, it's on now and I'll write for a while until it's ready for me. The water here doesn't come out in a torrent, I'm afraid.

Thank you so much for the money; I got an acknowledgement from the bank this morning, together with your letter. This morning I bought a season ticket so can save 50 per cent in fares as it doesn't count all the times I run backwards and forwards on that line – and if I want to branch off somewhere, it only costs me a tickey[31] extra.

I'd better go and see to my bath now; it's probably running over the edge. Oh hell, where's Rose? I wish she and Niña would come back as there's such a scary programme on the wireless and I'm beginning to get rather frightened. I've washed the dishes and, according to the BBC, someone's just been hit by a rock. Just let me have my bath now and then I'll carry on in bed. Oh thank God the rock hasn't killed her, only squashed her though. Thank goodness, here come the others – what a relief.

4 March 1959 (to sister Annabel)[32]

I'm scribbling this in bed before getting up on Wednesday morning. I must hurry though as it's already 8 o'clock and if I don't step on the gas I'll be late for class.

---

31. A South African term for a three-penny coin.
32. Annabel was still living with the Sucklings.

After a marvellous spell of sunshine, it's raining again and from heaven I've come down to earth with a bang. It's amazing what the weather can do to one's spirits. I don't think I'll go to de Vos this morning because there I work for 3½ hours without a break and I'm rather tired. I'll go to Dimitri Rostoff, and then this afternoon I'm going to have my hair styled at Harrods – madly extravagant but I feel like standing myself to a treat. On Monday night I saw *Swan Lake* at Covent Garden with Beryl Grey. It was lovely. Gosh, but the dancers there really are marvellous. I haven't a hope in hell of getting into that company. Jobs in London are very scarce, so when I have worked for a while here I'll probably go to the continent and try and get into a small company there. I'd rather be in a small ballet company than in musicals, which somehow don't appeal to me. I think you'd love London Anna, for the shops are full of the sorts of clothes you like and rather cheap too. I've seen quite a few things that immediately make me think of you. By the way, I got your first letter on Monday evening. It only had a 3d stamp on it, so was sent surface mail. Anyway, better late than never, so thanks a ton. Rose, Niña and I might be going to Cambridge for Easter. Write soon.

Wednesday 4 March 1959

This morning when I woke up I felt tired, so instead of going to de Vos I decided to do a shorter class with Rostoff instead. I enjoyed it very, very much. After class I had lunch with Cornell in Baron's Court and from then on to Harrods. Yes, I did my first extravagant thing since I've been here – I had my hair done, and I must say I look terribly posh.

People in London don't seem to dress up at all in the evenings and when we sit in the gallery we wear exactly what we wear during the day. When I saw Grey I wore my grey costume and when I saw Fonteyn I wore my tweed skirt and twinset. The people sitting in the posh seats though usually wear a frock with a stole. I suppose it's impractical to dress up in London because most people go to the theatre before going home.

I'm writing to you in bed and it's only 9.15. I'm having a really early night tonight so that tomorrow I can work my very hardest. I've eaten much too much supper and feel like a stuffed pig about to burst. Rose made supper tonight and is very generous with her helpings. We have very good food here – perhaps a little too good. Well, I'll say goodnight now until tomorrow.

Thursday 5 March 1959

On Thursday morning I went to class with de Vos. I didn't enjoy it though as I was tired and couldn't concentrate. Afterwards I went to a dingy café in Notting Hill Gate and was astounded at the bill – 6/- for cold meat and salad and a cup of coffee – I'll never go there again.

Anyway, after that extravagant meal I went to class with Dimitri Rostoff and enjoyed it very much. After class Rose and I met Julian Bolt at Richmond station and he came back to have supper with us. Oh Margie, I've never laughed so much in all my life. You should have heard his amusing reports about the musicals he's been in – he's certainly been around and has made the most of his experiences. He is so much more poised than he was before he left Cape Town.

Friday 6 March 1959

This morning I went to class with de Vos, and guess what? When I arrived Beryl Grey was having a private lesson – she's lovely.

After class I went to Soho, which is the place to shop. It's so full of atmosphere, character and life and I can get a meal for half the normal price. In future I will buy everything there. Tea there is 4d a cup, and in posh London between 9d and 1/-. Vegetables are between ½ and ¾ the normal price.

After my expedition to Soho I went to class with Rostoff, and guess who I met there? You can hardly believe it but it was Patricia Miller's[33] sister, Sheila. She looks very like Miss Miller, but hasn't got her good figure. She's sweet though and we spoke of home and Oakhurst.[34] She said that Oakhurst was her favourite school and she thinks a lot of

---

33. Patricia Miller (b.1927), ballerina with the Sadler's Wells Ballet Company, came to South Africa with her husband Dudley Davies (1928–2014), and joined the staff of the ballet school while Selina was still there. They later moved to Durban to direct the NAPAC Ballet Company there.
34. A state primary school in Rondebosch, which Selina attended as a child.

Miss de Schmidt.[35] When I arrived home from class, Rose said, 'Guess who I met today?' She said she was walking down Shaftesbury Avenue when suddenly she heard someone calling her. She looked around and it was Mr Johnson – the ballet school pianist. Really, we seem to have seen practically everyone.

Did I tell you that Peter Cazalet is joining Festival Ballet in two weeks' time? Gosh, but it's wonderful for him.

Sunday 8 March 1959

At the moment it is Sunday morning at 11.00 and I'm all snug in bed. I've just had breakfast in bed and when I'm finished writing to you I'm going to spend the rest of the day making the flat look nice and washing my clothes. I'll try and get the whole bang shoot done today.

Yesterday morning I intended going to class, but unfortunately by the time I arrived in Leicester Square it was too late, so instead I shopped in Soho in the pouring rain. Afterwards I went to the studio to meet Rèna[36] and together we went to Covent Garden to see *Swan Lake* again. Beryl Grey and all the soloists were on top form, but the corps de ballet danced appallingly. Well, after the matinée, Rèna and I came back to the flat to prepare dinner for the two of us, and for Rose and Niña when they returned from a Spanish rehearsal. Rèna and I settled down in front of the gas fire and told each other all about our own countries. She told me all about Athens, the Greek government and how the Greek people lived and I showed her a whole lot of pictures of South Africa. She's terribly nice and Niña and Rose both like her very much.

While we were waiting for the latter, Juliette [Serrurier] appeared on the scene and stayed for about an hour. She is spending her days at the Sadler's Wells School and boasts of spending every night 'pub crawling'. Apparently, she and other girls from Alexandra House go around to all the pubs, having a couple of drinks at each. She says she

35. Miss Lettie de Schmidt was the progressive headmistress of Oakhurst who came out from England because of her arthritis and introduced something she called the 'activity method'.
36. Rèna Sanikou, a young Greek woman whom Selina met at Anna North-cote's class and befriended.

never gets to bed before two and is enthralled by 'life'. I'm afraid that
that girl irritates me rather with all her big talk. Whenever I see Juliette
she depresses me terribly, I can't think why. Nothing's hard for her –
she doesn't miss home, scorns us for not having a char, never goes to
bed and works like a Trojan all day. Somehow I'm so glad I'm living
with Rose and Niña as they both have such sound approaches to life.
I find it disheartening to find that while I am finding the going hard,
someone else in the same field is finding it one long holiday. Rose says
I mustn't worry about Juliette because having everything on a plate
doesn't necessarily build the best characters.

Well, after Juliette left, Rèna, Rose, Niña and I had a lovely dinner
and an amusing evening.

Tomorrow morning I am going to the professional classes at Sadler's
Wells. I'm terrified as they say the girls there are terribly stuck up and
snobbish and I've been given due warning not to talk to them because
they won't answer. Margie, you've got no idea how awful and ruthless
the average English ballet student is. Quite frequently I've tried to open
a conversation and all I get in return is a disgusted look and a back
turned on me. Rèna said that once she was walking home from the
Sadler's Wells School when she happened to see two girls who had just
done the same class as she had. She quickly walked towards them and,
as they saw her coming, they turned round and spoke to each other
with their backs to poor Rèna.

Gosh, but it's a miserable day today. I guess I'd better get up now
or else I'll be up till midnight with my chores.

I've turned so patriotic – it's quite painful. The government is the
only thing that isn't faultless in South Africa, and when anyone asks
me about it I just rave about the sunshine, the scenery, the wonderful
people and the cheap fruit. If there weren't so many continentals in
England I don't know what I'd do, as they are the only people who
seem to have any feelings of kindness.

Wednesday 11 March 1959

For the past three days I've been rather busy, so I apologize for not
writing about Monday and Tuesday in detail, but I will tell you everything of importance. On Monday morning Rose and Rèna took me

along to the Sadler's Wells School to do the professional class. Barbara
Fewster[37] took the class; she gave me a lot of corrections and I enjoyed
it very much. In the afternoon I went to Rostoff as usual.

On Tuesday morning I went to the Wells again and did class with
Errol Addison.[38] He too was nice to me and praised and corrected me
quite a bit. Then, after Rostoff's class in the afternoon, Rèna and I
went back to Craven Hill Gardens, where she stays, and the two of us
had great fun cooking our meal over the gas ring in her room. We
made a gorgeous stew with rice and peas and I've discovered something marvellous. Next time you have rice you *must* squeeze lemon
juice over it – it's too gorgeous for words. Apparently, that's how the
Greeks always have it and I can assure you that it's well worth trying.
Rèna and I then talked for ages until it was time for me to make tracks
home.

This morning I got up early and went to Mr Rostoff's 10 o'clock
class. There were only five of us there and I felt that I'd worked well.
Then from there I rushed to the Royal Ballet School and did another
class with Miss Fewster. She gave a terrific class and I really enjoyed it
to the full. She gave me far more corrections than she gave anyone else
and I think the other girls got rather fed up. Anyway, I don't care
because now I have so many faults to correct and things to remember
that I'm happy just to know I can improve. I'm learning so many new
things I didn't know before – all the little things that seem to make all
the difference – if you know what I mean.

This evening Rose, Niña and I went to dinner with Mrs Khazam.
She is a charming, quiet, refined Israeli woman who lives in a fabulous
flat in Kensington. She has three lovely children and the eldest girl of
five is on the verge of being trilingual. We had a lovely dinner and
afterwards sat and talked and watched television. I'm not too keen on
television though. I'd rather pay 5/- and go and see a good film instead
of £200 to watch a vile film every night. The English radio is excellent
and all day one can hear really good programmes – much more
pleasant than television. My eyes are slowly gluing shut so I'll end off

37. Barbara Fewster OBE, teacher at the Royal Ballet School.
38. Errol Addison (1903–1982).

here until next time. I should say goodnight but somehow it's corny as you'll probably be reading this in the morning.

Thursday 12 March 1959

This morning when I got up I spent a couple of hours making the flat look spick and span and then I went to class at the Royal Ballet School. Pamela May[39] took class and I enjoyed it very much. At class I met Rèna and she said she had a surprise for me. Someone had given her two invitations to go to the BBC TV and watch a show being put over the air. Margit Muller was dancing in it and Virginia McKenna was to sing. So after Mr Rostoff's class this afternoon Rèna and I went along to Shepherd's Bush to the TV studio. We had the very best seats in the front upstairs and were so excited we could hardly sit still. First of all a man told us all about how the various cameras worked and how to applaud and when. There were all sorts of cameras, lights and various gadgets and, dotted around the recording room, were quite a few TV sets, so we could see the show over TV as well. Then for a couple of minutes there was dead silence while we all waited for the exact second to come onto the air and with a sudden crash the orchestra started up and the show had started. The cameras fascinated me because suddenly you would see this colossal contraption sailing silently towards the artists and then silently out of the blue it would extend upwards and poke its head over the pianist, singer or whoever was performing. The show was very good I thought, and Margit Muller did the *Don Quixote* solo and a lovely demi-charactère of a little girl trying to catch a bee. Then we had Virginia McKenna (the film star on the back of the Rice Krispie packet) singing a song accompanied by her mother on the piano. We had a couple of excellent opera singers and a jazzy blonde who sang blues popular songs, which of course I adore. You know what I mean – catchy tune and interesting words. We had a solo pianist as well and the band was very good. It was a wonderful opportunity I must say, as now I have a pretty clear idea of how it all works and not everyone can get into those shows. Margit had given the invitations to

39. Pamela May, OBE (1917–2005) was a Trinidad-born British dancer and teacher of classical ballet.

another dancer, Jenny, who was unable to attend, and as Rèna was there she seized the opportunity and offered to go instead. I'm back in bed now, and Rose and Niña are dancing Spanish in a cabaret at a hotel tonight, so won't be back till later on. So I think I'll go to sleep now as it's only 10.30 and I *do* appreciate an early night occasionally.

Friday 13 March 1959

Olé! It's my anniversary today. Yes, I've been here for exactly a month now and it was a sunnyish day to crown it as well. By the way, thank you so much for the parcel. It arrived the other day and I adore the evening coat and dress – I had no idea that they would be so gorgeous and thank you too for the other oddments as well.

This morning I did class at the Royal Ballet School and it's thrilling to see the stars in person. When I went to the office to pay for the week's classes, Pamela May was there. She asked me where I came from and when I told her she said, 'Oh, I thought so yesterday.' She remembered me anyway. I don't think I have a hope of getting into the company, but my next move will be to write to Peggy van Praagh[40] and ask her advice. I thought of catching her at an odd moment, but on second thoughts I think it's better to write because then she has time to think about it and perhaps we can meet for a talk sometime.

Class today was taken by Errol Addison and afterwards Rèna and I felt disinclined to do another class, so we went to a cinema in Piccadilly instead. The film was excellent and the funniest thing was that Virginia McKenna,[41] who we saw on TV last night, was acting in it. After the film I felt naughty so I popped into a little gambling place, put 6d into a slot, pointed some arrows towards, 'Libra' and 'female' and picked up a receiver. The modern fortune teller then proceeded to tell me my fortune over the phone – most glowing. She said that all

40. Dame Peggy van Praagh (1910–1990), dancer, teacher and ballet mistress who ended her career in Australia. Selina had met her in Cape Town through her ballet teacher Pamela Chrimes when she was about twelve years' old.
41. Virginia McKenna, OBE (b.1931) is a British stage and screen actor, author and wildlife campaigner.

the little things that I'd been working at in the past were going to take shape and that I was going to meet some people who were going to have a beneficial effect on my future. It was worth 6d because I walked away feeling much happier for it.

You know what? This morning I got a letter from someone in Cornwall and I don't know who it is. I wonder if you could find out for me if I gave you all the clues as I would so like to contact her and reply to the letter. Her address is Heligan House, St Austell, South Cornwall, and her name looks something like Moira Durno. Do you know anyone called Moira Durno, or something like that? She says she has a suite in a large old house and is looking for a suitable small house. She says they are going to Scotland early in June. She goes on to say, 'I do wish I could do something for you, perhaps I shall be able to one day – if and when we come to London I will let you know.' Haven't you any clues? It's an early night for me tonight – so good night until tomorrow when I will continue with the next epistle.

Saturday 14 March 1959

Rose is ill today so she spent the day in bed, but I hope she will be well again tomorrow. I don't quite know what the matter with her is, but she feels terribly sick and bilious.

This morning I did a very nice class with Mr Rostoff and afterwards went back to Rèna's room and together we made lunch over her gas ring. We had an omelette, peas, potato chips and a gorgeous pineapple instant pudding, which I made. We then sipped Nescafé around the fire and finally finished our meal at about 4. Afterwards we went to Bayswater to do some cheap shopping and there we met Niña, on her way back from a Spanish rehearsal. The three of us went back to our flat for supper and now, at 11.15, Rèna has just gone home. I'm feeling very happy at the moment and am enjoying working and living in London very much.

Sunday 15 March 1959

Today, as on most Sundays, we stayed at home making the flat a little more respectable and doing relays of washing, cooking and ironing. At 11.00 this morning Rose came up with a bright idea. 'Niña, Selina', she yelled, 'let's have coffee outside because the sun's come out and it's lovely.' Niña then prepared herself by wrapping a scarf around her ears and a fur coat around the rest of her and together we went out, shivering, to enjoy the sunshine: I had just got round the corner and stepped in a couple of puddles when, plop, the coveted ray of light disappeared, so the three of us sauntered back into the lounge to enjoy our coffee around the gas heater.

Soon after that I started washing and ironing and washing and ironing and washing and ironing and tomorrow I'll do some more ironing. The afternoon was gone before it had started and just as Rose and Niña were tripping off to church, Julian [Bolt] appeared on the scene. I went to church last Sunday but didn't like it much because the vicar made us sit in a ring and tell him the names of bible personalities beginning with Z. I didn't know any, so I didn't go this evening. Anyway, Julian came so I had company. I then decided to start supper but when I started to investigate what provisions we had in the flat, I found that we only had parsnips, which neither Niña, Julian nor I like. Julian then tootled off on his bicycle, which he bought yesterday, and came back about ¾ of an hour later bearing a beaker full of peas. 'Victory', he exclaimed as he made his grand entrance in the front door – I didn't ask what he'd done to gain this victory on a Sunday evening. In the meantime I'd done all sorts of things to try and contribute to our skimpy fruit salad. We only had one banana, one orange, one lemon and about six apples; so, to make juice I squeezed in some Juicy Joe, added marmalade, sugar and undiluted orange drink. It turned out quite nice.

We were in a crazy mood and almost rolled about the floor laughing, as we discussed our past life at the ballet school. We laughed and laughed and laughed and even our underwear on the clothes horse seemed to be reacting to the hilarity by staying wet.

Rose and Niña are busy sewing Spanish costumes for Saturday is the big day at Festival Hall, and it's all rather trying when one has to make a Spanish costume-cum-summer frock, as of course they can't waste the material. Rose's is black with blue chandeliers and yellow and pink lights on it (it isn't quite as bad as it sounds) and Niña's is navy with white spots (rather sweet).

Monday 16 March 1959

Today I only did one class as I was rather tired. Barbara Fewster took the class but although I enjoyed it I didn't feel in top form. Rose, Niña and I have gone on a campaign this week. Early nights and more nourishing food. I've been eating too many sweets and it's having drastic effects on my skin and figure. Instead of going on a diet I have decided to change my routine. A good breakfast with cereal, egg, toast and coffee and then straight after that do an early class instead of staying at home picking at things in the cupboard. Then I'll go to the Royal Ballet School for my second class at a quarter to one. At two I will have a very light lunch – yoghurt and fruit, or something like that, and then instead of going to the 4 o'clock class, I will go home and do my chores then so that I can get to bed early. In the evening we always have a good meal with cooked meat and vegetables. Fish is terribly expensive here and quite difficult to get. I won't eat anything in between meals and hope that that will give me a complexion of peaches and cream, a figure like a sylph and the energy of a race horse.

Before, I used to hang around in the morning picking at food and doing housework, which could be done in five minutes. Then I went to a 12.45–2.00 class and another at 4.00–5.30. I used to arrive back at 7.00 dog tired and then would spend half the night cooking supper, washing up, bathing and so forth and never getting to bed until very late. Anyway, for a week I'll try the new 'early to bed and early to rise' routine and see how it works. This morning I bought myself a pair of shoes. Navy blue leather with a T-strap; very sweet I must say. I had to get another pair as my brown ones were looking terrible and badly in need of a visit to the shoemaker. It's now 10 and I'm tucked up in bed ready for sleep, so goodnight and *totsiens* until tomorrow.

Tuesday 17 March 1959

Today, I did both my classes in the morning and I think it worked out much better that way. After the second class I went to the bank and then, quite spontaneously, went to the National Art Gallery, and saw an exhibit on nineteenth-century French art. I have never been to the gallery before, but loved it and will certainly go again. It is in a gorgeous building in Trafalgar Square.

I think that Trafalgar Square is the nicest of the lot because it's got so much. The pigeons, lovely statues, St Martin's cathedral, which is lovely, the gates and pillars leading up the Mall are really beautiful; the art gallery and, tucked in a corner, is the loveliest little Georgian house. Also, from Trafalgar Square one can see Westminster Abbey, Big Ben and Regent's Park. Piccadilly Circus is nice but all it is really is the statue of Eros (which I love) and a whole lot of modern shops and lights.

Today was bitingly cold and I felt rather 'poor little me-ish' as I have got a large grog blossom at the side of my mouth and it makes me feel madly unattractive. Anyway, I'm having another early night and am already in bed.

This morning Errol Addison took class and I felt such a fool because just after I had done a step he stopped the whole class and said, 'none of you gets an inch off the ground, you don't even try. Now this girl Selina, she's got good elevation but I tell you, the good Lord didn't give it all to her. She tries to get off the ground, and does, but she puts some effort into it.' He then made me go first from the corner and boy did I feel a prune. Thank goodness I can jump though because it's the one thing that I can do better than average and I just hope that eventually when I try to get a job that that will counter some of my other faults.

Wednesday 19 March 1959

Today when I went to Mr Rostoff's class there were some dancers who belonged to Ludmilla Tchérina's company, which is opening at the Cambridge Theatre in London on Thursday. I think I'll try and see them on Saturday afternoon as I'm interested in these little companies from the continent, as it's into a company like this that I'd like to worm my way sometime.[42]

I enjoyed class at the Wells too but still like Mr Rostoff the most. He has a wonderful eye for seeing the cause of a difficulty and is so very nice and kind. He speaks in the most broken, broken English and

---

42. Ludmilla Tchérina (1924–2004) was a French ballerina, sculptor, actor, painter, choreographer and author of two novels.

has really got something special to offer. I'll be disappointed when Anna returns from America and he has to leave.

Monday 24 March 1959

Oh dear, I've been so lazy – I've let Thursday, Friday, Saturday and Sunday just slip by and haven't written a thing. Wednesday and Thursday were rather uneventful days and by the time Friday afternoon came Rose and I had both had enough so we stood ourselves to a film at the Empire in Leicester Square. It was *The Journey* starring Deborah Kerr[43] and Yul Brynner[44] and was excellent. It was all about some people fleeing Hungary during the 1956 revolution and I found it really realistic, especially as I know Margit Muller, who fled from there at that time. How she managed to get out just beats me.

On Friday evening Rose's boyfriend Neil and his flatmate Mike came to call and took the three of us out for tomato juices. On Saturday morning I went to class, couldn't do a thing and felt most end of week-ish. Afterwards, Rèna and I met Juliette and the three of us went to the matinée of Tchérina's company. I found it interesting but couldn't stand Tchérina. She plasters expressions onto her face, which seemed insincere and rather irritated me. It was all terribly new and odd and some of the ideas were rather clever and effective, others were overdone but still it was interesting to see it. That evening Rèna and I went to Festival Hall to see Rose and Niña dance their Spanish number. They all danced beautifully and at the same time there was an ordinary dance going on. Mike appeared on the scene and so I spent most of the evening dancing with him. English dances are very different from ours. English girls seem to go to public dances alone and then stand against the wall in the hope that someone will notice them – no thanks, I'd rather die than do that.

On Saturday afternoon we gave a tea party in our flat – tea, pancakes, chocolate cake and chocolates. It was a roaring success.

43. Deborar Kerr (1921–2007) was a Scottish-born film, theatre and television actress.
44. Yul Brynner (1920–1985) was a Russian-born US-based Eurasian actor of stage and film.

Our guests were Cornell, Julian, Deanna [Blacher],[45] Rèna, Neil, Mike, Ronnie, Dave (Neil's flatmate) and a girl called Gerda. We had a wonderful time and didn't even notice the rain outside. Our flat was so warm and full of life and laughter. Everybody loves coming here and once they come they always come again and again. Over the Easter weekend we are going to have a smashing time. Rèna is coming to stay and Rose is going to Devon. On Saturday afternoon Mike is going to take Niña, Rèna and me to the Oxford and Cambridge boat race and afterwards there will be a party. Then on Sunday, the three of us (Niña, Rèna and I) are going to Cambridge. We will find a cheap room and it's bound to be divine.

Today Barbara Fewster took class at the Royal Ballet School and I enjoyed it very much indeed. We've just had a good meal of Bird's Eye fish sticks and veg – I like them better than Frikkie fish sticks as they have no bones. Rather extravagant I must say, but it's only the second time I've allowed myself the luxury of fish – on Saturday after Tchérina I stopped at a roadside barrel and had 6d worth of cockles and mussels and a piece of eel – now I'm really initiated! By the way, thank you so much for the parcel. All arrived safely and the blouses are lovely and so useful. Thank you very, very much.

18 March 1959 (to father, Peter)[46]

Thank you so much for your letter. It was sweet of you to say those nice encouraging things to me – they help a lot, but you mustn't expect me to get on straight away. It might take a long time before I manage to get myself into a company, but having seen every one else here I don't see any reason why I shouldn't eventually get the sort of job I

45. Deanna Blacher (b.1940) was a contemporary of Selina's at the ballet school in Cape Town, though more interested in Spanish dance than ballet. She went to Australia with her family in 1983. She settled in Perth, and established Danza Viva Spanish Dance Company and Academy. In addition to her teaching and choreography she is an acclaimed castanet recitalist.

46. This letter was sent to Foxwold, which is where Selina's grandparents lived at the time near Stellenbosch, so the family back home seemed rather dispersed, having let the Cape Town family home, Rowan House, to the Godfrey family.

want, but I'd rather be patient and get into something I really feel I can belong to and improve in rather than flit from one musical to another.

I'm working hard, keeping my eyes and ears open and leaving the rest to fate. It's difficult to get into a company these days without money and influence. You find that a lot of the dancers who get on are either director's wives, or have fathers who put up money for the company. But still, if I get on it's not going to be that way, so therefore you must be patient – give me time to improve enough to be taken in for my merit. I'd rather like to get a job on the continent, but until I feel ready I'll continue training in London, and if I run short of money I can always find myself some sort of job – working part-time in a shop or something like that.

I love London, but find living here heavy going and rather tiring – so much housework and travelling and one wastes so much energy walking from the station and doing the daily shopping.

After I got your letter I wrote to Barbara Hawthorn[47] and Nina and I are thinking of going to Cambridge for a couple of days over the Easter weekend. Rose is going to stay with friends in Devon and Nina and I thought that it would be rather nice to go up to Cambridge and get a cheap bed-sitter for the night. Brigitte Knight is leaving for Norway on a two-week skiing tour on the 30th and before she goes she has invited me to go down to Kent for the day, which ought to be very nice. There's so much I'd like to see and do here, but I'm frightened of spending too much money at first and then having no reserve when I need to travel to get a job or something like that.

Sadler's Wells seems impenetrable as there again you have to go through the school, which costs the earth. But don't worry, I'll be all right – I'm terribly good at looking after myself and organizing my life.

Thursday 26 March 1959

Well, today is Thursday and from tomorrow the fun will start. Rèna is spending the Easter weekend with us and is here already. She made

---

47. Barbara Hawthorn was Selina's sister Annabel's godmother and she lived in Cambridge.

supper tonight and we had a gorgeous Greek recipe for meat balls. Rose is leaving for Devon at 5.30 tomorrow morning and Niña, Rèna and I will spend the rest of the weekend together. There's not much point in telling you all that we are going to do as I would rather tell you about everything as it happens.

This morning I did class with Mr Rostoff and then went back to Rèna's room with her for lunch. When we had finally finished eating and she had packed her bags it was about five so we made a move towards getting to Richmond, which we eventually did. Now we are nicely settled around the fire and when I've finished writing to you I will darn a pair of pointe shoes, have some skoffie[48] and go to bed. The Royal Ballet School is on holiday now until 13 April.

Sunday 29 March 1959

At the moment I am sitting with Niña and Rèna in the waiting room at Liverpool Street station, waiting for the train to take us to Cambridge for two days.

The Easter weekend so far has been terrific. On Friday morning at about 5.20 Neil came to fetch Rose and she went with him to Devon for the long weekend. While Niña went to church on Friday morning Rèna and I cleaned the flat and I washed the yellow nylon curtains, which had turned grey and the difference in their appearance is unbelievable. Now the whole room has lightened up and they give an illusion of sunshine and brightness. We made ourselves a nice lunch and then, at about 2.45, Mike and his brother Charlie came to fetch us to take us sightseeing. We picked Niña up in town and from then on had a wonderful afternoon seeing all the things I'd been longing to but just hadn't had a chance to see. We saw Buckingham Palace, drove through Hyde Park, went to the Tower of London, drove past St Paul's, Houses of Parliament, Westminster Abbey, Downing Street, and generally all over the place. Then we went back to their flat, had tea and from there went to the cinema and saw an excellent film about an artist called *The Horse's Mouth* and when that was over we went back and grilled steak for supper. After supper we danced, talked, and argued

---

48. Skoffie was a very bland instant coffee made out of chicory.

for hours before finally being driven home at about two o'clock in the morning.

On Saturday afternoon Mike took us to the boat race at Putney and that was one of the most exciting things I've seen and experienced in London. We milled our way through the thick crowd to the boathouse and got a really good view of the river from the balcony. I got a little Cambridge trinket as I thought that, considering that Peter went there, it was only proper that I should stick up for them.

Everybody was getting terribly excited as the time of the race grew near and then suddenly it started. The two boats shot forward, the crowds yelled and the boats were followed by a surge of motor launches packed full of people and following the race in order to get a good view and also for television cameras.

As soon as the rowing boats were out of sight we went into the boathouse and watched the rest of the race on television. Oxford beat Cambridge by four lengths. After, we had tea in the boathouse and then, as it was getting rather stuffy, I decided to go onto the balcony to look at the river. The sun had just come out and caught the sails of yachts, which were being launched, and it all looked so lovely. The bare trees on the other side of the river and the swans swimming in the river made an absolutely perfect picture and owing to the surge from the launches the river began to rise and overflow onto the road, so we had to leave quite soon afterwards to avoid being trapped in the boathouse.

We then went back to the boys' flat and Eric, Mike, Charlie, Niña, Rèna and I had a gorgeous supper. Rèna and Mike made it and it was absolutely super – spaghetti with meat sauce, red wine and for pudding jelly with oranges in it and cream. We then put on some nice records and relaxed in front of the gas fire. We were rather tired by then so went home fairly early.

I'm now in the train and we're heading out of London for Cambridge. We haven't got into the countryside yet, but jolly soon we will.

Tuesday 31 March 1959

There must have been a hold up in the post because six letters arrived this morning. I must say I was getting quite desperate but my heart is at rest now and I'm happy again. Thank you so much for your air letter. It meant a lot.

I'll go back now to Sunday where I left off. We arrived in Cambridge at about lunchtime and immediately caught a bus from the station into town where we got off and lugged our luggage around looking for Maid's Causeway where Mrs Unison was going to take us as bed and breakfast 'paying' guests. Just as we arrived at the front door it began to rain and it was miserable and we were all so tired. Mrs Unison escorted us up some rickety stairs into one double and one single bedroom. There was no heating and barely enough blankets for one person let alone three. A large towering wardrobe leant ominously over the bed every time we ventured to move and of course there was the traditional marble topped washstand and jug and the chest of drawers dressing table with a mirror. The curtains were made out of red plush with orange, brown and yellow stripes on them and it was quite the most uninviting room I have as yet seen in England; but, we didn't care – it was all part of the game and it was fun. We were so clapped out that we all climbed into the double bed and slept soundly for a couple of hours. Then, feeling much better, we got up and went out in the pouring rain to see Cambridge. We staggered as far as the cinema café in a most awkward stance as there was only one umbrella and so, to avoid getting our heads and inside rumps wet, we walked in a rather uncomfortable position.

We were dying of hunger so went into a café and had a very special Easter high tea. It was lovely and warm and cosy in the café and we had a divine high tea for very little money. We started off with cakes, which were on the table when we sat down, and just couldn't sit and look at and went on to have fried eggs, chips and peas and a huge pile of hot toast and jam and then lots of boiling hot tea. We just didn't savour the idea of sightseeing in the rain so we committed an unpardonable sin – we went to the cinema. It only cost 1/9d and in London the cheapest is 5/- and the film was not at all bad, in fact most fascinating. After the film we went home again, put all the blankets onto the double bed and climbed in for the night. In England any squash is better than being cold.

The next morning, *Monday*, we woke up to a cup of hot tea and a biscuit and then at about 9 o'clock we were each given a jug of hot water to wash with, the bath was just an ornament.

This was followed by a gift from heaven – an English breakfast. I just must tell you what we had.

1) Post Toasties with sugar and milk.
2) Two pieces of toast covered with scrambled eggs and fried tomato.
3) Two more slices of toast, butter and blackberry jam.
4) One apple and a cup of tea.

I must say the breakfast was marvellous. After that we left the boarding house and caught a bus to Huntingdon Road to see Mrs Hawthorn [Annabel's godmother]. Oh, she and her husband are so sweet and such fun. We just seemed to hit it off straight away and had the most wonderful morning with them. Mrs Hawthorn reminds me a lot of Zoe[49] – you know that sort of amusing, gay, yet ladylike type, and they have an awfully nice house and big garden. You can tell Anna that she has the pick of the bunch and we had a good laugh when I told her about the mysterious aura that surrounded her in our inquisitive minds. They had a lunch date so Mr Hawthorn took us back into Cambridge to see the colleges and to dump us off at the rowing boats. He looked up Peter's name and found that he was at Downing College and was really so sweet and interesting.

After he left us, Rèna, Niña and I went into a pub and bought hot dogs, sandwiches and chips. We then hired a boat and went, laden with our food for a wonderful cruise along the river. We had a boat all to ourselves and rowed past all the colleges and it was so beautiful that I can't explain it in words. The most beautiful buildings I've ever seen and green, green grass coming right to the edge of the river and then clumps of daffodils and all the various spring flowers. All the fruit trees were in blossom and Monday was a perfect spring day.

Afterwards we had another high tea and then came the highlight of the day – a visit to King's Chapel. By mere chance I was standing

49. Margie's cousin and Georgie's mother.

Selina's father Peter as a young
man at Cambridge.

outside and saw some people going in so asked if we could too; we did and do you know what? We went right up onto the roof and saw the view of Cambridge from there. You know, there aren't only a few beautiful buildings but they are all so beautiful that at times I thought I was dreaming. How the students can look at books when they've got that to look at just beats me. We caught the evening train home and today is Niña's birthday so we had a little party with just the four of us. Champagne, cake and pudding were extras and of course we ate by candlelight.

Rèna is spending tonight with us and tomorrow Mr Goubé[50] from France is taking class. He is a leading French maestro, maître de ballet of Tchérina's company, and reputedly one of the best teachers in Europe.

2 April 1959 (to Annabel)

Thank you so much for your letter. Now just let me tell you all my news. First of all I'm loving ballet here and have had a lot of encouragement from quite a few important people and Peggy van Praagh said she thought that I could do well in Rambert's company, so I will stick around for a while and hope for a vacancy.

Anyway, I can but try and I would really love to join that company. The Royal Ballet is a dead end. I haven't a hope of getting in this year anyway and will never get in without going through the school first and

50. Paul Goubé (1912–1979) was a French dancer, choreographer and ballet master. He and his wife, Yvonne Alexander, who was also a dancer, worked closely and later, in 1969, they together established the Salle Pleyel.

also there are too many people who would be given places before me.
Actually, I have no desire to dance with the Royal Ballet Company as one
can never get on there, but if only I could get into Rambert Company I'd
be very happy. If I can't get in there I will go and live in Paris as M. Goubé
(leading Paris maître de ballet) took a class and his wife told me that I
should train in Paris and try to get work there. She says she will help
me in every possible way. I will give Rambert a bash first, though.

On Sunday and Monday, as you probably know, we went to Cambridge but Margie will tell you all about that as I told her every single
detail. I'm happy here and feel that I'm settling down well. London is
the most exciting, wonderful place on earth and I feel so inspired to
work and improve. Whether I'll ever get into a company or not I don't
know but I'll try my hardest and let fate take its course.

The boat race was wonderfully exciting. Oxford won and Cambridge is now hiding its head in shame. Your godmother is super and
is one of the most terrific women I've ever met. She's more like Margie
than anyone I know and told me all sorts of things about Peter's
undisclosed past, motorbikes, boxing. Really Peter, you never told me
about those vices. Apparently, Virginia was a bombshell at Cambridge
and Peter was quite a KAZ-BOY. We looked up his college and he was
at Downing. Honestly, I had no idea that Cambridge could be so
wonderful. I'm going back there at my very next opportunity.

Rèna spent a whole week with me and she's a real honey. I've never
met anyone before with whom I felt I had so much in common. She
looks just like a Greek – small, nicely rounded body, dark hair which
she wears in a chignon, huge dark eyes and a Greek (or is it Roman?)
nose. She's really super. I hope you have a wonderful time at Miller's
Point. I'm sure you will. Gosh, I miss you all so much and whenever I
see a little child in the street, I pick it up and run along the pavement
with it, turn it round and round and take it back to ma. Perhaps I'm
going off my head. Never mind.

Saturday 4 April 1959

It's about 2 a.m. on Saturday morning, but I've just come home to a
letter from you and have also had some Nescafé so am wide awake.
Why I'm really writing to you now is because I feel so happy that I

want to preserve that feeling forever. Just let me tell you my news step by step from Wednesday where I left off because if I don't calm down you won't be able to decipher a thing.

Well, the last thing I told you was that I was going to do a class with M. Goubé. I did the class and enjoyed it so much that I'm seriously thinking of going to Paris and studying with him there. He's the most marvellous teacher on earth and makes me feel as if I possess the whole world – you know that 'ugh' feeling one gets when you want to go on dancing forever. Anyway, after that class Rèna and I were so clapped out that we went to a film in the afternoon and saw *The 39 Steps*. It was not bad.

I don't know whether I mentioned it to you but I wrote a letter to Peggy van Praagh for advice and she replied by asking me to do a class at the Royal Ballet School on 2 April. So, on Thursday morning, I went along, an absolute wreck, and found myself in the 'Theatre Class' with all the various prodigies. The class wasn't too bad and afterwards she told me to meet her in the canteen an hour later as she had another class to take; and that is what I duly did. She was very sweet to me and seemed bent on the idea of me trying to join Rambert's company. She says I am just her type and thinks I would do well in the company. On the other hand, she may take a violent dislike to me and in that case I'll try something else, but Rambert will be my next step. Van Praagh says they have a lovely repertoire and are an artistic company offering good possibilities. The only thing is that before I can hope to audition for the company I have to go to the school, so this afternoon I applied for an audition to the school and will take that on Tuesday afternoon at 1.30. What a laugh if I fail to get into the school! By the way, I've also got my name down for an audition for Festival, but that's pretty impossible really. It may shock you but I'd rather not join the Royal Ballet, even if I could. They take their dancers, put them into a machine, drain them of their individuality, spend years in the school and then, after charging them £200 a year they say, 'Sorry dear, but your ears are the wrong shape.' If I were a prodigy I might consider it, but I'm not. A small, more compact company appeals to me more.

Yesterday morning I got up, washed the dishes, tidied the flat, walked to the station, renewed my season ticket, caught the tube, changed at Hammersmith, got out at Leicester Square, went up the escalator, showed my ticket at the barrier, went up the steps onto Charing Cross Road, walked along Charing Cross Road and straight into M. Goubé and his wife. They stopped me and Yvonne (his wife) started to talk to me as he doesn't speak English. She asked for my address and said she would write to me if there was anything going in Paris. Oh Marg, I can hardly tell you everything. M. Goubé thinks I'm a very good dancer and actually stopped me in the street to tell me so. They say they will help me as much as they can and Yvonne kept on telling me how impressed her husband is with my work. Oh Margie, just think GOUBÉ, the one and only Goubé noticed me – they never said it to anyone else. I'm so terribly, terribly happy as I've had so much encouragement and when it comes from such sources I want to run all over London at top speed telling everyone how happy I am. I think I must be considered a bit eccentric because when I'm happy I charge around like a wild bull and cackle at the top of my voice.

This afternoon Rèna made me laugh so much. We were in the bus when we started to discuss various English words. Now, her English is not quite 100 per cent or even 85 per cent and she has just learned the word 'bob' for shilling. She turned round in the bus to me and, in her loud rather odd accent, said 'Selina, do you say two bobs or two bobbies?' I almost fell off my seat I laughed so much. Last night, she, Niña and I went to see Walt Disney's *Fantasia.*

I'm still walking on air because today has been just as nice as yesterday and the day before. This morning I did a very nice class with Mr Rostoff and afterwards Rèna and I went to a café and had a cup of coffee with three other girls. I then went back to Rèna's room for lunch and slept for a couple of hours in the afternoon to prepare myself for a Goubé class at 6. There were seven of us at the class and it was super. I'm telling you, he's the most fabulous teacher that ever was, and he took a lot of notice of me too. His wife has got my address and I have theirs and so if ever I need any advice about Paris I'll contact them. They say that if there is a place going that they will write and let me know. Margie, I'm so happy – I'm just waiting to come down to earth with a bang, but am making the most of it while it lasts, as I find I can work so much better when I feel like this. I hope you are all having a wonderful time at Miller's Point.

13 April 1959 (to Frankie at Miller's Point)

Do you still remember your big sister? Anna sent me some pictures of you and the others and whenever I see anybody I show them to them and they all think that that you and Martie are such clever boys to fish so nicely. Won't you draw a picture for me?

14 April 1959 (to Annabel)

I thought I'd better write to you as I've been rather bad about writing this last week. I just haven't felt like it but I will soon, so tell the folks not to worry. I'm still alive.

I went to an audition for the Rambert School. I was the only one they accepted and they said that although they were chock-a-block full, they would make a place for me for next term; there is no vacancy in the company and no chance of one occurring this year, and even if there is one they won't guarantee I'll get it. The classes there are terrible and I can't afford to go to the school without a part-time job, and I'm sorry but I can't work morning, afternoon and night. So I've decided to throw that chance away, get a part-time job, stop drawing from my capital and in a few months' time, or when I feel ready to, go abroad and try there. I want to go to France and study with M. Goubé – he's marvellous and told me he likes my dancing very much. There's so much I *can* do and look forward to so I'm not really in such a hurry to get into a company at the moment.

I'm sitting in a café in Charing Cross Road, it's a lovely day and the Salvation Army is grinding out a soppy song outside the window. Yesterday I went to Gamba to buy pointe shoes and they gave me two free tickets for *Roar Like a Dove*. I'm going to it with Niña tonight. It is supposed to be an excellent play and we are in the best seats 19/6. The man at Gamba said he'll give me free tickets for shows any time I want them. Never again will I pay good money to see shows.

Monday 20 April 1959

I give you full permission to slay me, discard me, never speak to me again. I'm sorry I haven't written for two weeks and I've got such a conscience that that in itself is punishment enough. You know, it's funny, but I just couldn't write any more letters. I'd written so many that the thought of writing another just sickened me – anyway, I'll try and make up for lost time now. The last two weeks have been quite eventful and things seem to have taken a rather odd turn.

At the beginning of the first week I went for an audition for the Rambert School. They didn't accept anyone but me, but said I wouldn't get into the company for a long time – September at the earliest – and possibly not until next year, perhaps never. They said if I'd come before I would have got in right away but they'd just filled up every vacancy and so my chances were slim. If I liked the school I would take the chance to go, but Margie, the training there is vile. There is no method in the classes and I couldn't hope to improve there. Also, I'd use up most of my money and then if I didn't get in I wouldn't have any money to go elsewhere. I'd also lose all outside contacts and if I did get in it wouldn't be the most marvellous thing on earth. I've spoken to a lot of people about it and they all say that the girls in the company are miserably paid. I'd rather try for a continental company. What attracts me is the Marquis de Cuevas Company. I think it's important to be able to work well and improve while waiting for a chance and I know that I couldn't do that at the Rambert School.

Instead, I've decided to work with Anna and anywhere else I please and get a part-time job so I can save my money for when I need it to go to Paris or abroad. I've found now that I'm managing to live quite economically. At first I spent quite a lot of money because I didn't know what was and what wasn't cheap, but now I do and I think I'll be able to live on about £3 a week not counting rent, fares and pointe shoes, which I pay by cheque. Actually, I've already got myself a job as a waitress in a coffee bar. It's a very smart coffee bar in a nice area. It's in Charing Cross Road near Tottenham Court Road tube station and also very near Anna's studio and Leicester Square. I've worked there twice already and like it. Discounting tips, which come to about 6/- a night, I get £1 a night. I work three times a week, which is nice because it doesn't interfere with my work too much – Tuesdays and Thursdays from 4 to 12 and Sundays from 2 to 11.

I get a nice supper for nothing and the fares don't cost me anything because I use my season ticket. The boss's wife is charming and the other two waitresses are fun and we have a lot of laughs. The one, an Italian woman called Mrs Bianco, is a scream and is always smuggling food around the corner for me (hot chocolate drinks, hamburgers, frankfurters, cakes and cappuccino). When I tell her I can't eat any more she looks at me in blank amazement and says, 'Aren't you hungry?' as if I hadn't just been given a large three-course dinner. She's a honey though and tells me all about the customers, 'You see that man over there?' Yes, I see a West Indian man sitting with a blonde English girl, 'Well, just wait till I see his wife – I'll tell her something.'

By the way, I must keep you informed on fashion. Cape Town is years behind and completely outdated. Everything is very waisty – a pinched-in waist with a nice wide belt and a full top and skirt – dresses just below the knees, some wear them above but it doesn't look nice. I think I must send you a French fashion magazine. The clothes in them are lovely and very suitable for Anna.

By the way, I've never had to pay duty on anything and neither have Rose or Niña and they get sent cakes, fruit and crates of all sorts of things. Can't John send me some fruit because it really helps the budget terrifically or how about some pineapples from Harry?[51]

Rèna is teaching me to cook so that the food tastes like something. When you see how she prepares her food you can't believe that people can eat like they do. For instance, ordinary cauliflower is delicious if you squeeze a little lemon juice over it and a little oil. Rice with lemon juice is gorgeous. We buy cheap mincemeat, which is awful, but make gorgeous meatballs out of it. You mix it with a beaten-up egg, salt, pepper, onion, and lemon juice. It's a wonderful sense of achievement to make a lot out of nothing. Rèna says that in Greece everyone cooks with olive oil and the food is nicer for it. It's so expensive here though, so we can't buy it, but even with Oxo the food is improved. The margarine here is super and looks and tastes just like butter.

Anna [Northcote] has come back now and Mr Rostoff gave his last class on Saturday morning. Gosh, but I'm sorry to see him go. On

---

51. Harry Judd was Selina's maternal uncle and a pineapple farmer in the Eastern Cape.

Friday morning Beriosova came to class. She walked into the dressing room and I didn't recognize her at first. I just thought, 'what a skinny girl'. She started to talk to me and asked me about Rostoff's classes. Only then did I realize who I was speaking to.

The other night I went to see *Salad Days* but it was rather spoilt as I went with such a boring Englishman, but I got a free dinner and the show was actually very good. On Saturday night I went with Rèna to see *Tiger Bay* at the Queensway Cinema. It was a super film, but before it they showed a vile Western film and the most shocking little boy was sitting next to me who bit his nails to the roots and smoked cigarettes. Shame, perhaps nobody loved him. I spent that night with Rèna in her room as Rose and Niña had gone to Cambridge. Rèna is super. I don't think I've ever found a friend I've had so much in common with before. My, but we certainly live!

The other day I was doing class at the Royal Ballet School when de Valois walked in,[52] spoke to Miss Phillips who was taking the class and walked out again. The girls in the school nearly went round the bend as they only had half a minute to show their talent. They all started practising madly, but unfortunately de Valois wasn't looking. I feel rather sorry for those girls in the school because they seem so anxious.

Aunt Virginia has asked me to visit her but I just haven't had a moment because of the job. Anyway, Marg I can't think of any more news for the moment, but I've written now and so at least you know I'm alive. I haven't seen Amelia[53] yet but wrote to the Overseas Club. I suppose I'll bump into her sometime.

27 April 1959 (to Annabel)[54]

I got your letter just before leaving the flat and now I'm in the tube, I might as well take this opportunity to write to you. I spent last week

52. Ninette de Valois (1898–2001), founder and director of Royal Ballet Company.
53. Daughter of Dulcie Howes and Guy Cronwright who came to England in 1959. She later married an actuary called David Brown and they settled in Johannesburg and had two children.
54. Annabel was staying at Marlow, Marlow Road, Kenilworth, which was where Dulcie Howes and her family lived, so perhaps the latter were away.

with Georgie in Stella's flat in Marylebone High Street, which is very near Oxford Street (with gorgeous shops), and Harley Street. While I was there we went to Kew Gardens, Madame Tussaud's, did a lot of sightseeing and went to a play called Not in the Book, which incidentally was very good.

On Wednesday it was Mike's twenty-first birthday. By the way, Mike is a chap whom I don't really like but who professes to love me, which is trying, especially since I can't help being beastly to him; for his birthday treat he took me to a posh lunch, to a terrific musical called West Side Story, and then showed me Westminster Abbey; on Saturday night he gave a Hobo dance, which both Georgie and I went to. Georgie has now gone to Spain and is living like a queen in the best of society; ME – the opposite.

I'm working in a coffee bar, which is fun. There is an Italian student working there called Mario and the two of us have a hell of a time as we are both equally inefficient. Actually, last night I didn't do anything wrong except that the boss was in a filthy mood and kept me waiting for my money so I missed the last train home. On Saturday afternoon Georgie and I went to lunch with Aunt Virginia and it was very nice.

I'm dead nips about going to Paris, but anyway I'll start making all the necessary enquiries soon, and as it is so near to London, I haven't really anything to fear because I can always come back if I'm destitute. You see it is difficult for me to get a job there because of the language and also work permits.

People say, 'Oh, you'll be miserable', but nothing venture nothing gain and if you are going to go through life trying to avoid all difficulties, one might as well hibernate. I've given up being scared of people – if they want to be nice they can; otherwise they needn't – I couldn't care less. I quite enjoy not knowing where I'll be or what I'll be doing next, but sometimes it gets one down though.

Thank you so much for the photos. I do love them, but if only you knew what a hag I was looking you would forget about 'London chic'.

Amelia [Cronwright] is spending Wednesday night with us, but I haven't seen her yet.

*30 April 1959 (from Amelia Cronwright, 48 Nevern Square, SW5 to
Margie reporting on having visited Selina in London)*

A very belated thank you letter – but for once (for me) belated on
purpose, as I did not want to write to you until I had seen Selina.
Now, however, I do want to say a very heartfelt and genuine thank
you for the really lovely stole. It was such a wonderful surprise to
find a message from the Purser in my cabin to call for a parcel the
next morning and to find it was not, as I feared, something I had
already managed to lose! I made great use of it during the voyage
where it was much admired.

Selina came to meet me at Waterloo, but couldn't stay until the
train arrived and after some frantic notes and telephone calling we
met yesterday afternoon at Holborn station for the first time. She
told me she had got much fatter, but she doesn't look it if she has,
which I doubt. She is her usual glamorous self and seems all in all
to be happy and well-adjusted in her life here. I went out with her
to the flat where we spent a hilarious evening chatting and eating like
14 horses apiece (I'm *huge* now) except Rose, who, poor dear, is
fatter than ever. I believe Patti [Miller] had a row with Selina about
saying she's fatter so please don't say anything to anyone but it is,
unfortunately, true.

The three girls have great fun in their flat, which is wonderfully
cheap and not at all badly furnished. I spent the night – Selina lying
on the mattress on the floor in the lounge and I on the remains of
the divan next to her. As you can imagine it was pretty hopeless as
far as sleeping was concerned as we talked too much to give it a
chance!

Today Selina has gone off to try with, apparently, *all* the other
dancers in London who are not in work at the moment, for an open
TV audition for dancers for a 22-week summer season. As nobody
knows whether classical or modern dances are required there is
much speculation and Selina has gone off determined to do the Pas
de Trois solo if she has a chance, or otherwise a rather curious modern dance she learned from a fellow student at Anna Northcote's
yesterday afternoon in about five minutes.

I haven't seen many shows since I've been here, but I have seen *At the Drop of a Hat*, *Seven Wonders of the World* – a Cinerama film containing some wonderful choreography – *My Fair Lady*, Merle Park and Gary Burne in *Coppélia* and *La Valse* and tonight I'm going to see Nerina and Blair[55] in *Lac* – big thrill. Even bigger, of course, is the fact that I meet Daddy [Guy Cronwright] tomorrow morning and Mummy [Dulcie Howes] sometime later. Although London is expensive to live in and shows are costly, there is so much to amuse one just pavement plodding, going to the National Gallery, British Museum, Hyde Park and Kew Gardens that there never seems to be enough time to do all that one wants. I am, however, very often homesick and more especially friend-sick as I know few people here as yet. Anyway, Mummy and Daddy come tomorrow and I'm longing to hear first-hand all news of home.

Selina sends her love and so do I to the whole family, including my dear little brat of a sister whom I give you full permission to beat on her bottom until she writes to me.

Sunday 10 May 1959

At the moment I'm sitting on Niña's bed listening to the wireless, talking to Georgie and writing to you on a beautifully sunny and warm Sunday afternoon. Rose and Niña have gone out for the day and Georgie and I have spent the day lolling around on the lawn, washing our hair and paging through magazines. The weather for the last three days has been fabulous – just like Cape Town. Georgie appeared with a friend at 3.30 on Wednesday morning through my bedroom window. They had arrived from Spain and had nowhere to sleep. I got a hell of a fright as I woke out of the depths of sleep, to hear someone climbing through the window. Anyway, we dismantled my divan – Georgie and Jill on the mattress and me under a coat on the springs. Georgie's been with us since then but goes back to Hartwell[56] tomorrow. She had a

---

55. David Blair (1932–1976), partner to Margot Fonteyn until ousted by Rudolf Nureyev.
56. Georgie was at Hartwell House, then a finishing school for young ladies in Aylesbury, but now a hotel.

wonderful time in Spain and brought me back a charming pair of earrings – Toledo earrings (black and gold).

You'll probably be glad to hear that I've given up the coffee bar job as it was too tiring and, since I will probably be going to Malmö in September, I can afford to live without a job until then. I want to work really hard and improve as much as I can before I go – if I go – and so have decided to give up everything and go at it flat out.

Anna Northcote asked me if I'd like to go to Malmö and of course I said that I would love to. Two men came to watch class and they said that they liked my work and would like to take me on – but then, on the other hand, I am not going to bank on anything until I've signed a contract.

Well, let me tell you something about Malmö. I don't know whether you've been there or not but it is a town in Sweden on the coast near Denmark. They have a lovely theatre and work in operas as well as ballets. It is an eight to nine-month contract, my fares over will be paid and apparently my salary will compare favourably with anything else you could hope for. I've met two girls who have been there and they say they had fabulous rooms and were looked after very well. From Malmö one can go over to Denmark for the day and I think that the company tours Scandinavia. I'm not sure though. If I can get the job it will be a gift from heaven, so please pray for me, as I don't know about it yet – they have the whole of London to choose from and they saw me first – so I don't know. Please don't say anything to anyone about it yet, otherwise I'll feel awful if I don't get it. I'll let you know as soon as I do for sure.

On Friday afternoon I had lunch with Gwen Harris at Harrods, which was lovely and she gave me the frock. I think it's too sweet for words; thank you so much. I went straight home afterwards and wore it that night when I went out with a typical Englishman – who was not really my cup of tea. After all, there are right and wrong ways of folding handkerchiefs, sitting in a tube or carrying an umbrella.

Georgie and I have just come back from a lovely walk along the river – along with crowds of other people out in their new summer clothes. The river was full of rowers, speed boats and swans and the sun stayed out until about 9.00 p.m.

Is Anthony[57] still at medical residence or is he staying at Marlow? I tried for days to contact Miss Howes and finally did on Friday afternoon. I sent the flowers and am going to see her tomorrow at 3.00. I spent Saturday afternoon with Rèna and we went to see *Emergency Ward 10*. She says she'll arrange to have her room left open so that I can go there, make my lunch and rest between classes. Richmond is too far from town and sitting around in cafés is both expensive and tiring. Now that I'm not working I'll probably have more time to write more frequently.

Monday 18 May 1959

I saw Miss Howes last Monday afternoon in her luxuriously furnished room in Portman Square. She seems to be enjoying herself in London. I'm seeing beautiful paintings, hearing beautiful music and going to first-class shows and theatre. Living in an environment of art and culture can't possibly be a waste of time. I haven't yet heard about Sweden and don't know when I will, but I'll just wait, work hard in the meantime and if that doesn't materialize something else will in time. If I begin to run short of cash there are plenty of coffee bars, cinemas and shops in which I can work and I promise I won't go below £100. People often come to Anna Northcote for dancers and, since I'm not lying desperate in the gutter, I'm quite happy as I am.

For the last two weeks we have had perfect weather and in between classes I've been going to Green Park to lie on the grass and enjoy the sunshine. This weekend is Whitsun, which is why at midday I'm still in my pyjamas and writing such a long letter.

Yesterday Cornell visited, so he, Niña, Rèna and I went to Madame Tussauds and afterwards to an excellent film called *Compulsion*. After class on Saturday morning, Rèna and I had a picnic lunch in Hyde Park. On Friday I met Pam Minty at Waterloo station and she was taking everything most calmly and methodically. I acted big sister and showed her exactly what to do and all the sights. In the evening we saw *Irma La Douce* at the Lyric in Shaftesbury Avenue. It was wonderful. Oh how

57. Anthony Molteno (b.1938) is Selina's older brother who was studying medicine at the University of Cape Town at the time.

I wish you could come to England and see the shows and plays – they are superb and if you sit in the gallery are quite cheap too. *Irma La Douce* is acclaimed by many as the best show in London, and I must say quite rightly too.

Pam is staying in the William Goodenough House and although it's nice as far as hostels go I'm thankful that I'm not in an institution – it would drive me round the bend. Pam is in the south wing overlooking the quad and 2/- a month must go towards house funds – doesn't it make you squirm? Pam likes that sort of thing though because she was at boarding school, but I just couldn't I'm afraid. Pam left the fruit at Southampton but has written for it – so thank you very much for it and as soon as I get it I'll let you know how it tastes. Please write – perhaps it's the post, but I never seem to get letters any more. What's happened to the family? I haven't had one letter this month.

22 May 1959 (to Anthony)

Well, I hope you had a nice twenty-first birthday – I wanted to send you a telegram, but it costs a couple of quid a line and really is rather too much of an extravagance.

I sent you a pair of gloves – have you got them yet? I bought them at a special shop which specializes in gloves in Regent Street, as I thought they'd be rather handy for your motorbike. You can take the inside lining out to wash and in summer and for goodness sake treat them with great respect as they are the best you can buy in London – I do hope you like them. Do let me know if and that you do.

We've just had two weeks of glorious summer weather, but now we're back to normal – raining and cold with occasional thunder storms and lightning. Tonight I'm going out to a very posh do about which I know very little except that it is the Great Ormond Street nurses annual ball – should be quite fun dressing up and pouring on the perfume again even if my New Zealander partner doesn't turn out to be Prince Charming.

I'm still walking around aimlessly looking for Cook, Troughton and Simms, but as yet haven't had any luck. Are you sure there's one in London? Won't you find out whereabouts because then I'll get all the information and dope that you want. Nobody seems to know where it is but then on the other hand what do ballet students want to know about optical glasses for!

I still adore London. Hell, but it's a super place. Much, much nicer than I ever dreamt it would be. There are some excellent plays on and the last one I saw was superb. You go into the theatre and come out richer. It's the most marvellous feeling.

I've visited the National Art Gallery a couple of times and the paintings there have to be seen to be believed. Oh, it's a super dorp – it really is and I know for sure that you would really love it.

24 May 1959 (from Gwen Harris, 33 Park Walk, Chelsea, SW10, to Margie staying at Marlow, Marlow Road, Kenilworth, Cape Town)

I have been meaning to write you a line for *ages* – but over here life is earnest, work and pleasure combined, and never a dull moment – the only time I seem to sit down is in a train! At the moment I am in York, but return to London tomorrow to collect some clean clothes and then down to Sussex where my family are on holiday. I have been up in Scotland and have the past few days been enjoying unspoilt parts of the country in the North Riding of Yorkshire – ruined abbeys, castles, hamlets and stately homes and no people or petrol pumps and the weather and the countryside unbelievably beautiful.

I met your Selina at Harrods one day and we had a bite together in the Silver Buffet and I handed over her dress – I enjoyed her thoroughly and she has absorbed in a very short time a logical and loving viewpoint of life in London (a rare happening to a South African) she gets a thrill from most things and plays everyone's game of learning to live on a certain amount and seeking and searching for the cheapest markets and knowledge and ideas of things attainable or procurable.

She has great poise and is starry eyed and were she mine I would indeed be proud of her! She longs to show you London! And I feel quite sure would bring a lump to any adult Londoner's throat with her enterprise and courage – she talks of the children and naturally misses them, but I am quite sure she is well and happy and the world is her oyster. I hope to see her again.

Sunday 31 May 1959 (to Margie from Pamela Minty, a friend from the ballet school and contemporary of Selina's who came to London a few months after she did and was staying at William Goodenough House in Mecklenburgh Square, WC1)

To think that it was a month ago that we sailed from Cape Town is quite unbelievable. Life has been such a whirl and so much has been happening that I feel I have been here for years although it seems just like yesterday when we waved to you all on the quayside. It was so nice of you to come and see us off and thank you so much for the money you gave me. I spent it at the shop, which really did have some gorgeous things. I suppose Selina has told you how I left your parcel and my tennis racket at Southampton, but the British railways are very efficient and they were delivered to my door on the Tuesday morning all safe and sound. Selina looks very well and really seems to be loving life. She is exactly as she was in Cape Town, full of vim and enthusiasm, only a little pale after an English winter. I was so thrilled that she met us at Waterloo as we would have been quite lost if she hadn't come. No sooner had we put both feet on the platform than we were whisked off in a taxi to Goodenough House. After lunch here we rushed into the heart of London where we spent the day trailing behind Selina who pointed out so much and took us to so many places that I found myself in a permanent daze and only took in half of what she said. She was like a tourist guide and I'm surprised we weren't run over or something as we didn't seem to realize there was traffic on the roads and just followed her blindly. That evening we went to *Irma La Douce*, a gorgeous French musical and sat in the gallery, which I found very strange at first but then got used to. We then looked at all the Piccadilly lights, which was most exciting.

Our voyage couldn't have been nicer, there being such a nice young crowd aboard. We all got together and had a hectic time, so that it was very depressing leaving everyone behind and feeling we'd have to start all over again, settling down and meeting new friends etc. However, Angela[58] got back from Bristol on Monday – after spending ten days there – and yesterday she moved into the room next to mine, which is so wonderfully convenient. We are quite settled now and have our pantry of supplies, crockery and cooking utensils as it is far too expensive eating out. We love planning our meals though and the other morning had hysterics in the grocer shop as we decided to lay in a stock of soups, so very carefully selected four tins of mushroom, vegetable, chicken and pea soup. We then discovered there was a cheaper kind, so promptly changed them all over again. Then Angela says, 'put those back, there are some here for 1½d.' This meant another change over by which time the shop assistants were quite crazed as we were in fits of giggles actually. We have been so tired during the last week that we get giggling fits at the slightest things and there is absolutely nothing we can do about it.

There is just so much to see in the theatre live that we just don't seem to be able to fit everything in. So far I have been to *Irma La Douce*, *Room at the Top*, *West Side Story* (Princess Margaret sat a few rows in front of us in a private party – very exciting). Carmen Amaya[59] and her Spanish company, who was terrific, Pilar Lopez[60] and her Spanish company who was not so terrific, and we have been to the Rambert Company at the Wells Theatre three times. We also went to the Royal Festival Hall to a concert there. There is no need to worry about Selina at all Mrs Molteno. She looks the picture of health and is so organized about everything she does. Please give my love to everyone and keep well. Also, thank you again for your gift. I was very touched.

Sunday 31 May 1959

Thank you so much for your last three letters. You've no idea what a difference they make to my life. I'm sorry I haven't written for a while,

58. Angela Rowe, another dancer and relative of Madame Rambert, who later joined that company.
59. Carmen Amaya (1913–1963) was a flamenco dancer and singer of Romani origin.
60. Pilar Lopez (1912–2008) was a dancer, choreographer and teacher.

but somehow I've been caught up in a whirl of activities and haven't had much time.

Shortly after I last wrote to you Niña, Rose, Brigitte, Pam and I had supper at the Chicken Inn in Leicester Square and Pam presented me with your parcel. Thank you so much for the fabulous contents. We have enjoyed and are still enjoying some of them and what a joy it is to indulge occasionally in the luxuries of life!

On the Friday before last I went to a fabulous ball at the Mayfair Hotel, and had a wonderful time. I wore my red nylon evening dress, my white brocade shoes, white stole and a pair of Rose's drop pearl earrings and felt marvellous. I went with quite a nice chap from New Zealand, which was a refreshing change from the usual. It was one of those all-night affairs with wine, a midnight spread and the 'Gay Gordons', which incidentally I have cultivated to a fine art, but when they started on the cha-cha-cha, which I can't stand, I stuck my nose in the air, insisted that colonial tastes differed and started to attack a chicken bone. Anyway, it's great fun to let one's hair down occasionally and I do *love* dressing up.

When John finally got me home it was already light and the next morning I made rather a fool of myself, as I just couldn't seem to direct my washing into the right hole in the Bendix, and as for starting it, well the man with the machine next to mine had to do that. The Bendix people issue you with bags, which are supposed to hold 9 lbs of washing. I arrived, fuzzy headed and sweating at the brow. I heaved my washing onto the scale and waited to be allotted a machine number, a cup of bleach and a cup of soap suds. Instead, I heard, 'Caw blimey, never in all my life did I find someone who can fit 13 lbs in *this* bag!' I had to leave out 4 lbs for next time. That afternoon Mrs Nicholson and Jennifer[61] came to tea with us at our flat and your biscuits were a stupendous success.

On Saturday night John turned up to take me to a party before leaving for the continent and we had a lot of fun, especially as I knew almost everyone there. We had a madly exciting evening because we

61. Jennifer Nicholson had been a pupil at the ballet school. She and her mother lived in a residential hotel in Kenilworth, near Wynberg, and thus not far from the Moltenos.

decided to have a séance and it worked too. Unfortunately, no dead person wanted to have anything to do with me, so I had to be content to appreciate other people's dead relations. It was fun anyway.

On the next Sunday morning Rose's cousin David Eaton came to visit us and the four of us went to Kew Gardens for the day. It was perfect weather and we took a picnic lunch with us and ate it there. In the evening we went to the Thames at Richmond, hired a boat and went rowing along the river. It was really glorious. When the sun shines England is the most perfect place on earth.

Last Monday morning Cornell came to class and in the afternoon we went along to see *The Mouse Trap*, the Agatha Christie play that has been running in the West End for seven years. It was a good play and very well acted.

On Thursday night Rèna and I went to the Sadler's Wells Theatre to see the Rambert Ballet. We sat in the gallery for 3/- and saw *Laiderette*, *Simple Symphony*, *The Two Brothers*, and *Gala Performance*. *Laiderette* was the one I enjoyed least of the four, but still found it quite interesting. It was written by Kenneth MacMillan[62] and was about a girl (danced by Lucette Aldous[63]) who, rejected by her parents, attends a masked ball. She's ugly and when she shows her face, her lover also rejects her. I feel he could have done more with that story. Also, Lucette Aldous is better suited to virtuoso parts. *Simple Symphony* was delightful – lovely music, costumes and choreography and a most enjoyable romp. Irene[64] was in it and danced very well indeed. She looked very bright and fresh. *Two Brothers* was written by a member of the company, Norman Morrice,[65] and I am impressed by his work. It had terrific understanding and sensitivity and the lead was danced by a lovely dancer, Gillian Martlew. She wore such a pretty frock of grey chiffon and danced really beautifully. The last ballet *Gala Performance* by

---

62. Sir Kenneth MacMillan (1929–1992) was a British ballet dancer, choreographer and from 1970 to 1977 artistic director of the Royal Ballet in London.
63. Lucette Aldous (1938–2021) Australian dancer with the Royal Ballet.
64. Selina thinks this is Irene Siegfried, a pupil of Cecily Robinson in Cape Town. She was very talented, but gave up ballet quite early on.
65. Norman Morrice (1931–2008) was a choreographer and director.

Tudor was very funny. It was about three rival ballerinas all trying to outshine each other at a performance. They were from Moscow, Milan and Paris and the whole effect was put across in a subtle, amusing way.

On Friday night I went to see Ibsen's *Brand*, fully expecting to see something way above my head. Instead, it was a really gripping and superbly produced play.

On Saturday afternoon Rèna and I went to a matinée of *Coppélia* by the Rambert Company. It was a good production and Lucette Aldous was absolutely charming as Swanhilda and I thought their costumes were very nice.

On Saturday night Niña and I went to a Beethoven concert at the Royal Festival Hall. We heard Symphony No 6, The Pastoral, Pianoforte Concerto No. 2 in B flat and Symphony No. 8 in F. It was the London Symphony Orchestra conducted by Josef Krips.[66] Germany's most respected critic, Stuckenschmidt,[67] has called the solo pianist Glenn Gould[68] the greatest pianist since Busoni[69] and this was his first appearance in England. I enjoyed the concert terribly and the Pastoral especially was lovely.

8 June 1959

I'm afraid I haven't chosen a very appropriate moment to write to you. The wireless is blaring and there's chaos all around as we are preparing to go to a midnight show of *My Fair Lady*. Cornell managed to get complimentary tickets and tonight is *the* night.

Friday 12 June 1959

I've got quite a lot to tell you but I don't quite know where to start. Well, I hope this arrives in time for your birthday and I'll try and make it as fat as possible. I have already sent you a petticoat by surface mail, so I hope you don't have to pay too much duty on it. I'm afraid it's nothing very spectacular but I thought it might come in useful.

66. Josef Krips (1902–1974) was an Austrian conductor and violinist.
67. Hans Heinz Stuckenschmidt (1901–1988).
68. Glenn Gould (1932–1982) was a celebrated Canadian pianist.
69. Ferruccio Busoni (1866–1924) was an Italian composer, pianist, editor and writer.

Last Sunday morning Rèna, Niña, Rose's cousin, David Eaton, and I went to Petticoat Lane. It was a lovely sunny morning and walking through the stalls in Petticoat Lane was one of the most fascinating things that I've as yet done. You should have seen some of the things they were selling. There was one chap trying to sell little machines for 2/- that made ten bob notes out of blank paper and another man selling shirts who drew the crowds by pretending he was being filmed. There he stood perched on top of a ladder wearing a hat with a cockade of black feathers sticking up and a pair of red trousers stretched around his rather bulbous middle. He was holding a sword in his hand and yelling instructions to the sky from where he was being filmed. He then beckoned and called the crowds closer so that they could get into the so-called film – he dropped tin trays for sound effects and when he finally got the desired crowd around him he began by hauling out a colossal pair of fleecy-lined pants, which were only joined at the back. He called these the 'ever open drawers' and a 'bus conductor's paradise'. After exhibiting these he went on to say 'and when the Liberals went out and the Conservatives came into power' – his face fell and he dismally brought out an even bigger pair of pants with each seam sewn up meticulously. After that he began to sell his cheap poplin shirts, which he had presumably stolen the night before. Oh, it's so difficult to portray the crowds, bustle, atmosphere and wit of the market and the innumerable cockneys all trying to outdo each other by using their humour to sell their wares. They sold everything from baboons to stolen silver and when a policeman appeared they merely scooped up their belongings and moved off somewhere else. Afterwards we went to a delightful little pub on the river at Wapping where smugglers used to offload their loot and one has one's drinks sitting on the wall at the edge of the river Thames.

Oh, Margie *My Fair Lady* was super. We left home at a quarter past ten and caught a bus and tube to Covent Garden from where we walked to Drury Lane and met Cornell there at 11.15. For a while we stood outside watching various toffs going in adorned in their medals and tiaras and then we went to our seats which were just behind Beatrice Lillie (the famous actress).[70] The show was wonderful and

70. Beatrice Lillie (1894–1989), actress and comedienne.

Stanley Holloway[71] and Julie Andrews[72] were superb. Funnily, it was very close to *Pygmalion*, which surprised me as usually they change them quite a bit when they turn them into musicals. The costumes were lovely and Eliza at the tea party and at the races was adorable. There she was in perfect English describing in detail how her father ladled gin down his throat. After the show there were of course no buses or tubes so we had to walk to Waterloo to catch a surface train home. We went via the Covent Garden market, which was just opening up and it was a thrill to see these cockneys at work so early in the morning. It was still dark except for the lights in the sheds and everything was quiet and everyone asleep apart from the workers who were rapidly unloading fruit and vegetables and they only stopped to greet us, flatter us and wish us a good morning.

What a wonderful ending to My Fair Lady, which was set in that very place amid those very people. We bought hot coffee and bacon sandwiches at a stand in the market and then wended our way along the Strand towards the bridge. As we walked over the bridge dawn began to break and we stood there listening to the water lapping against the edges of the moored boats, and the night was only disturbed by a tug, which moved silently up the river and under the bridge like a dark shadow.

From the bridge we saw London lit by lights and the first red bus going along the Embankment. Waterloo station had already woken up or rather it never went to sleep and officials were pacing up and down, loading mail and milk and preparing for the thousands of newcomers into London the next morning. Our train left at 3.30 and when we got to Richmond dawn had already broken and the birds had begun to sing. It's a shame that one always misses the loveliest part of the day.

Last Monday afternoon I went along to the Sadler's Wells Theatre where I did an audition for the opera. The ballet master said he liked my work very much and if there was a vacancy in August he would take me on. So, if Sweden doesn't materialize, I'll try and get into the opera. Cornell, bless his heart, arranged it all for me.

71. Stanley Holloway OBE (1890–1982), English stage and film actor.
72. Dame Julie Andrews (b.1935).

On Wednesday morning Miss Howes watched a class at Annas. She told me that she thought I had improved quite a lot and afterwards took me to lunch at Simpsons – and what a lunch – I certainly tucked in well. I hope that after that she'll be able to afford her passage home.

Yesterday afternoon I went with Rèna to see a film called *Count Your Blessings* starring Deborah Kerr, Maurice Chevalier and Rossa Brazzi. It was taken from Nancy Mitford's novel *The Blessing* and was very good indeed. I enjoyed it as much as I did the book.

I've been enjoying classes lately and feel I've worked hard and well. Please thank Frankie for his drawings. I just love them and whenever I look at them I get a lump in my throat. I miss you all so very, very much and sometimes the longing to be able to come home to a family each evening becomes so acute that I want to scream.

21 June 1959

I'm so happy in London and my only wish is that I could share all my experiences and happiness with you.

On Friday afternoon I went to an audition for a Western Theatre Ballet opera. At the last moment the opera was cancelled but they held the audition to spot dancers for the company should they happen to need them. I didn't feel I had a hope. Angela Rowe was there, a lot of dancers from the theatre class at the Royal Ballet School and thousands of others as well as many with beautiful bodies and faces. I thought, 'a free class – I'll enjoy it.' I gave it stick, jumped my highest and put as much into it as I could. Afterwards they told the class they could go except for three girls and two boys – a girl from the Royal Ballet second company, another who had previously been accepted into the company but refused because of an already signed contract and me. Margie, I'm so happy I could scream. Me, me, but why me? I'm not as good as Angela or the others. I don't know what to say to you because I'm going to blow my top any minute. They say they'll contact me when they have a vacancy. Even if they don't I don't care. They picked me out of about fifty good dancers and the compliment is enough in itself. That evening I met Rose and Niña at Hyde Park Corner and ran all the way up the escalators. I couldn't stop running because I was so happy. We had a sumptuous dinner with the Taylors' Khazam friends.

I bought a pair of ballet shoes on Friday morning and was given four free 16/6d tickets for the *Prodigal Wife* at the Winter Garden Theatre next Saturday night. The Gamba[73] people have been really kind to me.

On Thursday afternoon Rèna and I went to a film in Notting Hill Gate called *La Strada*. It was an Italian film with English subtitles and was really very good. The leading actress was convincing in her impersonations of a simple semi half-wit.

Tonight is midsummer's night and the sun will set at 11. It's 8.30 now and it could easily be 4. Tomorrow I'm starting to work part-time in a shop in Victoria selling lingerie. I will work there until either Malmö, the opera, or Western Theatre Ballet materializes.

Yesterday afternoon I went from class to have lunch with Rèna in her room. It was so hot we just lounged around talking. I'm sure you would like Rèna a lot. She's so intelligent, open minded and interesting. Afterwards we went and sat in Hyde Park for a while and then I left her to join Niña and a girl called Pam at Covent Garden to see *Ondine* for the last night of the season. Fonteyn and Somes[74] were dancing and I enjoyed it very much. We saw Pam Minty, Angela Rowe and Pat Power there.

On Tuesday evening Gwen Harris is having a cocktail party to which she has invited me. There's a very nice French girl called Marianne who comes to Annas and she is sharing with Mary Jane. Marianne and I quite often go to the park together after class. She's a very talented dancer and such a nice girl too. I practise my French on her but unfortunately her English improves more rapidly than my French does and now our conversations make more sense in English.

Last Sunday, Rose's cousin Dave took Rose, Niña and me to Maidenhead for the day. Maidenhead is a little country village west of London on the Thames and we spent a whole day on the river in a rowing boat. The weather was lovely and all we did was lie in the boat, which Dave rowed, ate and admired the lovely scenery. We had a good laugh

73. Gamba is a maker of ballet shoes, so presumably Selina is referring to the shop that sold them.
74. Michael Somes (1917–1994) principal dancer of the Royal Ballet and frequent partner of Margot Fonteyn.

though when Rose fell in. We all took a turn at rowing with Dave. Niña was most heroic and rowed superbly. Dave said my rowing had good style, but unfortunately the boat drifted backwards with the current when I did it. Rose put a lot of vigour into it but made no headway whatsoever. Dave was putting more and more energy into his oar as was Rose until we realized that she was rowing the wrong way around and so counteracting Dave's efforts. Dave's brother John then turned up so we were relieved of our tiresome task. Oh, but what a lovely day we had!

Margie, thank you so much for the lovely cake. It arrived safely and was delicious; in fact the nicest fruit cake ever. I suppose you can gather from the past tense that the cake is now a pleasant memory. We had the remainder for tea this afternoon. Moira Durno sent me a tin of shortbread biscuits. She is so kind and sweet to me, which I find somewhat odd because she's never even met me. Georgie has gone to Paris with John [Molteno] for the weekend. I tried to contact him at St Ermine's Hotel before he left, but I was too late. I don't think he would have liked to have seen me though as he must be very busy with meetings.

Rose and Niña leave for the continent in July sometime and Rose returns to South Africa in August. Niña then goes to Norway. While they are on the continent I'll try and get Rèna, Amelia or someone to stay with me as a guest for a couple of weeks and if I don't go to Sweden I'll get a room nearer London. I'd like to share a double bedsitter with Rèna if possible, but I'll see to that when the time comes.

We're still waiting for Mr Kruuse from Malmö. He's due any minute now but whether he'll take me or not, I can't tell you. I got the job in the shop because, although a job seems likely to materialize some time, I would like to have a little money to live on between engagements in the future. Every dancer has to face periods of unemployment and I might as well save as much as I can for them. I think it's nice to have a little to fall back on if necessary.

I spent today lounging around at home playing cards, listening to the wireless and reading *Women* magazines. They keep playing terrific tunes on the wireless. 'I Can't Stop Itching'. Now they're playing 'You've Got Uh! Personality'. It's fantastic and all my spelling mistakes and grammatical errors can be put down to 'being sent'. Right now they're playing 'Don't Throw Bouquets at Me, People Will Say We're in Love'.

I'm glad you like staying at Marlow. Have you made any plans for when Miss Howes comes back to South Africa, or will you be going back to Foxwold? How are Kulu and Apa? Do give them both my love and say that I'll be writing to them soon.

Friday 26 June 1959 (to father, Peter)

Today is a very special day. It's Friday 26 June and this morning I signed my first contract for a post as ballet dancer at the Malmö Stadsteater from 1 September 1959 to 30 April 1960 with a possible extension to the 15 May for touring Sweden. I will be paid 550 krone a week (approximately £10) tax free. Return journey London–Malmö paid by Malmö Stadtsteater.

My contract starts by saying – 'Föreningen Malmö Stadtsteater u.p.a. (har nedan kallad teatern) anställer härmed Miss Selina Molteno (har nedan kallad den anstallde) såson DANCER vid teatern på foljande vilkor.' Doesn't it sound gorgeous? Mr Kruuse came to watch classes and, after seeing me once, said he would engage me. He took me to coffee three times, told me all about Malmö and the third time I signed the contract. So far I'm the only one he has picked, so I feel honoured to be his first choice. Mr Kruuse is an extremely nice decent man and his wife is very nice as well. He was pleased when I said that my cousin was marrying a Lewenhaupt. He says that they are charming, rich and refined people. He said that he would be pleased if you would write to him, acknowledging that you are aware of my movements and that you are pleased I have got the job. Just write a nice friendly letter to him as he's extremely nice, eager to please you and has been very good to me, and I'm sure will be in the future.

Anna Northcote has been wonderful and it is through her really that I've got this job. She's so kind, fair and sincere and doesn't flash around diamond tiaras and the right people. She's so nice and uncomplicated and I know that under her tuition my work has improved a lot.

Mr Kruuse says I can go to Malmö either by boat to Gothenburg and then by train down through Sweden to Malmö; or by boat to Denmark, train to Copenhagen and then ferry to Malmö. Which way do you think is best? What do you think I should do about my money? Should I transfer about £20 to Malmö and leave the rest in London on fixed deposit, or is it best to have it all in Malmö. I thought that I might lose a bit by transferring back and forth in and out of krone. Perhaps it's best to have a current account in Malmö only. Do let me have your advice on the subject? Mr Kruuse's address is Mr Carl Gustav Kruuse, c/o Malmö Stadsteater, Malmö, Sweden. I'm so happy and excited.

29 June 1959 (to Cecily Robinson)

Thank you for your letter. It was super hearing from you and, by the way, 'congratulations', you never told me that the *Pink Lemonade* had been written for you. Miss Robinson,[75] you're so modest. You make me feel ashamed of myself because this letter's going to be one big swank.

Oh, Miss Robinson, I've got a job in Sweden. I've already signed an eight-month contract and I'm so terribly thrilled. At the moment I'm spending the day in bed with a sore throat and cold and I'm not surprised. The excitement at No. 2 has been such that I haven't slept a wink for a week and now that I've finally signed the contract I just have to relax. Oh, Miss Robinson, it's wonderful. I can hardly get it all out I'm so excited. Now just let me calm down and tell you properly. First of all what it is and then how I got it. I have got a job as a dancer at the Stadsteater, Malmö, in Sweden. Malmö is a university town on the west coast of Sweden directly opposite Copenhagen. They have a beautiful theatre there and produce not only straight ballets but also operas, operettas and musicals. They give a class in the beautiful theatre rehearsal room every morning and shows in the evenings and of course some matinées.

Instead of Sundays we have every Tuesday free and for a few shillings one can go across to Copenhagen in a ferry in under an hour. I will be paid £10 a week in kroner and they provide shoes and other theatrical requirements. They will fix me up with digs and pay for my passage there and back. Mr Kruuse, the maître de ballet, says I can

---

75. Cecily Robinson (1916–2003) was an inspiring ballet teacher in Cape Town with a strong interest in Spanish dance.

Malmö Stadsteater (Municipal Theatre) in 1959.

book my own passage and go either through Denmark or down through Sweden. The contract can be extended until 13 May for an optional tour of Scandinavia with another company. Although both the Sadler's Wells Opera and Western Theatre Ballet said they'd take me when their next vacancy occurred, they are both uncertain and I think that eight months' experience abroad is always beneficial and after all a wonderful way of seeing the world.

I feel so happy as so many people wanted the job. Clive Hicks is interested in going so perhaps he'll come as well. He wants to take four girls but has not yet chosen the other three. However, all of those who are trying are very nice and I'm sure we will have a lot of fun together. I am doing classes with Anna and adore them and it's through her that I got the job.

Mr Kruuse had written to ask for girls and it was she who recommended me to him. He then came to London with a view to selecting dancers by watching them in classes. Before I signed the contract he asked me to show him some character and modern. I threw myself into a czardas, mazurka and jota and, when I showed him my Antonio farruca, he started to laugh. I did the kwela for modern. He said that I was versatile and could adjust to different things, so he gave me the contract. I saw Irene [Siegfried], Deanna [Blacher], Cornell [Senekal], Angela [Rowe] and Pam [Minty] yesterday.

Irene leaves on Friday and Deanne, who is looking happy and poised, has a lovely room in South Kensington. Brigitte goes to Canada quite soon and Niña is going to Norway.

3 July 1959

I've just got half an hour to kill before working in the shop so I thought this would be a good opportunity to start writing to you. The mad, unbounded excitement about Sweden has passed and now I'm happy and contentedly looking forward to it and will try and make the most of my next two months here. Although I'm honoured to have been the only girl picked, I'm also disappointed as I'll probably be the only English girl there, but quite a nice boy, John Massey is going too.

I've bought a *Teach Yourself Swedish* book and, with the help of Niña's Norwegian, am getting on famously. I study in the tube and in the evenings if I'm home and find it interesting, absorbing and fun. After nine months of living in Sweden I should be fairly fluent by the end. Once I have mastered Swedish, Norwegian and Danish apparently come quite easily. What an opportunity I have been given, but it tears my heart to see the row of disappointed faces of the other girls.

This morning I got a postcard of congratulations from Miss Howes and she seems thrilled about it. I don't much like working in a lingerie shop but the hours are good, it's relaxing and Mr Felton is kind and interested in my welfare. I get £3.10 a week and feel that I should try and stick it out till the end of the month anyway. After that, for a month before I leave, I'll do the shows and galleries flat out so that I've at least got something out of my six months here. I am seeing shows all the time and every weekend and on some week nights I go out and see or do something of interest.

Last Tuesday night Gwen Harris's nephew Nigel Marsh took me to a very good French film called *Mon Oncle*. You really must see it if it comes to Cape Town because it's very funny and superbly acted. It has got English subtitles. I'm going out with Nigel again on Monday night and on Saturday afternoon Josephine [Molteno] is coming to visit us.

This morning there was a shocking holdup with the tubes, so I was so late for class that I missed it altogether. Instead, I went to Dolcis and bought myself a pair of walking shoes – a nice plain cream shoe with a medium heel and pointed toe. The newest line is a point with a square on the end, but I'm not madly keen on them just yet. I would like to send you a pair of special stockings they have in our shop. They are rejects and are selling for 6/11 instead of 14/6d. They are called Taylorwood Lifelons and are supposed to last about six months. I'll send you a pair and do let me know how you like them, and if you do perhaps we can stock up the family. I haven't tried them yet, but Rose's haven't laddered at all and the customers rave about them. The only thing is, they are not terribly thin and also have a seam, but they are quite thin enough for everyday wear.

Josephine is coming to stay in the flat with me when Rose and Niña go to the continent and if she doesn't then Rèna will. In fact Rèna will in any case. Yesterday I went to the bank to cash a cheque and who should I bump into but my Bloemfontein hostess, Mrs Hart. She's been touring the world and seemed full of the joys of spring.

Lately, I've been doing very nice classes with Anna Northcote and she says I've improved and I feel I have. I hope Anna isn't cross about the delay of her present; I sent it off yesterday so she should be getting it in a couple of weeks' time. I personally think it's charming, so I hope she does too. I won't say what it is because I want it to be a surprise.

The temptation in Denmark is going to be terrific. I can just imagine ogling Danish tea sets and so forth, because I know how much you love Scandinavian things. Have you had any luck with selling my motorbike? I could do with that little extra cash.

Up until this week we've had lovely summer weather, but it's awful again now – worst luck.

After Work
Thank God that's over. I've just coped with a smelly old woman who said she wanted a pair of pants, but just for convenience. I had to go out because I couldn't control my mirth.

I was rather hoping I would get the sack, but no such luck. I was promoted to Mayfair (Berkeley Square) instead – quite fun though to mix with the high class. Mr Felton wants me to become first class he says, but unfortunately I have no such ambitions.

Miss Nathan, the head of the Victoria branch tells me I'm such a clever girl to tear up some old dockets and throw them away. 'Now that's a really good job done,' she says with a sickly grin on her face. I know I'm horrible, but it irritates me. Anyway, she gave me time off to go to a travel agency and find out about the fare to Malmö. It's £10.6s.6d through Copenhagen and about £14 through Sweden from Gothenburg. Apparently, the latter is nicer because you spend two days at sea instead of one and I believe that the Swedish boats are out of this world.

I'm writing this letter in the tube from St James's Park to Richmond and there's a funny man sitting opposite me. Every time I look up he tries to catch my eye, so I guess I'd better keep looking down.

I suppose you know there's a printing strike on in London and the papers are getting thinner and thinner. Next week we may not have any at all. I walked past a newspaper seller this morning and instead of yelling 'Evening Standard,' he said, 'Buy now and take home to put in the freezer; you won't get any next week!' I'm crazy about the cockneys – they've got tremendous character. The printers use up all the printing ink by telling us that it's all getting used up. Silly isn't it?

We're at Hammersmith now and a whole lot more people are getting in. 'Heave ho! – can't any more squeeze in? That's not a nice armpit to have in your face.' It's not too bad now though because I got off work late and the worst of the rush hour is over.

Today a woman came into the shop with a dog like Crackers. It didn't have any hair and shivered all the time. When she walked to the other counter she pulled the lead and the dog slid across the floor on all fours. Ugh! I was nearly sick. You know Marg, when Miss Nathan was out, I tried on a pair of Lifelon stockings and they are all too short for me in the leg, so I don't think it will be worth getting them. Sorry if I raised your hopes, but any stocking will go if it's too short and has continuous pressure from the suspender.

Next weekend I am going to the coast to stay with Nigel's parents and there's going to be a party. We're at Kew Gardens now, so I'd better pack this away because I get off at the next stop. I'll finish off at home.

What a wonderful joy it is to have a radio in the flat. I'm quite, quite sure that my life wouldn't be half as enjoyable without it.

Last Sunday night we went to a wonderful concert at Festival Hall. It was Mendelssohn, Mozart and Beethoven. Before the concert we went to St Paul's and the Tower of London and then we had tea with Deanna Blacher. Cornell [Senekal], Angela [Rowe], Pam [Minty] and Irene [Siegfried] were there as well and we had a super time. Irene left for America today for five weeks.

Poor Rose, I think she feels rather sick about going back to South Africa when we are all trotting off to new exciting countries. Niña and I will be quite close together so we are going to try and meet for Xmas and at various times. I'd better end off now. I'll let you know about Mrs Knight as soon as I can get hold of Brigitte but she's away at the moment. She's going to go to Canada quite soon. Write soon please. I hope you've all recovered from flu.

13 July 1959

How nice it was to get such a flood of letters from home last week and thank you so much for that gorgeous parcel – the food is wonderful and the blouse charming. Rose and Niña have gone onto the continent; they left this morning before I arrived back from Kent and so now I have the flat to myself for the next ten days. Josephine was going to come and stay with me but instead she's got a job picking cherries in Kent. I may ask Rèna to come if I get lonely, but I don't think I will. Georgie's coming to spend next weekend with me and on Friday I'm going up to Aylesbury to meet her. I've been given two weeks' vacation from my job and will be back at the beginning of August for a few weeks before finally quitting.

I'll use these two weeks to book my passage and generally settle my affairs for Sweden. I spent the weekend with Brigitte in Bexley. It was lovely. We went out on Friday evening from Charing Cross and as Dr and Mrs Knight are on the continent we had the whole flat to ourselves. On Friday evening we made supper, watched television and then went to bed; on Saturday morning, we went to the hairdresser and then after lunch went for a long walk across the fields. The weather was nippy and fresh and it was gorgeous. That evening we went to a film in Bexley and on Sunday we got up at four o'clock when we had lunch. After lunch we went for another walk, this time in the opposite direction. We went to bed quite early on Sunday because this morning we had to get up at 6.30 to catch the early train to London.

The weekend was such a wonderful change and it was super being with Brigitte again. I'm afraid Mrs Knight is coming back to South Africa very soon, so I'm afraid that renting her house will be out of the question.

Thursday 15 July 1959

I'm thoroughly enjoying being in the flat alone as I've been so busy, and having the flat to oneself for a while is wonderful. On Monday after class Cornell and I went to see *Mon Oncle* again. It really is such a good film and before it we ate our lunch on a bench in Soho Square. After the film Cornell came to Richmond and had supper with me and we spent a pleasant evening, believe it or not, playing cards. I'm still fond of my cards with the *Pendennis Castle* on the backs and occasionally take them out and have a good game.

On Tuesday I booked my passage to Sweden. I leave St Pancras station by the boat train, Swedish Lloyd Special at 3.00 p.m. on Saturday 29 August. The train takes us to Tilbury where I will leave on the *Suecia* at 5.30 p.m. The crossing takes two nights and one day and I arrive in Gothenburg at 6.00 a.m. on the morning of the 31st. I catch a train from Gothenburg at 1.31 p.m. and arrive in Malmö four hours later (5.31 p.m.). I'll have about seven hours to kill in Gothenburg so am waiting patiently for addresses of eligible parasite bearers! How about it? I already have Marina's address and am going to write to Penelope Molteno and tell her a long sob story about 'poor little me, only 18, going to Malmö all alone for nine months, and I don't know a soul.' I'll go on to suggest that 'surely your husband will know a few people I can contact there and I do hope you have a LOVELY wedding.' She'll have a conscience about not inviting me I'm sure, so will probably make a meagre effort. After all, the more Swedish counts the merrier. After I booked my passage I went to a huge toy shop in Regent Street and bought Frankie his birthday present and in the evening had dinner with Nancy Cartwright.[76]

Friday 16 July

Oh dear! I've got so bad about writing letters, but it's just not letter writing weather. It's about 6.15 in the evening and I'm sitting on our scruffy little lawn all alone in my blue and white striped sun frock in my red apron and bare feet writing to you and baking in the sun. I spent today alone and spring cleaned the kitchen and bathroom – the other two rooms are a mess, but I'm sick of housework at the moment. I don't feel like writing either but I dare say I'd better do something. I've been doing and going to so much lately that I can't possibly recall it all and London at the moment is so hot that I haven't worn a jersey for days – not even when I'm outside in the middle of the night.

I've been out with quite a lot of different people lately, but none has been particularly inspiring. The nicest were a group of Germans but they've all gone off to Scotland.

Gwen Harris's 25 year-old nephew seems to have taken a shine to me but I don't find him at all attractive, which makes me feel rather guilty, for I don't want to be unkind to him. I went up to Aylesbury on Friday and Hartwell House is lovely. The grounds are out of this world. I saw Susan Little[77] there. Yesterday John [Molteno] took us all over the place. We saw *Mon Oncle* (for the third time) and in the evening dinner at Simpsons and afterwards *Irma La Douce* (for the second time) – I adored it. Georgie left for Windsor this morning with John. I met Pippy Eriksen[78] in a café yesterday. She was with Trish Dennisten.[79] I've only got a few more weeks in London. I do love it so much.

---

76. Nancy Cartwright was one of Selina's godmothers.
77. Susan Little had been a neighbour in Rowan Avenue and she and the Molteno children played together. She went to Hartwell House with Georgie and later married a naval officer.
78. Daughter of Pam and Sven Eriksen from Elgin.
79. Trish Dennisten was one of the group of young women Selina knew from Elgin, where the Moltenos farmed apples.

John Gilpin[80] was in class on Friday. On Thursday evening I went out with Amelia and Maryam.[81] We saw *How Say You*. It was an excellent play and the next morning the leading actress came to Anna's studio to do an actresses' limbering class with some man or other and I had quite a long chat with her.

Amelia and Maryam are spending Tuesday night with me in the flat.

I haven't the foggiest idea what sort of parts I'll get in Malmö, but I won't get solos because they have their resident principals. The boy he was taking is going to dance in his other Stadsteater in Gothenburg.

22 July 1959

Life is fine. In fact I'm terribly happy and the only thing that saddens me is that soon I'll have to leave London and I do love it – in fact I adore it. The thrill has never worn off; it just gets more and more intense and sometimes I feel as if I'm going to burst. I've never enjoyed working as much as I do with Anna and every day I look forward to class – a good clean slog with no nastiness, no unpleasantness. Everyone comes there to do a class and no one worries about who's childish, who's fat, who's thin and Anna is fair, fierce and sincere. Everyone adores her and I'm no exception.

Yesterday Rèna and Juliette came to collect me at Anna's class. We ate some cartons of yoghurt on a bench in Soho Square with Cornell, before going on to see a comedy called *The Grass is Greener*. I was rather disappointed considering it had been given such a boost, but it was quite funny. Afterwards Rèna came back with me and we prepared ravioli for ourselves and Amelia who turned up soon afterwards. Now that I'm in the flat alone it's spotless. Rose and Niña have no home pride and don't mind a mess, but I do. I've removed all the bits of fern and ornaments and the flat's now looking fairly respectable.

I loved having Rèna and Amelia with me last night and, to top it all, a friend called John called round and took us all off to a little pub for a lime juice.

80. John Gilpin (1930–1983) was a leading dancer with Festival Ballet (now English National).
81. Maryam was presumably a friend of Amelia's.

Thursday 23 July

Last night John took me to see *South Pacific*, which was rather Americanized but striking and the music was gorgeous. Afterwards we had dinner in a restaurant in Soho. When I arrived home I found that Rose and Niña had returned from the continent. They had had a lovely ten days, so were full of beans and enthusiasm.

The glamorous film actor David Knight[82] came to the actors' physical jerks class at Anna's studio this morning. I do so enjoy bumping into celebrities. After class this morning Cornell and I met Rèna and the three of us went to a café for a chat and iced coffee. After that Rèna and I lounged around London and chatted. She's going to go to Paris for three weeks from 7 August. Cornell is also going there for a holiday.

Saturday 25 July

At the moment I'm sitting on the swing seat in the Marshes orchard. The weather is lovely and I've at last seen the English seaside. Not quite the same as ours but a wonderful change from London. I came down yesterday afternoon in a semi coma as London was unbearably hot and I had a hangover from the night before when I'd gone out with Tony.

Last night I went to bed straight after supper and slept for 11 hours non-stop. It's wonderful to be able to have as much as you like to eat without thinking, 'well I'd better have that because it's cheaper.' Mrs Marsh is very sweet and kind but dotes rather on Nigel. I think she's trying to pair me off with him, for she tactfully disappears all the time, which amuses me, though I couldn't be less interested in him. Nigel is so terribly English though that I am sure he'd run a mile if I said 'boo'!

I've had my first swim in the English Channel, which was beautifully warm and have also been to the club where I met quite a few people. The only trouble is that I don't feel I can escape from Nigel

---

82. David Knight (1928–2020) was an American-born actor of the London stage and British cinema during the 1950s, but who later focused solely on theatre work in the USA.

when I'm staying in his house. However, I'm feeling rather smug because I cured his grandmother of diarrhoea with burnt brandy.

Did you know that John Molteno is in hospital in Windsor? I don't know what's wrong with him but Georgie says she thinks it's what his father died of. I have an idea it was pneumonia. If that's the case there isn't much cause to worry nowadays.

I met a very nice Swedish girl on the beach and she gave me a lesson. She leaves for Sweden on the boat before mine. What a shame as she really is awfully nice.

Sunday 26 July

It's Sunday morning and I feel a wreck. Last night we went to a few pubs and then on to a club to dance. The evening would have been wonderful if I'd gone with someone a little more inspiring than Nigel. The worst thing about it is that he and his mother always call each other 'dear' and are hyper super polite. It irritates me. Anyway, the weather is wonderful, so until next time.

25 July 1959 (to Anthony)

I wish you'd learn to type as I have such a struggle deciphering your letters. Anyway, when I finally do I enjoy them very much and appreciate that you show some interest in the welfare of your little sister all alone in this big world. Don't worry, I adore it. At the moment I'm spending the weekend in Sussex recovering from all my late nights.

Guess what, I'm the only blancmange in London. Everyone else has a tan and it makes me sick. This summer is the best they have had here in ten years and it is just as hot as ours. I've got four more weeks in London and it's going to break my heart to leave.

Anthony, London is super, and terribly exciting, so whatever happens don't ever, ever turn down an opportunity to come here. A lot of the English of course are bores, but London is full of foreigners and has that wonderful cosmopolitan atmosphere. Niña and Rose have just spent ten days on the continent and seemed to have had a nice time. They went on a coach tour, which personally I'd hate. Did Martin get his ice-cream in hospital and how did he react to having his tonsils out?

Selina, Anthony, Annabel, Vicky and Sigurd (dog) at Rowan House c.1948.

Saturday 1 August 1959

Josephine spent the last two nights with me before departing for Norway this morning. She appeared out of the blue from Kent and the other night I came home to find her sitting on the floor writing letters. We brewed coffee and talked and laughed for hours. We had hysterics about the people of Kent and their weird way of talking. 'Shut your cake hole or I'll bash your brain box in and use your guts for garters.' Charming, isn't it? I saw her off at Victoria this morning and her case was so heavy that the two of us tottered to the station dropping it every few steps. The first night she stayed here Niña and Rose were still here so we had to share my little bed. I slept like a log but I have my doubts about whether she did. This afternoon I thought I'd do all my washing so with a lot of effort I lugged it along to the Bendix, only to find it closed for the August bank holiday. I was mad because now I'll have to do it all by hand as Saturday afternoon is the only time I can go along, and next Saturday I'll be in Sussex.

Monday 3 August 1959

Today was a public holiday and I spent it with Rèna. I adore that girl and we had a super time. We made lunch in her room and then in the late afternoon went to the Queensway cinema to see *Ferry to Hong Kong*. I enjoyed it very much.

4 August 1959 (to Martin)

Happy birthday, happy birthday, happy birthday. You never thought that when you turned nine you wouldn't have any tonsils, did you? Well, I've remembered your birthday and haven't forgotten to send you a present either. But you have to be patient for that because it has to come a long way and is inclined to take a long time too. Don't worry though, you'll get it. Just remember that it's coming and I've already sent it. What is it? Never you mind. You can just wait to see. Has Frankie got his yet? He should have by now.

Ask Peter to send you over to me for a few weeks. There's such a lot I want to show you and I promise I'll look after you very well; and won't even make you go to school. I've only got three more weeks in London and then I go to Sweden. Oh gomma man I'm nips! How about another letter or have you forgotten your favourite sister? Be good. No don't – be naughty.

Thursday 6 August 1959

Let me start by telling you about last night, which I spent with Brigitte, who is working in a travel agency just near where I am working in Berkeley Square. Well, she came and collected me at 5.30 and it was so super to see her as I haven't seen her since Kent. Together we walked along to the Piccadilly Lyons Corner House. Oh! How I enjoy London at that time and at this time of year. The streets are full of hurdy-gurdies grinding out tunes, street singers, violinists and the most fascinating road stands where you can buy 'wimpies' (like hamburgers with onion, tomato sauce and mustard), lovely ice creams, toys, fruit and all sorts of fascinating things. On the way we passed a man selling toy monkeys and I got one for Frankie. I'll send it off some time. We finally got ourselves to Lyons and with a lot of effort pushed our way through the crowds and into the café, which as usual was choc a bloc full of every conceivable type of person under the sun. We then stood as close as possible to two people who looked as if they were nearly finished and as soon as they got up to leave we pounced on their seats and had the traditional 'Lyons supper' – a wimpy and a whispy. A whispy is a divine sort of milkshake.

After that we went along to Leicester Square where we got tickets to go and see *The Nun's Story*. While we were waiting for the film to start we went and sat in the square, which we did in a similar way to acquiring our seats in Lyons. We walked round and round the square until one of the benches acquired a vacant spot.

At seven o'clock we went along to the theatre and for an hour before the film started, instead of having news reels, there was just a concert, which was lovely. The film was wonderful and afterwards when we came out into the square we walked into someone playing a squash box, which naturally took our attention for a couple of minutes and then when we looked round we noticed a huge crowd congregating outside the Empire. Naturally we burrowed our way to the front and who should get into a car right next to us but Jayne Mansfield.[83] I stood about two foot from her. We then walked back to Piccadilly Circus and caught our respective trains home.

I've quite enjoyed working in the shop today because there's a hurdy gurdy playing outside and it is rather divine. Today I had lunch with Brigitte. This morning I went to the dentist, which was free because I am under 21, but as usual there was nothing wrong.

83. Jayne Mansfield (1933–1967) was an American film star and major Hollywood sex symbol of the 1950s and 1960s who was tragically killed in a traffic accident at the age of 34.

On Tuesday evening Rèna and I had our farewell outing and we went to see a very good film called *The Complacent Lover* with Ralph Richardson in the lead. We could only get standing room for 2/6d as the 4/6d had gone, but fortunately we ended up in the front row of the dress circle due to the generosity of the charming French usherette. Rèna left for Paris at 9.30 this morning and she gave me a lovely purse. I gave her a Blue Grass cologne stick. When she comes back I will be in Sweden so I probably won't see her again for at least nine months.

Hoorah! Fame at last. Buy the August edition of the *Dancing Times* and see for yourself. Scan it carefully and somewhere towards the end you will see my name in bold print. I think it is page 563 but I'm not sure. On Sunday John came round and took me to London airport and from there down to Windsor, which incidentally is gorgeous. We saw Windsor Castle, Eton College, the long mile to Ascot and Ascot – in fact the lot. We had dinner at a very olde restaurant called Nell Gwynne House and on our way back again we popped into the aerodrome to see it all by night. People were waiting to leave to all parts of the world and planes come in and go out literally the whole time. Tomorrow evening I'm going to Sussex for the weekend again. I only hope that I don't brain Nigel before the end of it as he irritates me so intensely. The other day Miss Howes drifted into the shop and we had a chat. Did I tell you that John took me to Festival Ballet, which was super? We saw *Napoli*, *London Morning* and *Graduation Ball*. Must fly now so that I can post this tonight.

Sunday 9 August 1959 (from Middleton-on-Sea, Sussex)

I'm spending this delightful weekend in Sussex and, except for Nigel, I've enjoyed it immensely. We came down by train from Victoria on Friday evening and as it was so full we had to sit on a bucket in the guards' van for about half the way. Then we went into the saloon where we had refreshments and drinks. We arrived at Bognor Regis station at about seven o'clock where Mrs Marsh met us.

That night there was a formal dance, so after a quick bite I retired to my room to prepare for this very special occasion – Mike Webb's twenty-first birthday party. The Webbs are fabulously rich and Mike has got three cars of his own, went to the Sorbonne and wears a beard for effect. Anyway, it was a lovely evening and the dance took place in the garden where they had a dance floor rigged up under an open tent, a divine band, out of this world food and an unlimited supply of liquor and cigarettes, neither of which I indulged in to excess.

I had one problem though – NIGEL – he's like a boomerang. There was lots of talent around and, for some extraordinary reason, it decided to hook itself onto me, which I can assure you put me in my element. There was one especially nice chap there called Mike Britten who's just returned from Cannes because his father's just died, but unfortunately he's one of Nigel's best friends, which made things rather awkward. At one stage during the evening we felt we had to escape so we made a quick retreat and bolted. Nigel wasn't staring into space after all and immediately appeared on the scene and had a rittletit. I was furious because after all one doesn't go to a party to sit next to the drip who happens to bring you. After that I danced with practically every man there, including Mike and Nigel. We laughed and joked and people were continually asking questions about Africa. I told them all sorts of tall tales, which they believed, and had a wonderful time. I said we rode ostriches, which in fact was the only tall story, and then I told them about how one became expert at catching fleas. They were disgusted and said that to them fleas were worse than bed bugs. The party finished at 4.30 and with a chap like Nigel what else can one do but insist on going home. Shame, I really am rather awful to him but he is so boring. His mother is the same and all they can talk about is what the neighbours are doing, and all they do as far as I can gather is eat and swim. They also go into raptures over the weather report, which is so silly because we can quite easily turn our heads and see that there is a slight glare in spite of the fact that the sky is covered with a layer of cloud of the medium grey type. Anyway, it was a good party and the next day I swam in the afternoon and went to another party that night. It was held in a huge barn and was good fun. This time Nigel didn't hold me on a lead, so I had a good time and met quite a few people, including Charlie Kunz's[84] son, who is a very nice chap. Today I've done blow all. I'd better go and have tea now as it's past 4.30.

84. Charlie Kunz (1896–1958) was an American-born British musician popular during the British dance band era.

Monday 10 August

I'm sitting in the shop and, although it's been raining, it's unbearably hot. I had lunch with Brigitte this afternoon and will meet her again after work this evening. After tea yesterday afternoon I went for a swim and then in the evening caught a train back to Victoria. John popped in to see me when I'd arrived home. This morning my official contract arrived by post and so has my ticket to Sweden and two labels. I suppose I'll have to cut them into tiny pieces so that each piece of luggage can have some labels. We are all beginning to sort out and think about packing as Niña leaves this Saturday. We are giving a farewell party on Friday night.

I'm giving myself a short holiday from classes and will throw myself back into it next Monday so that I'll be fresh and working well when I go to Sweden. I'll spend this week more or less preparing to go. Georgie is coming to stay with us in a couple of days' time and as far as I can gather so are fifty other people. It's good fun though, even although I always have to give up my mattress and sleep on the springs. Work at the moment is very slack, but I enjoy watching people walking past the window. The landlord wants to throw me out of the flat on the 20th. He's welcome if he wants to pay for a room for me in a West End hotel.

15 August 1959

You break my heart because you are such a bad correspondent. I'd better lay off and continue when I'm feeling in a better mood. I'm going to Lensbury[85] for the afternoon and so will try to get a letter to you when I come back. I've been leading a gay, hilarious life, so will have lots to tell you.

19 August

I'm sitting in bed as I've just woken up and I'll try and make an effort to finish this time. This minute I've just received a letter from Penelope Molteno and it's made me very happy. I'll copy it out for you.

---

85. Lensbury is a sports, leisure and social facility in Teddington for Shell employees.

What a surprise it was to get your letter and to hear that you are going to Malmö where my fiancé works, and which is only a few miles from where I am going to live after my marriage in September! You must come and visit us often, as I shall be only too delighted to talk English as my Swedish is non-existent, although I have been trying to learn with the aid of linguaphone records. You'll probably pick it up much quicker than I will, as I find it awfully difficult.

Congratulations on getting the job at Malmö. Do you know where you will be living, i.e. have you got an address where Claes[86] can contact you? I'll write to him and perhaps he could meet you at the ship, or at any rate arrange something with you. Is the name of the ship Suecia or Snecia I can't read what you have written? Please write and tell me your address, if you have one, so that I can tell him. He will be coming over here about the 6th or 7th I think, as we get married on the 9th. Then we will be back in Sweden about the 23rd or 24th.

I'm so glad you wrote to me – we certainly must get together. I shall be living in the tiniest house you ever saw, but you will be very welcome!

I was thrilled to get it and I hope you are too. At last we've got the flat and landlord sorted. On the Tuesday before I leave I will move across the road and stay as a guest with Mr Christian's blind brother and his wife and they will put me up AND feed me free of charge. John has offered to get my luggage to St Pancras for me, which will make it so much easier than trying it get it there by train and taxi.

Last Friday night we gave our farewell party and it was a great success. We had lots of rolls with cheese and sausages and gallons of

---

86. Penelope Molteno married Claes Henrik Graf Lewenhaupt in 1959. He was a Swedish aristocrat and had to get permission from the king to marry a commoner. They were living in Malmö at the time but moved to Stockholm when his father died. They had a son who was killed in a tractor accident in Germany as a very young man and a daughter with Down's syndrome. Selina became close to them in Sweden.

punch. We danced, sang, and generally had a *lekker* time. That night, our flat was full of female corpses and the next morning Neil took us all down to Victoria station to see Niña off. She's gone to Paris, Madrid and then on to Norway for a couple of years perhaps.

After seeing her off a very nice South African girl called Sylvia and I went to Soho to snoop around. We found a divine little antique curio shop and browsed around for ages. After that we went to a wonderful film called *The Seven Wonders of the World*. It was fascinating and we both enjoyed it very much.

On Sunday afternoon we went to the boys' flat and a crowd of us went to Lensbury. The boys swam in the Thames but we reckoned it looked rather grim and afterwards shocked this frightfully high-class club by letting our hair down and playing rounders. What fun we had! We then went back to their flat and Roger and I produced the supper. It was divine – spaghetti *à la* little bit of everything and red wine. We had hysterics in the kitchen as it was both Roger's and my first effort with spaghetti and we kept losing worms when we were testing for flavour. One would keep watch while the other rescued portions of the supper from under the stove. After supper the others washed up so Roger and I danced for a few hours and then he brought me home in his younger brother Peter's (who lives in the flat) car. It was such a ramshackle old jalopy that I'm surprised it made the journey.

Last night I went out with Mike Britten, whom I had met in Sussex and what an evening we had! First we went to a little underground pub for a lime juice and after that we went to an excellent play in the Haymarket called *The Pleasure of His Company*. Afterwards Mike said he would take me to a night club called the Blue Angel, so we set off and walked there. On our arrival, we went down miles of steps and finally arrived in this divine underground night club. It was beautifully done out and we were served scampi followed by a juicy tender steak. We danced to a fabulous Negro[87] band and at about 2.0 there was a cabaret. It started with a blonde girl in a frock covered in sequins

---

87. I have retained Selina's original descriptor 'Negro', as it did not carry a negative connotation at the time.

singing and playing the guitar. She was South African and among other things sang *Sarie Marais* and *Daar Kom die Alabama*; you've no idea what a thrill it gave me to hear them. We left the club at about 3.15 and walked to Waterloo, which is quite a long way. We got there at about 4 and then Mike and I parted company. I crawled into the train and went to sleep as the train only left for Richmond at 5.20. No sooner had I lost consciousness when a bobby came along and said 'what are you doing here?' I said, 'sleeping, are you going to arrest me?' 'Me arrest a young girl like you, never, but you are committing a criminal offence.' I said, 'surely sleeping isn't an offence.' 'Ah yes,' he answered, 'but you've got your feet on the seat.' After that we chatted until the train left. When I got home it was six o'clock and already quite light.

G.B. Wilson, the chap who gave me my write up in the *Dancing Times* is arranging for me to meet someone from Malmö today. Goodie, goodie, gumdrops.

By the way, what's your new address? I've been waiting to get a letter but no such luck so I hope Miss Howes gets this to you. Rose leaves tomorrow and so chaos reigns. Georgie may come and stay with me when she goes. I met Mr and Mrs Serrurier in the tube.

I've told Nigel to vamoose and he has got my Swedish book so my progress has become somewhat stilted!

23 August 1959 (from Highbourne House, Marylebone High Street, W1)

I've come to the conclusion that the searing gap I left has now filled up and so perhaps my letters are superfluous, so kindly let me know if you wish to carry on this one-sided correspondence! Anthony is my only faithful boetie so if you want to know about me, ask him. I know all about the post mortems at the mortuary, but I don't know where you live!

Anyway, at the moment I'm residing in Stella's flat as Mr Christian has virtually turfed me out of mine. Georgie is lying on the bed and looks charming in her blue and white shortie pyjamas. Rose has left for South Africa and I have now left my job. I've got one more week in England and 101 things to do in that time. I'm feeling frightened, lonely and miserable, so don't take any notice of this letter; if only, if only, if only I wasn't going alone. Anyway, I daresay I'll survive. I've done so much lately but it hasn't really meant much to me because I can't help wondering if all is well at home. Please tell me if it isn't, or if it is.

I've had dinner on a pavement, been to a couple of films, been to see Amelia, entertained Pam and Angela for lunch, attempted to find a bed among the rubble caused by Mr Christian in the flat, swum in the Thames at Lansbury, seen Brigitte and tried in vain to get my clothes cleaned, washed and sorted.

This afternoon I gave a whole lot of junk to Pam and Angela for their new flat in Chelsea (it's rather fun).

I'm tired now. Write *please* to Stadsteater, Malmö, Sweden if it's after the end of August. I'll write again when I've heard from you.

Chapter 3
Sweden

6 September 1959 (from Stadsteater, Malmö)

Well, I've arrived here at last and I don't quite know where to begin. I think it's best if I tell it to you as a story from when I left London. I spent the last few days in London with a couple living opposite us in Townshend Road and Georgie and Amelia came too. The day I left was very warm and I wore my yellow linen frock. John took me and Amelia to Soho for lunch and then on to St Pancras station from where I left. Pam, Angela, Anne Darnborough and Julian Grenville were there too and, until the train pulled out, I felt fine. Then I went and sat down in my compartment and from London to Tilbury I didn't utter a word as I was unique in the knowledge of the English language. Once I was on the boat though people began to talk to me and I had a wonderful voyage. The journey across was rough but I managed not to get sick and the food was very good indeed. The last night on board was especially good fun as it was so beautiful – the sky was full of stars and in the distance we could see the lights of Denmark twinkling on the horizon. We sat on deck, each individual wrapped in a blanket like a cocoon and sang songs to a guitar played by a young Swedish boy. Most of the people on board were Swedes, but there were quite a lot of Finns too. One Finnish boy called Matti gave me a charming pair of little drop earrings made out of wood.

When I arrived in Gothenburg there was a card waiting for me from Georg Bie and at 8 o'clock he picked me up. I can honestly say that the Bie family are the nicest people I have as yet met. They made me feel like one of them right away and I'll never forget their kindness. First, Mr Bie arranged for me to go on the evening train and then took me home to have a bath and meet his charming wife. He then had to go to the office and his wife and I painted Gothenburg red. We went on a coach tour, then to a restaurant for lunch and then in a small canoe on the river and into the harbour.

I must tell you that when I first arrived at their house Mr Bie proudly led me into the lounge and pointed at a skin hanging on the wall – 'Your father gave that to me' – he said. 'He shot it himself' and he showed me the two little holes I guess Peter cut out with the bathroom scissors. He says he shows it to all his friends and boasts about his wonderful friend from South Africa. Later that afternoon Mr Bie's daughters came home and we had supper together at their house. After that Kirsten and I went to Liseberg, which is the equivalent of the de Waal Park fete in Gothenburg but much nicer. It was beautifully done out with lights, lamps and statues and there was a funny little man who cut out your silhouette. I had mine done and am sending it to you with this letter.

After Liseberg I parted company with Kirsten and caught the bus to the station. The buses in Sweden are peculiar. They run on rails, are single storeyed and have two coaches joined together like a train. They have three doors each which open automatically – two exits and one entrance. On this bus I met two South Africans from Pretoria, which was a coincidence and they carried my luggage for me.

The overnight sleeper left at 11.00 p.m. and arrived in Malmö at 7.00 the next morning. I had a cup of coffee and waited at the station for two hours and then took a taxi to the theatre. I walked in and nobody greeted me. There were people all over the place speaking Swedish and German and I felt like a flea among a herd of elephants. Finally, an oldish man came up to me and asked me in broken English if I was for the ballet and on receiving my reply led me to Fru Necké's office and deposited me there among a crowd of babbling females – Fru Necké was on the phone so I just stood and bit my lip. When she had finished she turned to me and asked me who I was and then filled in lots of forms. Some dancers came into the office and I was introduced to them and whether they spoke to me in German or Swedish is still a mystery. I got through the morning somehow and met a Turkish girl called Dreta Kruize who said I could come and live next to her – no accommodation had been fixed up for me, so Dreta's appearance was like a star from heaven.

Claes then came to the theatre and took me and Dreta out to lunch and then to his house for supper. Claes is very nice but a little shy at first. The countryside where he stays is very beautiful and we had a terrific evening. I haven't seen him since – I think he has gone to Scotland to marry Penny.

The classes at the theatre are nice and I am sharing a solo in *Troubadore* – it's the leading jester but I don't know yet whether I'll have a chance to do it. If I don't I'll be an ordinary jester. But that means little to me – all I care about is being friendly with the people, but they just don't want to know me. I feel terribly lonely. A few can speak English but they don't want to and I'm beginning to get desperate. I feel as if there's lead in my head and it gets heavier every day. When I order things in the canteen they get irritated because my Swedish is so bad and I take so long to get a sentence out and even then they can't always understand me. They aren't a bit eager to help and I feel stupid, boring, hopeless, and only wish that something could happen to make life more pleasant. I am studying Swedish – I really am, but I can't speak yet so I dare say I'll just have to resign myself to the fact that, until I learn it, I will be ignored completely.

Without Dreta I would have died, but Dreta has a boyfriend in Malmö and though they sometimes take me with them I feel like an intruder. Anyway, the language is the first barrier and I'm determined to learn it. I can't go on like this for nine months.

On Sunday, Dreta, Bengt (Dreta's boyfriend), a friend of his called Akka and I went to Copenhagen and the moment I set foot on Danish soil I felt happy again. The atmosphere in Copenhagen is marvellous and I adore Danes – I think they are far more my type than the Swedes. We went to Tivoli[1] and had a really wonderful time. We went on all

1. Tivoli Gardens (or simply Tivoli) is a famous amusement park and pleasure garden in Copenhagen. It opened on 15 August 1843 and is the second oldest amusement park in the world after Dyrehavsbakken in nearby Klampenborg.

the various things like the train that charges down a terribly steep hill at top speed and then up an equally steep one again, through narrow tunnels and then drops down a hill in pitch darkness. It was terribly nerve racking but great fun. Tivoli was marvellous and the Danes are happy friendly people. We saw some monkeys performing and they could have been people; we saw a man do the Charleston on a tight-rope and another perform on top of a high pole, which was swinging backwards and forwards – it was wonderful. Please won't you send me the addresses in Denmark because we have a lot of free time from the theatre and I want to get to know some people?

I've sent you a couple of jam jars. I was just walking in the streets of Malmö the other day feeling terribly lonely when I saw them and just had to buy them for you – I hope you like them. There is one big one for the whole family and a smaller one for you.

7 September 1959

I've been here a week and haven't written and feel awful about it, but can assure you that there's a book on the way. I got both yours and Peter's letters – *tack så mycket* [thanks very much] – and the case of oranges in London – they were lovely. The Bies entertained me for the whole day in Gothenburg and were super. I came down on the over-night sleeper.

Claes has gone to get married. I had supper with him the first night and he is sweet. I'm the only English-speaking person in Malmö and am struggling frantically to speak Swedish. Most of the girls in the ballet speak German and can't utter two words in English. The theatre is beautiful. On Sunday I went to Copenhagen and adored it. We went to Tivoli and had a wonderful time. I have a room quite near the theatre, but have to move out at the end of the month.

I'm terribly, terribly homesick and desperately lonely. It's a terrible feeling to be out of contact with friends. I think that the Swedes on the whole are very cold and unfriendly and don't really care whether or not their friends are happy. I don't know – perhaps I'm wrong. Please write to me often because I really need your letters. The next long, long, long letter will arrive very soon. Did Martin get his present from me? It should have arrived by now.

8 September 1959

I feel happier now because my Swedish is coming on nicely and I think I'll be speaking quite well within a couple of months. People have suddenly become more friendly and sometimes help me when I'm sitting in the canteen studying Swedish. Such a difference in a couple of days – it's unbelievable, and when I can speak I'm sure I'll be happier. Today I went out and bought my supper in Swedish without looking up one word, but I practised at home for at least half an hour before going out. Every morning when I arrive at the theatre I say, '*Har dett kommit någon post till mig idag*' and when I have my lunch in the canteen I say '*Jag skulle vila ha lunchen*' and then '*hoe mycket är kostan dett.*' I'd better get on with studying – so until tomorrow goodbye and tell Frankie that he is a *snelle pojke* (a good boy).

Friday 11 September

Yesterday I stayed in bed because I had rheumatism in my back, but it is better now so this morning I did class. I liked the class, which was taken by Mr Kruuse's sister-in-law Karen. The only thing is I feel so lonely here and wish I knew some people. Dreta has got another room from the beginning of the month so I hope and pray that when the Zadig family come back from their holidays they will let me continue to stay here. I'd rather stay with a family than on my own and Fru Necké says they are very nice. He is an artist and she was in the theatre and that they have a few children.

This afternoon I had an interview with the press because this *bobbejaan* [monkey] from the jungle – by being from Sydafrika – is arousing considerable interest in Malmö. Anyone would think I was from Mars, and the big joke is that I haven't yet seen proper snow – that will probably be the headlines in tomorrow's paper.

There are some nice German girls in the ballet but they don't speak any English or Swedish and that's frustrating. My God! What can I do? '*Vad är det? Det är en pojke. Vad är det? Det är en flicka.*' It's driving me mad!

15 September

Yesterday Dreta and I each bought ourselves a bicycle for 50 crowns apiece. Mine is huge, terribly rusty and rackety and Dreta's is almost a

UNGA på scen
Kvicksilver från Sydafrika väntar på snön och tomtarna

— Får jag två varma hundar — med bröd och senap.

Koryförsäljaren studsade till. Varma hundar. Vad man kunde beskylla honom för men inte affärer i hundar. Och varma till på köpet.

På andra sidan disken — alltså på trottoaren — stod 13-åriga Selina Moltina och såg konfunderad ut. Förstod att det var nåt som var galet. Men det hette ju hot dogs och hot var het och dogs var hund. Det är inte lätt att hänga med i alla svängar när man nyss kommit hit från Sydafrika.

Selina Moltina kommer från Kapstaden. Där har hon gått i skola och där har hon lärt sig dansa balett. Tvåspråkig redan från den tidiga barndomen har hon inget bekymmer med engelskan.

Hon är ekorrpigg. Mörk i håret men ljus i hyn. Skrattar gärna och ofta, tittar med skälmska ögon på omgivningen och njuter i fulla drag av vistelsen i Malmö, som började för ett par veckor sedan.

Selina hör till stadsteaterns nya balettfynd, en smal och smäcker liten dam, som nyligen arbetat sex månader i London, som tycker Copenhagen är en underbar stad och som fladdrar omkring på teatern och ute på stan med en svensk textbok i handen. Efter bara tio dagar kunde hon hälsa och vara artig på det svåra svenska språket.

Fyra års balettutbildning dansa, dansa, dansa dagarna igenom. Det är ett hårt yrke som fordrar både kroppslig och själslig balans, kondition och ett glatt humör. Och att Selina har gott humör, den saken är alldeles klar.

Vad väntar sig nu en 19-årig flicka från Sydafrika av Sverige?

Att arbetet på teatern skall gå bra, att hon skall få tillfälle att uppleva ett ordentligt snöfall, att hon skall få se jultomten.

— Sverige är ett underbart land, kvittrar Selina. Här är så vackert, människorna är så snälla. Men varför spelar dom inte — och sjunger?

Här ser man ingen som går på trottoarerna med instrument. Det är alldeles för lite sång och musik på stan. Selina är lite förundrad över det. Kan inte riktigt förstå varför det inte är förenligt med god sed att sjunga och spela på gatan. För henne är sången och musiken ett uttryck för människans inneboende livsglädje, och livsglädjen skall man kunna visa varhelst man befinner sig. Livsglädjen är väl ingenting som man visar först när man stängt in sig.

Tre månaders relativt kylig väderlek med regn har varit hennes vinter hittills. Undra på att hon är mycket spänd på den dag, då det kommer något från himlen om man kan ta i sina händer. Att handerna sedan blir valna och frusna har hon aldrig tänkt på.

Selina har en beundransvärd energi. Det försäkrar hennes kamrater. Så får hon en ledig stund från repetitionerna för Trubaduren tar hon fram sin svenska bok. Och ute på stan vill hon hjärtans gärna försöka krångla sig fram med svenska ord.

Efter bara några dagar gick hon och "handlade på svenska", berättar hennes kamrater vid teatern.

Teaterledningen knyter stora förhoppningar till det sprudlande lilla flickebarnet. Hon är ung, ser bra ut, dansar bra, är energisk och har en otrolig aptit på livet.

Om ni ser någon som kommer in i en affär och med något ovanligt ditong artigt men sammanbitet säger:

— Kan jag få köpa en tidning så är det Selina Moltina.

fairy cycle and shiny and blue. After the purchase we went for a long ride and parts of Malmö are really beautiful. We rode along to the beach and looked out over the bay at the buildings of Copenhagen. The big, orange sun was just resting on the horizon and there was a ferry in the sea heading from Malmö to that wonderful city. It was so beautiful that we parked our bikes on the bank and just ran down the huge grass bank to the sea – just for the sake of running. I'm so pleased I bought the bike because Malmö is flat and with no effort at all you can go to all sorts of super places and literally everyone rides a bicycle – even Baron and Mrs Kruuse. When we came back we cooked our supper and then Bengt and Akka came and took us to the cinema.

I can now speak Swedish in a fashion and am still learning hard. As far as the work in the theatre is concerned I'm sharing a solo in *Troubadore*, or at least learning it, and have a nice part in *Carmen*. Classes are really very nice indeed and they take quite a lot of interest in my work.

Today I got a letter from Kirsten Bie and Mr Bie put a postscript on it telling me to phone him tomorrow as he has a sister in Malmö. I'm terribly pleased as it's impossible to make friends here without an introduction – everyone says so and I'm inclined to agree with them. Swedes on the whole seem to lack warmth; and yet the Bies are the warmest people imaginable, so one can't really generalize. All I know is that if I do manage to make some friends here, I will have broken a record. I'll try though because I really love people and it only takes nice people around you to have really terrific times. You can fry an egg with nice people and it can be the funniest, most exciting, entertaining and wonderful thing on earth. But do the same thing with a bore and you want to die!

Thursday 17 September 1959

I got your letter this morning and Peter's yesterday and was really thrilled to get them. I will answer Peter's soon but this one is really for you both – in fact they all are.

Today the most marvellous thing happened to me. Mr and Mrs Bie came to Malmö all the way from Gothenburg just to see me, and were really so kind. Just look on your map and see what a really long way it is. They came to the theatre at 3 o'clock and picked me up and we went and had coffee together – then Mr Bie got a whole lot of addresses and we went around in his car looking for a room for me as he says he forbids me to stay in my dreadful room a moment longer.

What we finally settled for was super. It's a room in a flat owned by a young married couple and the husband has gone to work in Gothenburg for a year so she is alone in the flat with a little baby. She couldn't be a day older than 24 and is bright, amusing and charming. The flat is modern and has a wonderful kitchen and bathroom and although the bedroom is small it is prettily done out and has central heating. The lounge is lovely and has a radio and I think TV. She speaks English and Swedish and says she works all day and if I like I can earn money baby-sitting instead of her taking the poor little thing to the clinic.

I'm thrilled and to top it off it will only cost 80 kroner a month – 10 less than my present room and the others we looked at were 125 kroners without cooking facilities. In fact this will be like sharing a flat with a charming girl and gorgeous baby for half the price of a mingy room. The Bies like this girl very much too. With my bicycle it's less than five minutes from the theatre and one minute to the sea, and a modern shopping centre is just around the corner.

After we had found the room we had a dinner in Malmö's swishest hotel and then went to the cinema and saw an English film with Swedish dialogue. It was very good. They bought me chocolates as well and also gave me a wonderful present – an umbrella that folds into something a few inches long and can easily be slipped into a bag when not in use. It's an absolute beauty.

I can't understand their kindness as they came to Malmö just to see me and spent a fortune and a whole day for some stupid idiot whom they'd met once in their lives before. Can you believe that such nice people exist? When I try and thank him he just says that he deserves no medal because if his daughter went to South Africa you'd do the same! Please do if Kirsten does come. Mr Bie said he could get Peter a good contract in Germany – but says he has written to him, so perhaps Peter knows about it already.

In the theatre we are now working on *Carmen* as well as *Troubadore* and I adore my part as a shoe-shine boy's girlfriend. I dance it with Charlie, who comes from England but who has lived in Sweden for quite a while; he is married and is the proud father of a son.

Did I tell you that I might be sharing a solo in *Troubadore* and we open on 3 October? My Swedish is coming on well – or at least I like to think it is.

Sunday 20 September 1959

I'm now sitting in my nice new room on Sunday morning – having had a good night's sleep, a bath and a hair wash. I feel that a dab of disinfectant behind the ears would put the finishing touches to my already immaculately clean state. In Sweden one never sees dirt and if I see a table with dust on it, I shudder and say 'ugh'. How can one be expected to have to look at that?

I like my new room though – it's very sweet. I have some storage space in a built-in cupboard near the bathroom so can hang up my blouses as well. The bathroom and kitchen are both ultra-modern and the bath, like all baths in Sweden, has a shower attached to its taps, which is wonderful for rinsing your hair. The kitchen has an electric stove and built in cupboards.

My room has central heating so two blankets are ample for the winter. I have grey and white wallpaper. Mrs Malmberg's baby daughter (14 months) is too sweet for words. She has just come into my room to say hello. She took all my earrings out of the jar and put them all back again. She looks so sweet in her white jersey, green dungarees and white leather boots. She has very little hair, but what she has is ash blonde and stands up in a little point. The rest of her skin is slightly tanned.

Last night Dreta and I went to a Swedish film called *Stänger på Slottet* – it was very funny although I couldn't understand a word. Before the main film there was a beautiful short on the midnight sun. I really must try and save so that I can go and see it – preferably before I go back to England – but I don't somehow think I can ride there on my bicycle – especially with the brakes as they are.

Evening: This afternoon Dreta and I went to the beach on our bikes and guess what? We had a swim. I got in somehow and when I got out again I could feel the blood in my body defrosting again but it was great fun all the same, and afterwards I bought two ice creams like you can get only in Sweden. I must describe the ices because they were really gorgeous. First of all, the cone: it was like one wafer, which had been wrapped up, so it had a seam. On top of that was divine ice cream. That went in and hung over the edge as well. On top of the ice cream was a dab of strawberry jam and on top of that ordinary cream. We then came back to my room and had coffee and went out again for another ride on our bikes. We came home again and made supper and played with the baby and then Mr Bie phoned me from Gothenburg to see how I was and invited me to go and stay with them in the country whenever I can manage a free weekend. He really is so sweet.

The Peking Opera has come to Malmö and tomorrow night we have been given tickets to it. They are performing in the Stadsteater and I heard them rehearse a bit. It sounds interesting and their music and voices are beautiful and, as far as I can gather, mostly in the minor key.

Last night Dreta and I rode past the theatre on our bikes and got a wonderful surprise because to celebrate the opening night the statue outside was on fire. Look at the statue on the picture and notice the big bowl that is held up in the air, well that was full of flames and the fountain was on full blast as well – what a glorious sight! It really sent a tingle down my spine.

I would really adore to get the newspaper from Cape Town each week as Rose did in London. I now really miss it as I don't understand the Swedish ones and am somma [kind of] losing touch. I only knew that the Russians hit the moon about a week after it happened! Rose is back now so won't you give her a ring as she doesn't know where you are living. I know that she'd like to see you. I must end off now as I'm rather tired and must go to bed. So until next time adieu.

26 September 1959 (to Anthony)

Thank you so much for your letter. I always enjoy hearing from you so much and thank God that at least somebody has a sense of humour.

Sweden is getting better. At least I've decided to adopt a different attitude. If they want to be a lot of heartless, cold icicles they are welcome. I'll read a book by a less heartless individual instead.

It's a terrible feeling though when you know that no one cares about you. Mr Bie came all the way from Gothenburg to get me a room and merely because the theatre couldn't be bothered. I think it's my fault though because a lot of people get fabulous digs from the theatre, but I'm always diffident and readily agree if someone suggests I'm inadequate. I won't any more though. Next time you see me I'll be a tyrant with icicles dripping from my ears and you'll be frightened to come too close in case you freeze. That's what the Swedes are like. They aren't only like that to me but also to their best friends – even their husbands and wives. When they smile they show perfect teeth and shoot daggers out of their glorious eyes. You can't believe how nice South Africans are and what sunshine does for one's mood.

I haven't got all that much personality but the Swedish press wrote an article in the paper about it. I'll send it home and you'll have a fit, and at the interview all I did was giggle because I couldn't understand what the man was talking about, but I never even had a giggling fit like I used to at Mrs Lillelund's Afrikaans lessons[2] – just polite laughter and it shook them. People here don't laugh or cry and you determine their mood by measuring the degree (in fractions of a centimetre) of the slope of their mouths one way or the other. I'm dying to go to Copenhagen again but don't think I can as my foot is giving me trouble again and I am running up bills with a doctor before I've even got my salary – I've already taken almost half of next month's money. Living here is expensive and one ice cream costs one kroner (1/4d). I've realized now that it's not because of me or especially to me that the people are unfriendly, but it still makes me feel miserable, lonely and different.

29 September 1959

Life in Malmö is more or less the same and I find myself up in the clouds one minute and so miserable the next I want to crawl into a hole. Recently, they had this ridiculous article about me in the paper,

2. At the age of about 12 or 13 Selina, with her classmate Betty Gerber, took extra Afrikaans lessons with Mrs Lillelund at her small flat on the Main Road in Rondebosch. She was a good teacher, but they used to collapse in hysterical giggles every time they met because, they claimed, she had too many ornaments. It was probably just because they were that age.

but I'm sure you would be interested to see it. In case no one can understand it, it's roughly about my zest for life, which is all rather odd and I don't for a moment think I told this to the reporter because I didn't and anyway he couldn't even speak English.

The people in the theatre I meet daily in the canteen have started to be really sweet with me. I am the only foreigner studying Swedish and making an effort and I spend most of my spare time in the canteen either learning Swedish or reading, and frequently have famous actors come and sit by me and help me with my lessons.[3] Practically everybody talks to me now, but only to hear me speak Swedish. I'm by no means fluent but I can make myself understood up to a point, which is terribly morale boosting, and I don't care anymore about being lonely so much because I have joined the library and will do a lot of reading. I've just read Pearl Buck's *The First Wife* – the China one – and really loved it. Everybody thinks that I'm a real scholar – little do they know how illiterate I really am, but I just use long words in English and they gasp and beg me to teach them.

The other day I went to visit Mr Bie's sister who lives in Malmö. She is charming, is married to a doctor and has three small children. We had a fantastic Swedish tea and her eldest son (Martin's age) was enquiring after the wild animals in Africa, and was fascinated to hear about them. Torben Grandt[4] wrote yesterday inviting me to come to Copenhagen to visit him. We have today off but I have no money. I have to go without one ore until then and hate it because I've borrowed and am so much in debt. I've run up an account for my food in the canteen, another at the doctor because of my foot and then on top of that when I get my money on Thursday I have to pay for my room and my wireless and I have to buy makeup for *Troubadore*.

It's a ridiculous idea paying us at the end of the month because for the first month I had so little and now when I get it it'll all be paid out before I've started. It makes me mad because I'd love to go to Copenhagen more frequently and on our salary I can, but also can't,

3. One of these was Max von Sydow (1929–2020) who became a renowned actor and was eager to improve his English at the time.
4. Torben Grandt was a friend of Selina's parents who spent some time staying with the family at Rowan House in Cape Town.

because I have to start off in debt and it's virtually impossible to catch up again.

We've started rehearsing on the stage already and it is so colossal that we all look like sylphs and can travel as much as we like, which is marvellous, especially as the leading jester is full of big jumps and jetées. The big theatre in the Stadsteater is fantastic because you just have to press a button and the auditorium concertinas in to seat the number of people likely to attend the show. The stage is the same. We can have it colossal but it can also be small. The orchestra pit is under the stage. The theatre has to be seen to be believed. Did I tell you that everything was under one roof and we even have our own makeup artist and wig maker? The theatre has quite a few floors and of course lifts. Everything is centrally heated and behind are colossal scenery building sheds, photographic studios, and the lot. There are two theatres – the big one and the other one called the Intima where they put on productions better suited to a smaller theatre.

At the moment *Dromspeler* is on in the big one and *En duft af Honning* is on at the Intima theatre. The latter is Shelagh Delaney's *A Taste of Honey*, which is on in London, and has caused an uproar in Stockholm because it is so immoral![5]

We can get free tickets for the shows if there are any over, but of course *A Taste of Honey* is booked out by other curious members of the community.

On Sunday afternoon I went to see *Jungfruburen* and the music in it was superb. It is an opera by Schubert. I had no idea that the man who helped me with my lessons could sing so magnificently and got applauded the moment he appeared on the stage.

Tonight I want to go to the concert there and this afternoon a singer in the choir has asked me to go for a ride on my bike with him. He only speaks Swedish so our conversations are mostly with the aid of my dictionary, but anyway it's good practice.

I like the classes we have. They are given by Karren Berggrem and Myram? (a Norwegian) and are very much like classes in Cape Town.

5.   The play is a kitchen-sink drama set in working-class Britain that addresses questions of class, race, gender and sexual orientation.

They aren't as difficult as they are in London but very nice, a little more difficult than Cape Town though – about Intermediate standard.

I don't know yet about what makeup we must do except that for *Troubadore* I have to put on a funny face.

Thank you so much for the letters and please thank Vicky for her letter and the earrings too. They really are sweet.

Wednesday, 30 September

What a wonderful surprise the cheque was. I'm so happy now. Thank you very much. I've decided to get some lappie [material] to do some sewing as it's always nice to have something with which to divert one's attention in our spare time. The grapes have arrived too and they are so delicious you've no idea. I also got a sweet pair of pyjamas from Brigitte[6] in London – white nylon with blue trimmings and all lacy and gorgeous. I really like Brigitte so much. She's such a good friend to me.

Last night I went to the concert at the Stadsteater after my bicycle ride with the singer and at the concert I sat next to a Frenchman called Jacques Dupréz who afterwards took me to a restaurant. It was so nice as he was a foreigner and we talked for hours about all sorts of interesting things. He is 32 years old and not glamorous, but bubbly and full of life. He speaks French, Swedish, a little Dutch and English, as well as German, so talking was not difficult, as we spoke in Swedish and the words I didn't know I said in English, Afrikaans or French. It's funny, but now I sometimes seem to slip into Swedish without even knowing I am until I find myself stuck for words.

This morning we had our first orchestra rehearsal for *Troubadore* and for the first time I saw the rest of the opera. It is beautiful and the music out of this world. We will give another performance tomorrow.

The weather here is getting colder by the day but I'm determined to make the most of my time here and if I can't find enough to do in the theatre I will read, sew and learn Swedish. Perhaps I'll do some knitting too. I'm dying to go and meet Torben Grandt, and I will very soon. Copenhagen here I come!

---

6.   This would be Selina's friend Brigitte Knight.

Tonight I'll try and get a ticket to *Ert Dromspeel*. They gave me a free ticket to the concert last night as a special favour as usually for the concert you have to pay three crowns.

Niña[7] has invited me to Oslo for Xmas, but I don't know yet whether I'll be able to manage to get time off. I doubt it, but I do hope so.

I do miss you all so much and feel so far away from the people I know and understand, but am happy to have the chance to travel and learn different languages. Since I left home I've developed such a thirst for life and interest in things that I'm sure that it's the nicest thing that someone of my age can do. You've no idea what a lot one begins to learn and understand in such a short time and feel that now I see things in a different light.

When one meets a person, either a Swede or an Englishman who has lived in their country all their lives and has never travelled you can pick them out straight away after talking to them for less than five minutes, and there are so many things they just can't see and understand and I know that it was the same with me in South Africa. I think it's only when you find yourself on your own in strange surroundings in a strange country and feel smaller than an ant that you begin to see things differently; now I just feel amused when I see people fretting about unimportant things like what parts they have and how important they can try and appear to others, and yet only a year ago (at least one and a half years ago) I cared more than anything whether or not I had a nice part in the ballet – now if I have it I like it and if I haven't I couldn't care less.

8 October 1959 (to Vicky)

You really are a shocking writer, but I often think of you and wonder how you are getting on with your music. Thank you so much for writing to me and sending me those sweet earrings. I really love them and they go so beautifully with my new handbag and shoes.

With the money Margie and Peter sent me for my birthday I felt that I really must buy something to remember it by, so I spent a fabulous afternoon in Malmö spending. First of all I got a beautiful pair of black

7. Niña Horne, the person with whom Selina lived in Kew Gardens.

shoes, a handbag and gloves to match. I also got a white petticoat and a new two-way, as my old one has big holes in it from trying to pull it on so often. I also got a nice pink lipstick, some face powder and a pair of stockings. I feel quite a different person now, especially with my lovely new scarves and beautiful shortie pyjamas from Brigitte and a blouse from Dreta. It's one of those that you can wear [tucked] in or out. It's a lovely oyster off-white too and goes with everything. Everyone north of the Equator seems to wear scarves and I've followed suit. I got the idea in England and now always do it, especially when I ride my bike. I feel so much better since my spree and don't get depressed so much anymore. Now it's every second day instead of every day.

I can speak a sort of pidgin Swedish now thank God and on Tuesday went to Copenhagen and saw Torben Grandt. He says he adores Margie, so if Peter gives her any trouble just tell her to come to Copenhagen. He recognized me straight away as he says I look like her.

Copenhagen's fantastic. I adore it. Malmö is cold and unfriendly. On my birthday Dreta gave me a little party and two Germans came too. The night before I went to a night club with a Swedish singer and saw a Negro strip tease. They had a terrific band and I loved it. It made having a birthday away from home more bearable.

Please write again soon Vicky and give Miss Seabridge[8] my love.

Sunday 11 October 1959

Please excuse the delay of this letter. I have a real conscience about it, but somehow the days have just slipped by so quickly and I didn't realize that it was so long since I last wrote. First, I must thank you for the wonderful cake. I got it the day before my birthday and it was so delicious. It's just finished now. I gave a little piece to the other girls and they loved it so much and I adored it. The writing in pink icing brought back so many happy memories of home and I had a super birthday. Dreta arranged a little party for me in her flat and we stuffed ourselves by candlelight and played records. It was such a nice birthday, but I really would like to have had it with all of you. The scarves and hankies are sweet too, and so useful as I've taken to scarves in a

---

8. Miss Seabridge was Vicky's piano teacher, and formerly Selina's as well.

big way lately. Please thank Frankie and Martin for me and I'll write
to all three boys soon.

Last Tuesday I went to Copenhagen and met Torben Grandt at the
boat. He is awfully nice. He took me to some friends of his – a charming family by the name of Maalon who have a daughter who dances
and I went and watched some ballet classes, which I intend to do
myself in future. Torben Grandt sends you all his best regards and
asks you to send me some photos of the family so I can show them to
him.

I went to Copenhagen again the other evening with someone from
the theatre and we had a fabulous dinner in a Chinese restaurant. The
ferry ride over from Malmö is always such fun and it's wonderful to
arrive in the bay in Copenhagen as it's really quite beautiful. I love
Copenhagen so much – it's so full of atmosphere.

At the moment I'm sitting in the canteen after a performance of
Troubadore and today I did the solo – it was quite fun. I did it last night
too. Yesterday afternoon I went along to the Swedish Turkish baths
and it was great fun.

If you really honestly have the urge to sew I'd adore to have a dress,
as I need something a little smart rather badly – something to wear to
restaurants, theatres and so forth, but not too posh, preferably
something I can wear in the day too. I'll find a picture of the sort of
thing I'd like and send it to you. Thank you so much for your kind
offer – it really would be greatly appreciated. The blue frock and
striped blouse you sent me have been so useful, in fact they are one of
the most frequently used garments in my wardrobe.

I'll write a longer letter soon, but I'm afraid my brain has petered
out and I'm dead tired, so I'll sign off now until next time and I promise
you that it will be very soon. The new house sounds such fun – did
you get the jam jars I sent you? Ask at the post office as I think I forgot
to say Main Road.

27 October 1959

I have to apologize for the shocking delay of this letter, but somehow
I've been caught up in such a rush of activity that the days seem to
have slipped by without me noticing.

At the moment we are working all day and every day on *A Winter's Tale*, which we are putting on soon and I enjoy rehearsals for it, not only because of the dancing but because we work with the rest of the play so much. In Malmö we have some of Sweden's greatest actors, singers and stars and it's fascinating to watch them work, and to work with them. I can get so much out of Malmö if I try, as we are entitled to see and hear everything in this theatre and in the Royal Theatre in Copenhagen for nothing. Last week there was a wonderful pianist here from England and I heard both the rehearsal and the performance of Beethoven's Fifth piano concerto and some Mozart and Haydn. What a relief it is to be able to speak Swedish now because now I have many friends in the theatre. A Chinese conductor is here at the moment from Brussels and I sometimes speak with him as he speaks no Swedish.

Last night I went to a film with the first violinist – Thomas (pronounced Thomaas) and we had a nice evening. It was pelting with rain and my feet were squelching with every step I took but nevertheless we saw a very good film. Thomas is a Dane of about 35 and has been terribly kind to me. He is going to get married quite soon for the second time and I quite often go to films with him when we are both free. Tonight I will go to a film with the theatre photographer. A lot of people ask me out, which I like, but it's only because I listen to their troubles. I really must get this letter off to you today as my conscience is getting worse and worse.

30 October

Festival Ballet has arrived on the scene and there seems to be such a lot going on. It's so nice to speak English again – and my South African colleagues have been wonderful to me. Len Martin sends you his love and Peter Cazalet and Ivan Baptie[9] are with them too. There are also a lot of other South Africans whom I've met and some dancers whom I knew in London. Yesterday Doug, a boy in the company (from Durban) whom I knew in London arranged for me to do a class with the company, which I did – it really was an awfully nice class.

9. Len Martin, Peter Cazalet and Ivan Baptie had all been at the UCT ballet school before coming to Europe.

Tonight is the opening night and I am seeing it from out front, and will see the wonderful Toni Lander[10] for the first time. I met her in the canteen today, but I've never seen her dance. Len Martin was surprisingly kind to me and says that when I get back to London I must ring him and he will try and do something for me. I think I'll stay in Malmö for nine months and then go on a summer, perhaps also winter, tour because then I can really see Sweden and although the work won't be up to much we at least can save a lot of money. If only Swedish people were nicer though – I don't think I could stay in Sweden for very long because the people are so cold. They are as nice to me as they can be – but still there's just that something missing. It struck me especially when Festival came and I saw these people against the Swedes.

31 October

Last night I went to the opening night of Festival Ballet and enjoyed it very much. They put on *London Morning*, *Concerti* and *Études*. The latter was really very lovely. The Danish ballerina Toni Lander danced the lead and I hadn't even imagined before that a dance could look so utterly beautiful. It's funny but I prefer Festival Ballet to the Royal Ballet. I would very much love to dance in a company like that, but to get in takes so much more than being a good dancer – there are some worse than me – but it means hanging around all the time being always ready to pounce at the right moment. Some girls even follow the company around on their tour waiting for the right moment. I can't do that – it's just not the way I'm made. I feel so happy to have these days with the company and they have been so kind to me and the dancers are always asking me to do them little favours because I can act as a sort of interpreter. One old bod called Aubrey (the musical director) came up to me when he first arrived and asked where the lavatory was. I didn't know where the gents was, so I took him to the ladies, and afterwards he told me that he had got stuck in there. He said he tried

10. Danish ballerina Toni Lander (1931–85) worked with Festival Ballet, the American Ballet Theatre and eventually Ballet West in Salt Lake City. She married the choreographer Harald Lander in 1950 and kept his name even after their divorce in 1965.

to climb over the top of the door but unfortunately got stuck in the
lock. He said that he didn't like to scream as he hated the idea of
someone finding a strange man, who couldn't speak the language, in
the ladies' lavatory. I didn't like to ask how he got out in the end.

Yesterday I got a letter from Penny[11] and will telephone her as soon
as I have written to you. I hope you aren't worried about me as I haven't
written for so long. I'd better sign off now; otherwise, I'm liable to go
on indefinitely. I'm so happy that Festival are here and that they are
being so kind and sweet to me. Len also gives his love to Kulu.[12] Till
next time, which I hope will be soon. Gosh, I do miss you so much.

3 November 1959

Thank you so much for your lovely long letter. Somehow your letters
bring me more pleasure in my life than anything else.

Today was Tuesday and supposedly our free day, but they decided
to give us a rehearsal this morning so my Copenhagen plans were
thrown off completely and instead I spent the afternoon and evening
with Penny and Claes and will probably be spending Saturday night
and Sunday with them too. Today was the first time I've met Penny.
She is awfully sweet.

8 November 1959

At the moment I am spending the weekend with Penny and Claes and
I have been enjoying the refreshing change. It is almost Sunday
evening now, so unfortunately it is drawing to a rather rapid close.

After Festival Ballet left I felt depressed and lonely again but I've
more or less got the nice people and company out of my mind now
and the Swedes in the theatre are beginning to seem slightly less grim
again. It's amazing what one can get used to. The work in the theatre
at the moment consists of long hours standing around on stage doing
nothing and the dancers are getting frustrated and irritated. It seizes
them all in different ways. Some sulk, which is the most natural reaction, Dreta (who incidentally irritates me and everyone else intensely)

11. Cousin Penny Molteno who had married Claes Lewenhaupt.
12. Selina's maternal grandmother.

shouts at everyone and makes quite sure that she is always the centre of attention; there are some who are satisfied with such an existence and there is one German girl called Elke who constantly whines, is clammy and when you try to help her, only whines more, complains more and lets off a revolting squeal if you happen to dry your hands on her towel, and refuses to lend a hairpin to someone in distress. There's a vile German boy who is married to one of the dancers. She is sweet, but he is fat and incidentally sucks his false teeth all the time. Some of the boys are quite sweet, but they are always asking to borrow my Blue Grass.

On 15 November I'm moving to another room, which is nicer than mine as it has so many more amenities and although Mrs Malmberg gave me the impression of being nice at first she turned out to be rather grim. I didn't like to say anything as I knew you'd worry but now I'm moving to something rather like a little flat in a hotel and it will be my own. Mrs Malmberg became so disagreeable that I hated to go home and so therefore only did late at night. I used to stay in the theatre and read or study Swedish or something – but you know Marg, although it was so cheap with Mrs Malmberg, I'd rather pay more and be able to use my room as a home. Mrs Malmberg wouldn't let me bring a friend home in the afternoon and I wasn't allowed in the kitchen until she was ready, which was sometimes so late. I could only put the radio on terribly softly and after a while I became so frightened of her that I dared not even use the iron or the kitchen.

This weekend with Penny has been marvellous. She and Claes picked me up after rehearsal on Friday evening and we went out to dinner with some of their friends at the home of Mr and Mrs Ascot [Ascor?]. Oh Margie I must tell you about it as it was so wonderful. They were all much older than me – in fact I was the only young person there but I felt happy to meet some educated, well mannered, well-bred and charming Swedish people.

They have a beautiful house in the country and we had a wonderful, beautifully served Swedish dinner. For the entrée we had eel and spinach – then some kind of cold meat with a salad done up with wonderful sauces and that was followed by an ice-cream pudding, which was covered in a type of delicious crust.

They drank sherry and wine with the dinner. I sat next to one of Sweden's top surgeons – a charming man married to a very rich Swedish countess and I spent most of the evening talking with him. Apparently, according to Claes, he will receive the Nobel Prize. You've no idea what a joy it was to speak with a really intelligent person. He explained to me what was wrong with the Swedish people and puts it down to the social system, which gives the people all they need for nothing and then encourages them to be as lazy as possible. The average Swede has (according to him) the mentality of a 12-year-old through mere laziness and he says that all this selfishness and perversion is because they have nothing better to do than think of themselves and apparently that is one of the biggest causes of madness. The children all have cars as soon as they can drive and the terrible Swedish youth is because they have so much money and such short working hours. Perhaps such a terrifically high standard of living isn't such a good thing after all, as surely it is more important to have good values than to have a Bendix, TV, a modern apartment and a car.

I don't know but somehow Malmö could be so nice if it wasn't for the people – but perhaps I just know the wrong ones.

Penny and Claes are very nice and I'm terribly fond of them both. Penny can't do a thing for herself and is rather spineless. She can't speak a word of Swedish, can't cook, can't sew and hasn't really learnt much about life, but she is oblivious to all that and is quite happy just to ride her horses and ask Claes whether to put one or two pinches of salt in the soup. She's been spared all the hardships and struggles of life and I hope for her sake that it'll go on like that. She's always had plenty of the necessities and luxuries and it's all just fun. She seems so charming, so naive, so innocent. I'm sure she's never felt insecure, desperately lonely or frightened – but on the other hand I'm sure she's missed a lot with all that wealth. It seems silly, but I somehow can't help feeling that she's a little sister who has never had a chance to burrow underneath into reality.

You've been so good about writing to me and your letters mean so much, but I'm so frightened of always being lonely – I just want you to explain to me that it's silly to think that. I can't seem able to tell myself. I have many superficial friends, in fact more friends than I can count and everyone says I have a natural talent for making friends, but I still feel lonely and insecure. I know that people like me as they are always saying so, but I also know that if it suited them they would cheat and deceive me and, worse still, abandon me.

Please give my love to everybody and ask Frankie to please send me a photo of himself. I loved the one of Anna – thank you so very much. She certainly is looking pretty! How about one of Martin, Vicky, Anthony and you and Peter?

15 November 1959

How terribly I miss you all at the moment, but I at least have a couple of consolations. One is that I've moved into my new room – another is that Diana, a friend from London, has come to stay with me and the third is that I've decided to make an effort to try and break my contract – but the latter I think is almost impossible – I think that I can get very good work in Stockholm for 1200 crowns a month and I want to go more than anything. The first move is to see if there is still a vacancy as the ballet master, Gaubier,[13] knows me and says he likes my work. Mr Kruuse[14] is such a cunning old sod though that I'm sure he wouldn't let me leave. The work here stinks – in fact there is blow all to do – somehow life in Malmö seems so futile compared with London and everything one endeavours to do is blotted out by someone's pessimism. Anyway, I'm sure it's going to be much nicer now that I have my new room. I was thinking of getting some posters from SAS and putting them on the walls and then I can invite my friends home and cook them lovely meals in my little kitchen cupboard.

Monday 16 November 1959

Today I did something that nearly bowled me over. I heard from Fru Necké that Gaubier really wanted dancers and me too at 1200 crowns

13. Albert Gaubier (1908–1990), a Polish Jewish dancer and choreographer who danced with the Diaghilev company and later sought refuge in Denmark and Sweden.
14. Carl-Gustaf Kruuse (1912–1964), the ballet master at the Malmö Stadsteater.

tax free, good work, and possibly a tour to Las Vegas and Paris and one of the boys I know has just started working there and says it's very nice so, considering I was furious with Kruuse for keeping us waiting the whole day for nothing, I marched straight to the theatre chief's office and let off steam *à la* Margie. He got so frightened that he just shook and promised to do his best to release me. Kruuse is the next obstacle and if it still goes well with Gaubier – well then soon I'll be in the money in Stockholm.

Tuesday 17 November 1959

Diana and I are off to Copenhagen now and so must fly – we are going to paint the town red – just in case it's the last time. It's super having her here. Life seems to have taken on a different hue altogether. I'll send some photos and things when I can find time to have them done, but first I must try and get myself out of this joint.

Tuesday 17 November 1959 (from Ansgar Mission Hotel, Copenhagen)

Today has been the funniest, most wonderful and craziest day I've had and just somehow everything has been so wonderful. Diana and I laughed until we were nearly sick – isn't it wonderful what Copenhagen can do to one?

First of all we left Malmö in the bitter cold to catch the boat to Copenhagen and, at 10.30, it pulled out of Malmö harbour and we settled in the warm, cosy dining room for a breakfast of eggs and bacon and hot coffee, and what should happen but two young American men from California came and sat with us and we had a fabulous journey over. They were wonderfully kind and chivalrous and even paid for our breakfasts. We talked solidly for the 1½ hours and they told us about their travels abroad in a very interesting and amusing way and somehow they were so light, charming and full of fun. When we arrived in Copenhagen the air was fresh and nippy and – guess what – the first snowfall of the year had fallen. It wasn't a very heavy one but it was my first and it gave me such a thrill to see everything covered with the white film of loveliness. The Americans found us our cheap room in the Mission Hotel and then the snow began to fall more heavily and Diana and I went out into it and made snowballs, which

The Ny Carlsberg Glyptotek in Copenhagen.

we threw at a couple of gay tourists walking in front of us. We all just laughed for the sheer joy of being alive in the snow in Copenhagen.

Suddenly we felt like obtaining some culture so we wended our way to the Glyptotek sculpture museum and saw sculpture that has to be seen to be believed. We saw the mother with all her babies and some really lovely Danish work – how I love Danish things – they always have such charm and simplicity. We also saw Egyptian mummies, Ancient Egyptian art and a fantastic collection of ancient Roman busts. It closed at three so we unfortunately had to leave before seeing the whole collection, but we certainly saw enough to fill quite a big gap in our education.

After that we went out into the nippy snow-dusted street and burrowed our way into a warm coffee bar where we had Danish pastry and hot chocolate drinks with cream on top. By the time we'd had our tea-cum-lunch, twilight had fallen and we saw Copenhagen at its best with its higgledy-piggledy lights, buzzing, smiling and full of sunshine even in the dark. We decided to go to a store so we did and looked at their wonderful things. All the Xmas decorations are up now and I felt that I wanted to buy madly for you all, but didn't have the money.

Oh Margie, I've seen so many things that you would drool over – absolutely charming chinaware with such a flavour of Denmark on it that I would have given anything to have had you there with me to enjoy it as much as I did. But I bought it all for you in my mind and one day I really will. What a sweet dining room table I saw all decorated with charming mats, candles and dinner sets and what sweet jewellery for Anna, toys for Frankie and Martin, jerseys for Vicky and fantastic cheeses for you, Anthony and Kulu, and cigars for Peter and Apa. What fun we had! We then went into a crowded apartment store, perched ourselves on high stools with loudspeakers pressed to our ears and listened to vile spirituals. Imagine Harry Belafonte singing 'God Got Angry so He Turned the Sky Grey And so Said to Noah, Build an Ark, bum, pum, bum, bum pum bum.' It was too camp for words but terribly funny. We then went out into the street again and bought hot dogs, which we consumed right there as we watched a woman squealing with laughter because she had dropped her shoe in the road.

In the evening we went to a very good film with Yul Brynner in it and after that we found ourselves in a café consuming *smörgas* and coffee. We were shortly afterwards joined by a couple of Italians. One was a surgeon and I don't know what the other was, but they took us to a fantastic little restaurant where we drank coffee and listened to someone playing the piano by candlelight. They were too funny for words as they were really trying so hard to get off with us. You know what Italians are like and we were jacking them up like mad. Eventually, we couldn't fight for our virtue much longer so we got out of the car and walked from where we were, which was such fun as the walk was really picturesque. Oh, but the Italians were funny, especially in their reasoning about Diana. 'But what does it matter; your husband's not here now?' They were perfectly harmless though – just full of fun and great fun to put off.

We walked home and now I am snug in my bed in a funny little double room in the Mission Hotel under a 'feathers' *à la* Brigitte Knight – remember?[15] What a wonderful introduction I had to my very first snowfall and my happiest day in Scandinavia to accompany it.

No more money in the bank
No cute babies to spank
So let's put out the lights and go to sleep.

---

15. Brigitte Knight was the only person Selina knew who owned a duvet, clearly the height of luxury at the time.

Wednesday morning

Oh hell! We are now packing to catch the one o'clock boat back to Malmö after a divine breakfast in the hotel. I can see the rooftops from my window on the other side of the road and there's only a little snow left from wonderful yesterday.

23 November 1959 (back in Malmö)

I hope you don't mind but I've broken my contract at the Stadsteater for a job in Stockholm, which somehow promises much more. I will leave here at the end of the month and will work at the Intima Theatre in Stockholm with Gaubier, and will dance ballet – on pointe – in an operetta called *Charlie's Aunt*, which, although it isn't straight theatre, has very much more ballet in it than we do here in Malmö. I will be paid 1050 crowns a month – tax free – which is about £16 a week, almost twice as much as I'm getting here.

Another thing about it is that Stockholm is the capital and therefore offers much more than Malmö. Malmö has only one theatre and in this theatre the ballet plays such a minor part and I now realize that however hard I worked here there would never be any chance of making one's mark and one is inclined to become rather disheartened through feeling that you're not really very much use in the theatre. I think I'll be happier working in this smaller theatre, which has a company of many different nationalities. So far, from what I've experienced from theatre abroad, is that the people working in it are not very nice on the whole and are so utterly selfish and self-centred that it's almost comical to observe.

I don't know how long I'll stick to ballet, for I don't fancy living my whole life in such an environment, but then on the other hand it's a wonderful way of seeing the world. I love dancing and know I have the ability to do it after seeing the standard in Europe, and I'm convinced that if I wanted to I could eventually get into a very good company, but the trouble is that I don't know if that's what I really want to do in the long run. I don't feel cut out for the theatre, but am unable to do anything else. I don't care what that is so long as I feel I'm making some sort of contribution and I'm not sure I'll be able to do that in ballet. Anyway, I'll try it for a few more years as I must have a lot of experience in it before I decide whether or not it's my cup of tea. Somehow I feel that now that the world has opened up, I wouldn't be scared to go to any country or to try something else. Anyway Marg I hope you are pleased I'm changing to a better job and have come into some money.

Last night Diana left to meet her husband in Stuttgart and it was the funniest farewell I've ever experienced. There were four of us – Diana, myself, and two Swedish men called Leonard and John, who have somehow shed their Swedish formality due to visits to the USA. We thought that the ferry to Copenhagen left at 8.00 but lo and behold it didn't. Diana's train left Copenhagen at 10.30 and our only alternative was to fly and, considering that we were all in a crazy mood, we decided to go together. We went to the aerodrome and booked our seats. It's only a ten-minute flight to Copenhagen and so we went in the tiniest little plane. It was terribly exciting rising up over Malmö and seeing all the lights and then descending again onto Copenhagen's aerodrome. We were driven in an SAS bus to the front door of the aerodrome and then took another airway bus to the central station where Diana caught her train to Hamburg where she changes. After seeing her off, we went back to the seafront and caught the 11.00 o'clock boat back to Malmö. It doesn't sound madly exciting, but I found it so because just to be in Copenhagen gives me such a thrill. I never knew that a city could have such an effect on someone.

I'm sorry that Diana has gone now as it was such fun having her here, but then again I'll be busy getting ready to go and before I know where I am I'll be gunning up to Stockholm. I couldn't be very much further from home, could I? But I'm so grateful to you for giving me the chance to come to Europe, to see the world and to live on my own. I think I've learnt more in these last nine months than I ever did while I was at school.

I'd better be signing off now as time is slipping and I have an awful lot of things to get through. I'll have to invest in some North Pole clothes as the winter is really setting in. Thank God for the wonder-fully warm houses in Sweden, for everything is centrally heated and that somehow makes going outside easier. It's always nice to know that you can just step into a shop and be as warm as toast in two seconds. From December my address will be Intima Teatern, Stockholm, Sweden.

1 December 1959 (from Intima Teatern, Odengatan 81, Stockholm UA)

Well here I am in Stockholm – tired, worn out, fed up and disinclined and unenthusiastic about starting a new job. But I'm glad I did what I did because I think that Stockholm is a better town to live in than Malmö and here too I can do good classes and even try for some television or something like that.

The Royal Theatre in Stockholm is almost impossible to join as it is nationalized and therefore they only take Swedish girls. Of course an exception to the rule does occur occasionally, but that I think happens in most countries. I'm glad to see Stockholm though and I'll try and get as much as I can from it and my stay here. On the whole, I'm disappointed in people as I seem to discover so many bad things and so few good things about them, but perhaps I'm just looking on the negative side of things because I'm tired. Last night we danced *Carmen* in Malmö and I enjoyed it and afterwards I said goodbye to the girls and Rudi Kristensen, an artist from Denmark, took me to the station where we sat eating squashed, rubbery hot dogs until my train came at 12.30. Rudi gave me a picture he had drawn of the boat to Copenhagen, but I was feeling so tired and fed up that I didn't really appreciate it as much as I should have, for it was really very nice.

Anyway I managed to get a sleeper and went to sleep in peace. The next thing I knew was the guard shouting '*Stockholm i en halv timme*' and my only reaction was 'Oh bother' I have to get up now. I didn't feel in the slightest bit excited or even interested. Anyway, I'm here now and already know that I'm going to be happier working with Gaubier than with Kruuse.

It's the second day now and I've already had two rehearsals – I will go on in one dance on Friday night and am being worked to the bone. Gaubier seems to like me, which is wonderful for me as to have a ballet master interested in you can make a lot of difference in this lousy world. He is teaching me to dance modern as well, and just tell Dulcie

Howes from me that unless she teaches her students modern they are next to useless overseas. I will learn a lot from him I know as he has something to offer.

The Intima Teatern is very sweet and has a lovely atmosphere and the ballet is very international. There are Greek, Spanish, Swedish, Danish, Finnish and Brazilians among them and a Japanese and English girl are leaving. My God, but Stockholm is dead. Here I am in a restaurant and if you could see the faces around me you would pop. They are playing *Patineurs* on the radio and not even that stirs anything in them. I've learnt to take it now and I don't care anymore – why should I? I'll dance and I'll work hard at it and I won't care anymore. Gaubier says that I'm very talented and after he's taught me what he can I'll get an even better job.

For Xmas I think I'll probably be with Niña in Oslo. Everything that is sent to the Stadsteartern is being forwarded to me.

Oh, how I miss you all and every five minutes I take out the photos of Martin and Frankie and Anna and gaze at them in awe. There's a little boy in Malmö who is going to write to Martin. He doesn't speak very good English. His mother is the dresser in Malmö and was very kind to me when I was there, so if he writes, Martin must write back too. I miss you all a lot.

December 1959 (Tuesday)

I just don't know when I'll be able to get this letter finished as somehow time seems so scarce, so if it happens to be rather disjointed, you will understand that it's because a few words at a time are being scribbled in between rehearsals, performances, cups of coffee and perhaps even in bed at night after a strenuous performance and in a desperate effort to keep my eyes open.

First, I'd like to thank you for the dress you sent me. It arrived the other day and it is charming and just the sort of thing I need most. What a lovely colour it is – thank you so much Margie, you are really so terribly sweet. I did get Granny's money and wrote and thanked her for it, so I hope she got the letter. I can't remember whether or not I wrote and thanked Anna for the jewellery box she sent me. It really is awfully nice and I'll be writing to her again soon.

I don't regret leaving Malmö one single bit and am so happy here in Stockholm. In Malmö the theatre was so big, cold and unfriendly and the staff or people in charge took no interest whatsoever in us personally. They made no effort to find me a room and the Kruuses never once invited me home or enquired how I was getting on, which I think is bad manners. One doesn't treat employees from a faraway foreign country in that rude offhand manner, especially as they were just about the only people who could speak English; and, as for the work, well that was a dead end as the whole organization was run around Kruuse and his wife who is a crank old dancer from the past and if the standard of the work is kept down by a fool who doesn't know when to retire and if you happen to be able to do one pirouette more puts you in the back row – I just don't think it's worth wasting my time over. I don't particularly care whether I'm in the back row or the front, but when you know you are kept back to let dear Inga have a fair chance, it becomes a bit aggravating.

Also, Kruuse is going through an off period and is doing vile choreographies at the moment. I made no trouble whatsoever – I just went to the theatre chief and told him I wanted to leave and why, which no one could deny, not even Kruuse, and they released me from my contract at the end of the month. Kruuse was grossly embarrassed by the whole thing and avoided me like the plague. I didn't have to refund any money and was even given 200 crowns extra for overtime work and holiday money. I lost nothing out of it and as soon as I arrived in Stockholm Gaubier refunded my fare up.

Wednesday

At the moment it's about 11.15 in the morning and I've just finished ironing some blouses. The radio is on (I'm buying one on the never-never system) and I'm sitting by the window in my room writing to you. My room is very warm but outside is just a maze of snowflakes and the street below is thick with a carpet of white, white snow. There are some cars parked in this street and they too are becoming covered in snow. Not many people walk along Grev Turegatan, so any tracks they make in the snow are quickly covered up again – it looks really beautiful and is so much pleasanter to go out in than the rain. Yesterday, it was too cold to snow properly, but the spray from the sea blew onto the land in little frozen icicles, but now it's snowing properly, so I hope that it's not that cold anymore; but it will be interesting to spend a winter almost at the North Pole and to have a 'white Xmas'.

From the theatre we are free from the 19 to 26 December and I think I will go to Oslo and spend Xmas with Niña there. Just so that you'll know where I am, her address is c/o Grieg Norstensen, Drammensveien 201 B, Bestum, Olso, Norway and I think she and I will have our 'Julafton' Xmas Eve with Odd Haanshuus, Rosenborggaten 15 B. Niña invited me long ago and it will be interesting to see Oslo.

I'm getting some Xmas presents together slowly but regret I haven't sent any off yet. I've had to buy myself a North Pole coat and so at the moment have not very much money, but will get it soon. I would also like to have a look at what they have in Oslo and so when Xmas Day comes just remember you have another Xmas in store from me. Is there anything you would especially like for your new house? Or, how about some silver spoons or something – you must always say if you want me to send you anything in that way, as the things you get here are so much prettier and it seems a waste not to make hay while the sun shines. Anyway, I only hope you will like what I eventually choose for you all.

Stella Firth is so sweet. Yesterday a parcel containing two books arrived from her. She's the most wonderful person to know in London, as besides being very intelligent and very nice, she has a flat right in the middle of London where one always feels welcome.

The Intima Theatre staff have been wonderful and the other night the director, Mr Jorgensson invited Ernesto and me home to meet his wife and family, and he also found me a room. There was nothing available in Stockholm for less than 15 crowns a day, so I will pay five and he pays the difference. I'm staying in what they call a 'pension' and I can eat here as well if I want to. It's quite nice and comfortable and then on the 19th when one of the dancers goes back to America I will move into her room in a flat with some of the others.

At the moment we are rehearsing every day and performing every night, so as yet I haven't done my classes, but I think I will start again at the beginning of next week. I have a choice of two good teachers, but will try them both out and then decide which one to take up.

In a way, Sweden has so much, yet it also has an atmosphere I don't like. Here one has financial security and gets paid more than I would in another country, so what I plan to do is work here until perhaps the end of March and save as much as I can and then return to London. There's no doubt that experience abroad is invaluable and I am impressed to see what Gaubier has done with a dancer who was with me at Annas [Anna Northcote]. She came straight to Gaubier when I went to Malmö. She was a little dead, but has now developed such a stage presence and style that it is almost impossible to believe. I know I can get a lot from him as he's willing to help and correct and certainly keeps your nose to the grindstone. At the moment I am dancing two modern dances, a classical waltz on pointe, in which I do a solo with fouettés and soon am going to do a *gota* as well. As soon as you master one thing, Gaubier pushes you into something else.

I like the others in the company. There is a Greek boy from Athens, a Spanish boy, a South American boy, a Finnish boy, two Danish boys, two Danish girls, and two Swedish ones. It's a small group, but I prefer it that way, and they are all very friendly and nice. The theatre is small and very sweet, but the dressing rooms are tiny, though we have nice showers with hot and cold water, so are not made to suffer unduly. The theatre is also nice and warm.

A German girl in Malmö gave me a letter to a German boy here and last Sunday I took it to him. He lives in the Gamla Stan, which is the loveliest part of Stockholm and he has been very kind to me. His parents are trapped in Germany in the Russian zone and once when he tried to get back, the Russians caught him and put him in a camp for three months and he has more or less fled to Stockholm, but in spite of having nothing in his pocket and no work permit he would be the first to help one if one was in trouble.

A Swedish girl attached herself to him. Her parents objected to his political views and so told her to leave him. She wouldn't and as her father is in a very high position in the country, he refused Hans permission to get a work permit and if he is caught, he will be thrown out of the country. I hate it when people use their power to ruin other people's lives. I must go to rehearsal now, so until next time 'Adieu'.

22 December 1959 (c/o Grieg Thorstensen, Drammensveien 201B, Bestum, Oslo)

At this moment I'm sitting in Niña's office, which overlooks the harbour of Oslo – what a lovely town this is and I feel so happy. I will be staying here with Niña until just after Xmas and then I'll be returning to Stockholm in time for a show on the 25th. Since I've left Malmö I've been happy in both my work and myself and life seems marvellous again. When I arrive back I'm going to dance the main 'Gota' girl as one of the dancers is leaving and going back to her husband in the USA.

Anyway, I'm in Oslo now and am very happy to be here. Yesterday a friend of Niña's – a charming girl called Janne – took me around Oslo and I bought something for you. I must tell you what it is as I just adore it. It is a hand-made Norwegian pewter teapot and in my mind it is just you – I hope you will like it. There is so much I'd like to get for you but unfortunately I haven't got enough dough and it's taking quite a long time to collect Xmas presents together, but sometime I will and then you'll all have to have another Xmas just from me.

Niña has a sweet little room where we are staying together and she sends you her love. The other day Marina Keet and her husband came to see me backstage and they are off on a trip to Russia. It seems funny to think of Stockholm being so close to Russia – as it always seemed so far away.[16] I like the Norwegian people very much. They seem friendly and hospitable and Oslo has a charming atmosphere, especially now that it is decorated for Xmas. The last of the snow has melted now and so I don't think that we'll be having any for Xmas, but I certainly saw my fair share of it in Stockholm. I like Stockholm very much and think it is because I've tried to keep my distance from the Swedish people. In the theatre, they are mainly Danes as well as people from every conceivable country in the world and I spend most of what I have of free time with a German boy called Hans Senger. He knows a terrific amount about art and literature and so usually we explore the Gamla

16. Marina Keet (born 1934 in Calvinia, South Africa) married Mikael Grut in 1959 and had a distinguished career as a Spanish dancer and writer about ballet and Spanish dance. She was at the UCT ballet school throughout Selina's childhood there.

Stad and browse around having a marvellous time as Stockholm is a very beautiful city and if Swedes didn't live there it would be paradise.

The journey from Stockholm was lovely. I'm so glad I went during the day because we passed through fantastic countryside and lakes. Of course, I bought the cheapest ticket, but after five minutes a Hollander came and invited me to sit in his first-class compartment in a luxury armchair. He bought me food and as a result I had a very pleasant and comfortable trip.

I would like to try some skiing sometime but won't as I can't risk breaking a leg just now. Last night Niña and I went to the cinema and saw an American film called *Some Like it Hot*. It was quite funny but nothing out of this world.

Oh, by the way, thank you so much for that box of food that you sent me. It's absolutely gorgeous and what a lovely surprise. I do like that dress you sent me so much and wear it often. Somehow I wonder how I ever did without it. It really is so sweet. I hope you all have a very happy Xmas and don't worry about me because I'm fine and perfectly capable of looking after myself. I miss you all a lot of course but whatever you do don't worry as you have no need to. Please give my love to everyone and have a wonderful Xmas.

Tuesday 5 January 1960 (from Intima Teatern, Stockholm)

I'm sorry I didn't write sooner. I feel bad about it but somehow I've been so tied up with rehearsals that I haven't found a moment.

Thank you so much Margie for those parcels – they were wonderfully welcome and I adore the frock. It is too chic and charming for words and one of the boys, a dancer from Rio de Janeiro called Ernesto Teccerari says that your cake is the nicest he has ever had and that if you are as wonderful as your cake is you must be something very special. Oslo was too lovely for words – everyone I met there was charming and I had a lovely Xmas. On the night of Xmas I went to see Betty Clausen and spent a lovely evening there. She is charming and made me feel so welcome. She showed me some pictures of Peter in his youth and still adores him. Afterwards her stepson took me in the car up into the snow to see the beautiful view of Stockholm from that famous ski jump, but even so it wasn't the same as having Xmas at home in sunny South Africa.

I think that Niña will be going back to South Africa in about a year's time as she seems to find it difficult to adjust to living away from her parents. Poor Niña, she is too good and too sensitive for this dirty cruel world. Practically everything I've learnt and seen in Scandinavia has been about the seamy side of life, but I dare say one loses nothing by seeing such things and people as it puts you in a better position to know what you want.

I must say I'll be glad to get back to London. I'm not sorry I came here, but I'll never come back to Sweden again; perhaps Norway and Denmark, but not Sweden. There is such an awful atmosphere in this country. It's a shame because Stockholm is beautiful: but what the hell – *que sera sera*. I'll be back in London sometime soon and then I'll see Rèna and all my good friends again. How wonderful that will be. I can't wait to see Anna Northcote again and to be back in that wonderful town. The other day I went to an exhibition of Spanish master artists and it was amazing. I especially liked a Rubenstein picture of an old man sitting in an empty room reading a book – it was lovely.

Marina Keet comes back from Russia around the 8th and then I'll go and visit her. Gaubier makes us rehearse from morning till night, which is very tedious.

18 January 1960

I'm sorry I haven't written earlier but I've been so tied up with work that an appropriate moment hasn't presented itself before now. I have three-quarters of an hour to spare, so I'll try and get it all in then.

In about a week's time we leave Stockholm for Helsingbörg, Halmstad and Malmö where we will be on tour until 28 February and then – thank God – I'm leaving Sweden and will never come back again. I've got a lift back to London by car with two people from the theatre called Jane and Antonio. That way, I'll be able to save quite a bit of my fare home and at the same time see Germany, Holland, Belgium and France. We will stay in Paris for a couple of days, then drive to the coast and take a ferry over to England. I'm really looking forward to it. When I arrive in London again early in March I haven't a clue what will happen, but I'll just have to see when I get there. Everything here is covered in snow and the pavements have a little space cleared where you can walk. I love the way snow squeaks under your feet when you walk on it. I spend most of my spare time with Ernesto, Antonio and Jane and together we have a lot of fun as Jane has a car. The other night we popped the popcorn you sent me and it was delicious.

I'm so looking forward to being back in London again. I will go back to Anna's and if I can't get a good ballet job I think that after seeing a bit of the continent, I'll probably come back to South Africa as somehow I don't think I'd like to make my home in Europe; and to float around in ballet companies is so sordid as theatre people are the dregs. I feel like taking the next plane to Cape Town, but don't want to until I've made something of being in Europe.

1 February 1960 (overnight in a hotel in Halmstad, Sweden)

At the moment I'm sitting in my hotel room all cosy in bed after two performances in Halmstad and later this morning (it's already morning now) we catch the train to Malmö where I'll be until the 28th. Only 28 more days in Sweden – what a thought!

Helsingbörg was a delightful little town and from my hotel room I could see Denmark and the other day Antonio, Jane and I took a ferry across to Helsingør, which is a very small old Danish town only ten minutes by boat from Sweden. We had such fun there looking at all the quaint little curved streets and trying to twist my Swedish into Danish. It's rather like Swedish except you take a little hiccup between the words.

The show was a great success in Helsingbörg, but personally I don't like it much; it's worth it for the money though as I've already saved 1000 crowns, whereas at the Stadsteatern I couldn't save any.

The journey from Helsingbörg to Halmstad by train this morning was lovely as the sun was shining on the snow, the sea was a brilliant blue and Denmark on the other side shone. The small trees were especially lovely as they literally glittered. It's bitterly cold though and when we buy hot dogs on the way home at night – by the time you've taken two bites of bread the rest has frozen and you have to thaw it with spit. I was afraid my ears would drop off, so I invested in a white fluffy hat to match my coat. The theatre in Halmstad is gorgeous and has a restaurant in it, so between performances we ate there and listened to rock-and-roll records on the juke box.

All over Sweden they have machines that dispense food throughout the night and we had many funny times in Stockholm trying to diddle them. Once we came across one that gave an unlimited supply of coffee for the price of one packet and then Antonio, Jane, Ernesto and I would go to his flat, brew coffee and listen to music. After doing this a few times Ernesto would ask me what music was on and now I've got Tchaikovsky, Beethoven, Vivaldi and Mozart taped, not to mention Callas, Fitzgerald and Marlene Dietrich as well. It was great fun though until the neighbours beat on the door and then suddenly Ernesto could only speak Portuguese, Antonio Arabic, Jane French and me Afrikaans and then in very broken Swedish we would say, 'Vi talar inte Svenska', which means we don't speak Swedish.

The main source of conversation among us vile foreigners is how much we hate Gaubier. Ernesto is almost fanatical about him and one night when we were driving in the Djurgården Ernesto referred to him as 'that little bitch'. 'Well, for goodness sake', he said, 'I can't call him a gentleman just as you can't call a cow a butterfly' – we laughed about that for days as it sounded so incongruous coming from him.

8 February 1960 (from Södra Teatern, Malmö)

I got your letter today and can't tell you how happy it made me, as I had been feeling a bit desperate, almost as if I'd lost contact with home after hearing nothing for so long. Anyway, I also got a letter from Rèna today who says that I can share a flat with her in London from April and that makes me very happy too.

Yesterday we had the day off, so Antonio, Jane, Rudi and I went to Copenhagen where we spent a very pleasant day just walking around. We caught the last ferry back to Malmö and afterwards Jane, Antonio and I went for a drive along the coast in Jane's car. The three of us have a very nice flat in Malmö where we are staying for this month and it works out much cheaper than staying in a hotel, which is what most of the others are doing.

12 February

Life is going on very much as usual. Get up at one, eat, do some housework, go to the theatre, have a performance, come home, Rudi visits and we eat, and talk till about 4 and then sleep. It's snowing today for the first time since I've been in Malmö but not so very heavily and it isn't really very cold anymore either. In Stockholm the snow was so high and thick that when one wanted to get one's car out in the morning you had to take a spade and dig for half an hour before you could budge it. Cars parked along the road looked like a wavy hump.

Today we took the laundry to the *tvättomat* and did a good load of it and at the moment poor Jane has hauled out the iron, turned the bookcase into an ironing board and is preparing to attack some sheets. Rudi gets me English books out of the library and since I've been here in Malmö I've read Steinbeck's *Of Mice and Men* and two of Saroyan's books, *Tracy Tiger* and *The Adventures of Wesley Jackson*. I've now got a Graham Greene and a J. B. Priestley to attack. I've developed a great love for reading now and do it all through the performance between my numbers as I find the girls in the ballet so dull and the novelty of speaking Swedish just for the sake of it has worn off.

We've been having such good houses here that Mr Gaubier is thinking of going for a few days to Gothenburg, which would be a help as on top of our salary we'll get ten crowns extra every day. It's difficult to save in Sweden as all the prices are standardized – there are no Soho style markets, but I have saved 1000 crowns already.

From what I can gather, a socialist government is awful. I know you hate snobbery, but I don't think I do so much, as everything is brought down to end up at a very plebeian level. The people lose their individuality and live like machines. You don't see poor people, but you don't see happy people either. If Anthony came here and was the best doctor in the whole country he'd get less money than the worst because he's 22 and the worst is 52. All the young people lose their ambition because they rise naturally with age, but no amount of striving helps and if you are the laziest thing on earth, well it just doesn't make any difference, you still have your car and TV set. As a result, the service in shops and restaurants is appalling, as there is no such thing as being fired.[17]

17. It is perhaps helpful to note that Selina's views on the demerits of socialism radically changed later in her life.

(No date or address but probably sometime in February 1960)

Just before I left Stockholm I went to the South African consulate to fix my passport – which didn't need fixing – and met a charming bunch of South Africans who invited me out and seemed disappointed I was leaving. I met there a Mr Grant Smith from Johannesburg who knows John Molteno,[18] and is Sue Collins's[19] uncle. He was very kind to me and gave me his son's address in London as he thinks he can help me get a cheap room. Sue is now dancing with a partner in cabaret in Spain.

I was so mad that Gaubier made us rehearse and perform every day including Saturday and Sunday so I never had a chance to go and see Marina. I saw her once backstage and she and I arranged that if I had a free day we would make an arrangement to meet but, believe it or not, except for my trip to Oslo we didn't have one. We used to get up at two to be at rehearsal at three, rehearse and perform and then entertain ourselves afterwards at night and get to bed around 4 or 5. I could hardly expect Marina to join us then.

I'm sorry about the messy paper but it's all I've got now. I can't sleep tonight, but I'd better make an effort or I'll never catch my train at 9.45 – ugh, what a thought!

22 February 1960 (from Södra Teatern, Malmö)

I've tried every remedy for going to sleep and as none of them has worked I've decided to put my time to better use. I've read half of a J. B. Priestley book, a *Readers Digest* and the *Cape Times*. I've been reminiscing like mad over my divine childhood and have gone through *Rendezvous*, *Swan Lake*, *Coppélia*, and *Patineurs* in my mind. During the last week I've been as sick as a dog with the most shocking cough and flu. Gaubier sent a doctor who irritated me intensely by being far more concerned about my low blood pressure than by my really effective rasp, which came almost from my big toe, but anyway I'm on my feet again and haunt the theatre like a ship's horn.

A girl in the ballet called Margareta Thulin has lent me her puppy for two days while she's in Copenhagen (tomorrow night we're free).

18. John Molteno was Selina's uncle and a major fruit farmer.
19. Sue Collins had been a student at the UCT ballet school.

His name is Schnobben and is terribly sweet, but makes suspicious noises, so I've just thrown him out of my bed. Poor dog, I'm not surprised as all we had to feed him on was very dry poppy seed rolls and wine and we'd be blowed if we'd part with the latter. We've been given quite a lot of very nice wine lately and enjoy it immensely even although it's a bit incongruous with our slip-shod meals.

Rudi, my Danish artist friend, comes to visit us most nights after the show and says he'll paint me a picture to hang in my room in London. He had a beard and we made him shave it off and then to celebrate we had oatmeal porridge at four o'clock in the morning.

Schnobben is tearing around the room with Jane's slipper and somehow or other has managed to turn it inside out! What he'll do next I hate to think. Oh God, he's found my jock belt and now he's added my tights to the collection. I'm surprised to see him so active, as at the theatre he always seems to be sleeping in a polythene bag.

The tour has been extended for another 14 days, which makes me mad as it has put my nice little visit to Paris out of sight again – but we get ten crowns extra each day, so I don't suppose I can complain. Rudolpho (a dancer from Argentina and a very nice man) has just had a son and is thrilled to bits, but Gaubier has sacked him because he missed an entrance and there seems such a hole without his witty remarks. Gaubier objected to him acting like a prima donna, but I couldn't see it – he just took everything too lightly. There's a girl still away with a fever, so I took her part in a classical pas de deux. Gaubier was pleased and said I will keep it when she comes back.

The heavy snowfall seems to have stopped in Malmö and just slush remains. It's cold and glum and bleak and miserable and every night I say a silent prayer to Granny's rug, which, together with the ironing blanket and a cushion, comprises my bedding. Oh hell, I wish my nose would stop running. Last night I went to a film called *The Five Pennies*[20] and cried the whole way through. No Swedes did and I think now that it must have been my low blood pressure because it wasn't especially sad, although it was a bit on the sentimental side. Jane's car

---

20. A semi-autobiographical film released in 1959 starring Danny Kaye and Louis Armstrong.

hooter goes off every time she tries to park and the Swedes lean out of their windows and throw snowballs at us from their window sills.

Friday 4 March 1960 (from Ljung Resande Våning, Ystad, Sverige)

I got your letter in Malmö – thank you very much. I got the impression you were annoyed because I hadn't been to see Penny and Claes, but I did contact them although I didn't pay them a visit; but I've been ill and, besides, there is no train or bus to their place. This tour is killing me and for the last three weeks I've been quite ill and so spend all the time I can in bed in dingy hotel rooms. Apparently, I have very low blood pressure, but I'll have it seen to in London where I don't have to pay. I've already spent so much on hospital bills and it's rather a waste when you're travelling around. It's keeping me nice and thin though, so I don't really mind.

At the moment I'm in Ystad[21] on the south coast of Sweden where we have *the* most beautiful theatre imaginable and got fabulous press reports. I've got a room in a grim hotel with no hot water and no bathroom. There was no bathroom in Kristianstad either. Talk about the high standard of living in Sweden! Don't let anyone spin you that yarn – its deplorable. Let's not be pessimistic though.

Ystad is an ancient little town with very pretty old buildings and narrow winding streets and, even although it's in Sweden, it has a sort of atmosphere about it and is much warmer than anywhere else I've been this winter. We travel around by bus, which steams up so much inside that you can't see out. Suitcases wedge your feet into a position that gives one cramp within five minutes.

Dick, a very queer dancer, has a portable radio and he sits cowering over it, making a pretty picture with his sprayed grey hair and pretty face, which sometimes shows traces of blue eye shadow, but it's nice because if you listen very hard you can sometimes hear a little music. Then of course there's Sten Gäster, a casanova, who's always telling the girls not to seduce him and rants and raves about how we all gossip and spread scandals about him. No one says a word and the only scandal I've heard in connection with Sten is what he's said. Maud

---

21. Ystad is where the TV series *Wallander* was set.

Elfisiö laughs loudly and coarsely about nothing and May-Lis sits bolt upright with a blank, prim expression on her face and looks exactly like a school teacher. Åna has thrown out his wife so he sits at one end of the bus smoking vigorously under a no smoking sign and poor Liz, his wife, sits at the other looking sad.

Margareta, my roommate, the owner of Schnobbin, looks very sweet cuddling her dog and Lennart never says hello without trying to flirt with you. Terry from Greece hardly speaks any English and no Swedish and is always saying 'Hur mår du – bra [How are you – good]?' which drives us up the wall. There are others too, but they all have something in common. No intelligence – no education – no values – no money – no illusions – no hope – and they very wisely don't trust a soul, not even themselves. Jane is intelligent though, well-educated and awfully nice and I'm going back to England with her – how or when I don't know, but we're going – probably on Tuesday or Monday. I've read so many books though and everyone thinks I'm a little odd and terribly, terribly learned. I read Nevil Shute's On the Beach and they are now all petrified of radioactive air and keep on asking my opinion on the destiny of humanity. I feel quite scared myself now. Tomorrow we're going to Kristianstad, and from there to Lund. Five more performances and then we quit. I don't know if I'm glad or sorry. I think I'm glad but just rather petrified of not being able to get work.

The house sounds most exciting[22] and if you would like me to send you samples or things from London I'll be only too glad to help.

I've sent a parcel of presents home and expect you'll get them at the end of this month.

I don't know what my address in London will be but write to me c/o Standard Bank of South Africa, West End Branch, 9 Northumberland Avenue, London.

I'd like to go on rambling, but I'm afraid I've run out of paper. So until next time keep happy and please don't forget to write.

---

22. Selina's mother was in the course of building Lane House in the grounds of Rowan House in Kenilworth.

Chapter 4
Back to London

*Undated postcard (**March 1960**) from a ferry called* Kong Frederik IX.

Am crossing the water from Denmark to Germany in the middle of the night. Today travelled from Malmö to German coast – we are all dog-tired.

15 March 1960 (from 44 Sydney Street, Chelsea, London)

Well, I've arrived in London at last and am staying with Josephine. I haven't seen her yet as I've just come down from Peterborough today where I've been spending a few days with Jane. Through no fault of my own my luggage has been mislaid in Sweden and I'm having a hell of a time trying to get it back – until then I suffer in silence smelling more and more each day. As a stopgap, I bought myself a charming suit in Upington for only £2.5s. It is mohair, a gorgeous blue and terribly warm. It is really divine.

We had a very pleasant drive back over the continent from Malmö to Copenhagen, down south to Gedser, ferry across to Germany – Hamburg – Cologne – Belgium – Lièges – Brussels – Ostende – Dover. I liked Belgium very, very much, but I can't exactly say that I was very impressed with Germany – the Germans were rude and the country is teeming with troops and, according to the Belgium customs, will have another outbreak within ten years. There's a colossal anti-South Africa campaign going on in England now – television programmes showing the maltreatment of the natives are prevalent and they're appealing to the public not to buy South African fruit.

I popped into Mary Feltons this afternoon and they offered me work again from Monday – I'll take it for the pocket money until I've found my feet again and can arrange my life accordingly. The position for dancers is getting worse, but if I can't find what I really want I'll go back to [Albert] Gaubier in September for a 2½ month tour of Scandinavia at an even better wage than before. The tour isn't certain yet though!

Everyone in London says I've changed beyond recognition and even London somehow seems different to me, but I'm glad I went to Sweden as it has taught me a lot. The bank clerk spent ages looking for a clean note for me whereas before they gave me whatever was there. All this ultra-politeness and respect does a lot for my morale and I feel more confident than I did before. I think that by travelling one gains more balanced values and learns to sum up people far more quickly.

23 March 1960

I went to the bank this morning and they told me you have sent me £20. Thank you so much Margie – it really was a lovely surprise and lifted me right out of the doldrums – but why, oh why haven't you written for so long? I wait every day for a letter from you and it just doesn't materialize, which becomes rather distressing after a while.

I'm sorry to hear about what's been happening in Langa, but it's certainly made everyone sit up. I only hope it's not too late to nip it in the bud (if you can still call it a bud).

Isn't it ghastly about the sudden increase of radioactivity in the air? A child in Britain has already died of leukaemia as a result of it and apparently if they don't stop experimenting with atomic bombs my children will too. I'm going through an awful phase of feeling that there's no future. Do you think the human race is heading towards extinction? I suppose everything must end sometime, but I only wish I hadn't seen *On the Beach*.

Josephine is a marvellous girl. She and I just seem to know and understand the same things and we get along like a house on fire. Last night she and I stood each other to a meal, went to a cinema and then she showed me a poem she had written about 'words'. It was very wonderful and very true too.

I've moved in with Amelia because Angela and Anne Darnborough were difficult about me staying there. They told Jo that they couldn't understand me anymore as I'd changed so much, but that doesn't worry me because I understand more than I did before. Going to Sweden taught me a lot and I wouldn't wish to have missed it. It's not pleasant finding oneself alone in an obscure place, but it makes you see things from a different perspective. Jo understands but the others can't see how I can be glad that I endured times that weren't pleasant.

I've started working part time at Mary Feltons again and am beginning to get back into the swing of doing classes again. Jo has found a wonderful boyfriend in Mike, who seems to be just right for her. Amelia and I are keeping our eyes open for a flat, preferably around South Kensington.

I wasn't at all well when I first came back here, but I'm beginning to feel better now. I think I lost too much weight too quickly. In fact, I never recovered from being ill in Malmö, but now that I have a chance to lay off and take it easy, it's much better.

Rèna is going back to Greece next month and is giving up ballet. She reckons that with three languages she should be able to get herself an interesting job. I think she's being wise, although I'll miss her a lot. Perhaps I'll go to Athens and spend a holiday with her sometime.

The weather here has improved, but it's still cold and, although my luggage is on the way, it hasn't arrived yet, damn it. You should be getting a Xmas parcel from me soon. I hope you like your coffee pot.

Amelia seems well and happy and is in the throes of trying to get a new job. I haven't seen Georgie or Stella yet – they're the next on my list. I think I'll try and fit Stella in on Sunday if she's free. It's funny she's so old and yet just like a friend. Antonio has got a job Spanish dancing here and will get £100 a week – but I must admit he's a jolly good dancer and Sweden did him the world of good.

I earn £3.10 at Mary Feltons. I'm using up all my writing paper and it's extravagant and, after all, you don't really deserve such a long letter considering how naughty you've been about writing. I'm waiting for some pictures from Sweden, which you'll get straight away if they eventually come. I missed all the auditions by about a fortnight, so I'll be very lucky if I get anything within six months.

2 April 1960 (to Anthony)

Thank you so very much for both your letters and what a treat it is to hear from you so frequently. I'm sorry I have been so bad about replying but I really will try to pull up my socks in future.

In a way I've hated coming back to London, as the novelty and magic of it has worn off and there seems nothing to take its place. It's gradually getting better, though I daresay I'll soon be able to adjust to a new existence again. I've come at a time of year when ballet jobs are virtually non-existent and so I'm doing classes with Anna from 10 to 11.30 every morning and then selling stockings in Mayfair until 6.00 p.m. I earn £4.10 a week (£4.2 with tax deducted) but am considering looking after Jane's baby instead. He is a sweet little three-year-old and at least if I do that I don't limit myself to subtracting 3/11½ from a pound all day. I can go to the library to read – in fact do what I like as long as he is all right.

Tomorrow I'm going to the boat race again – sounds awfully blasé doesn't it? But I went last year and when I exclaimed in surprise, 'but there are only two boats,' someone indignantly replied, 'they're only two universities!'

My luggage still hasn't arrived back from Sweden and it's getting me down. I just hope to God that it comes eventually. London is full of South African news and there have been protest marches outside South Africa House in Trafalgar Square, which caused obstructions and lots of trouble. I miss you all so much. In fact I feel more homesick now than I ever have before. London at the moment is grey, cold and everything drips – from your nose down to the four-day-old washing hanging over your bed.

6 April 1960

I'm sorry about the scruffy air letter but I found it at the bottom of my bag and as I have time to kill I feel it is a waste not to write to you.

At the moment, today and Friday, I'm working on TV in a dancing programme called *Cool for Cats*. It's terrific fun. Today we are rehearsing at TV House in London and on Friday we go out to Wembley for the shooting. I think the programme is on the 18th. How I got the job? Well easy. The producer just phoned up and asked me. No audition – nothing. In the meantime I'm still at Mary Feltons, which is monotonous but helps funds. Anyway, two days' work is better than nothing. Jo has gone to Cornwall for two weeks and so I've moved into her room and now sleep in a bed instead of a stretcher, sofa or floor.

Last night Julian Grenville and I went to see a fireworks display outside Buckingham Palace to commemorate the state visit of de Gaulle. It was one of the most spectacular things I've seen and London is in a whirl because of it. On Saturday afternoon I went to the boat race. Oxford won and Princess Margaret and her fiancé nearly rode over my foot. I'm seeing Georgie tomorrow night and then she's off to Lebanon for a holiday. Last Sunday Amelia and I went to see Julian and he showed us some slides of Cape Town and the ballet. We were reminiscing. I like Amelia very much and enjoy being with her. I think I'll start entering the pools. I'm in the mood to make a fortune because I want to come home for a holiday sometime and I also want to live in Park Lane. Something's got to happen – I'm getting into a rut. The air in London is so thick and filthy that one feels perpetually tired and ill – unless of course you live in Park Lane and can go for midnight walks along the banks of the Serpentine. I've been to a couple of good films lately and on some rather uninspiring dates. No, my luggage hasn't arrived from Sweden yet, and I did get Kulu's postal order. I wrote and thanked her for it and gave the letter to someone else to post. They must have failed to do so, so I'll write again soon. Give them my love.

Tuesday 24 April 1960

I've been trying for days to put off writing to you in case your reply to my last letter came with the next post, but I'm sorry I can't wait any longer. Anyway I've got lots to tell you. I hope I can remember it all.

Don't faint, but I'm going to Copenhagen on Sunday until the end of August. It's rather short notice I know, but I only knew today, so I couldn't have let you know earlier. Gaubier turned up at Anna [Northcote's] class today and persuaded me to go. Rehearsal period is from 2–20 May and then we perform every day including Saturdays and Sundays with one performance on Mondays, one on Fridays and two every other day except 5 June, which is a national holiday, until 14

August and a possible prolongation until 21 August. From 2–20 May I'm getting £1.15 a day, and from then onwards £2.10 a day. That means I earn £255.5 in all and I reckon I should be able to come back to London with a nice little sum of about £135. I haven't touched my capital of £100 in the bank and hope to add about £30 to it before leaving.

The work should be rather fun as we will be 20 minutes outside Copenhagen by the Bellevue beach and I will be dancing the same sort of things as I did before. I don't really like Gaubier much, but I do adore Copenhagen and four months shouldn't kill me. There are very good classes in Copenhagen too, so I won't have to let them slip.

I've definitely made up my mind that the theatre isn't really where I'll find most happiness but as it's my only means of support and spasmodically is quite a good one, I feel I should carry on a little longer and at the same time try and cultivate other interests and hobbies. When I'm in Copenhagen I've decided to try a little amateur writing; partly because I enjoy writing, partly because it makes one observe and notice what's going on around you more than otherwise, partly because I'd like to keep impressions and experiences alive and partly because I personally feel that it is a good escape from self-pity and depression which seemed to have dominated my life to a large extent in Sweden. Instead of observing these people as an outsider might and being amused and interested in them, I let their unfriendliness get the better of me and by the time I came back to London I'd lost any incentive to see or learn more, in fact I had no particular desire even to live, but I've got over that now and I'll try not let it happen again. It's hopeless to let unfriendly people affect you and I'm sure they won't as drastically again.

My address in Copenhagen at the moment is c/o Mr Waldorff, Nytorv 9, Copenhagen, and I wonder if you could get me Torben Grandt's address again as I've lost it, and any other people you happen to think might not mind too much if I contacted them.

This afternoon I popped round to see Hallam, who is staying just around the corner, and we had a long chat. He is such a nice man.[1] I

---

1. Hallam Elton was Selina's maternal grandmother's brother who farmed in what was then Rhodesia. He was also an aspiring writer.

got a letter from him a little while ago, but as I've been working in the shop all day and have been out practically every night I didn't have a moment until now. He seems happy and looks well and I only wish that I wasn't going to Denmark so soon. Anyway, I'm going to take him round to meet Stella before I go and introduce him to Jo[2] as they are staying so close together. I met David Elton and his wife too and she said that what Americans hear goes in one ear and out the mouth.

Why don't you visit Copenhagen this summer. We will be on the beach while I'm working you can visit night clubs with Torben. I will keep you there if you can pay your passage. We can get a tiny flat just out of town and cook Danish delicacies. We can feed the pigeons in the square and go to matinées of English films. We can send postcards of the little mermaid to everyone we know saying 'Having a lovely time. Must fly now. Luv us,' and anyway you are my mother and I want to see if I still approve and perhaps you want to see if you still approve, which is far more to the point. And after all you don't want to miss the flea circus and throwing ores into the wishing pond at Tivoli either. It'll be open all the time we're there – Oh come on Marg be a sport. It'll do you good and you need a holiday. If you can't make it perhaps I'll be able to come home for your next summer in September. You know, catch a whaling ship and pay you a visit, for a few months and keep my money tucked away in the Standard Bank of South Africa for when I go back again. I don't want to come back for good yet but I would enjoy a visit and then I could return to London for the summer.

Right now spring has sprung, the air is clear, the streets are lined with blossoms and Jo and I walk under them with our heads up so that we can see into their full pink and white faces; and all the trees are bursting into bud, curtains are being pulled, windows flung open, coats and grim expressions shed, we all feel prettier, the men have started whistling, the hurdy-gurdy in Berkeley Square has started up, people are visiting each other again and the bus conductor calls you ducks. It is marvellous! I want to live again, learn again, see things again. I feel young again.

2. Selina's cousin, Josephine Molteno, married Mike Macrae and had two children, but tragically committed suicide at the age of 34.

At the weekend we spring-cleaned the house, sang songs to *King Kong* blasting from the house into the street and had little coffee picnics on the carpet. Our regular friends came round and told us how nice we were. I told Jo how nice she is and she told me how nice I am, and as a special treat I let her cut my hair. It looks like rats' tails, but feels just dandy. A boy called John and I went on the Aldermaston march but they can't blow the world up now because spring is here and life has begun anew. That means new ideas and not blowing up and killing and hating ideas, but loving and giving and improving ideas instead. I saw Georgie and she gave me a petticoat and a compact. She's gone to Lebanon and has cultivated a peaches and cream complexion.

Jeff Patterson is giving a party on Friday night and last night Eric and I went to see *Once More with Feeling*. We sat in the cheap seats and ate Turkish delight. We laughed when it was funny and were moved when it was sentimental and though that Kay Kendall and Yul Brynner were divine. We went to a Chinese restaurant, talked about life and then walked home making up stories about everyone we saw in the streets. We walked through some stinking mews, past some sweetly scented blossom, we looked in a hotel window and saw a woman standing absolutely still and a man drinking and we decided that inside that glass window was the aftermath of a tragedy. We looked through Hallam's letterbox to see if there were any letters for him but didn't ring because it was after one a.m. and when I went to bed I went to sleep until today when Gaubier floated in, grinned and sat down. He gave me a fabulous lunch of curried chicken and rice and we spoke for three hours before I decided to kick up my heels and vamoose. Leave London, Anna's class, selling stockings and poverty. I can always come back to it can't I? One can always stay alive in London but a chance to be in Copenhagen for the summer doesn't happen every day. As far as I know, only in April in the 1960s.

My luggage will come. I got a letter this morning saying they put the wrong name on it but that their error has now been corrected. It'll probably come on Monday just after I've left, but Jo, dear Jo, will send it to me I'm sure. Did you ever get a parcel I sent you from Malmö at the end of February? It should have arrived by the end of March. Jo has given me a suit – I must take it in, but otherwise it's rather nice.

For the Easter weekend everyone went away except me. I was sick.
The doctor came and diagnosed bronchitis, flu and, believe it or not,
tonsillitis. I've been under the weather for a couple of months now,
but now that it's spring I'll never be sick again.

It's a pity really that I leave just before Princess Margaret loves,
honours and officially obeys her photographer Antony Armstrong-
Jones, the first Lord Snowdon.

Give my special love to all I love and sit down now and write to me
in Copenhagen because you never know, perhaps spring hasn't sprung
there.

Chapter 5

Denmark

5 May 1960 (from Skodsborg Strandvej 260, Skodsborg, Denmark)

I'm desperately happy here in Denmark and I have so much to tell you that I don't know where to begin. I left London from Liverpool Street on 1 May and took the train to Harwich. It was a fairly pleasant trip except that I was put in an apartment with a deadly dull Hollander who spoke about his career as an unsuccessful lawyer and nearly sent me crazy with boredom.

We arrived in Harwich and I climbed onto the ferry, which pitched and rolled furiously and, as a result, I spent most of the journey clutching my middle and feeling ghastly. I had the biggest sole in the world for lunch, which an English Royal Navy chap bought for me. He also bought me my supper on the train in Holland, so I can't say I did too badly. The Hoek of Holland was grim and cold, but once we were in the train and heading towards Rotterdam we passed through glorious countryside and I saw all the things one is supposed to see in Holland – dykes, tulips, windmills, houses on stilts and Hollanders.

After a while it began to get dark and I made a rather unsuccessful effort to sleep in a corner under my coat, but we were interrupted the whole way to Grossenbrode Kai by people getting in and out and officials coming in to stamp passports and look at tickets.

We arrived at Grossenbrode Kai at 5 in the morning – the train drove into the bottom of the ferry and what a joy it was to go up and wash and eat. I bought myself a bottle of Carven Ma Griffe and started to speak Swedish again. Now I'm learning Danish, German and French and am getting on fine. Danish and German are both easy to learn and I hope that by the time I leave I'll at least be as fluent in Danish as I am in Swedish.

We arrived in Gedser (southern port of Denmark) at about 8.30 and from the most beautiful Danish boat on earth we ventured into a filthy, packed train again, in which we travelled for three hours all squashed together with Swedes, Danes, Germans and Americans. A fat German woman gave me German lessons and some American beatniks told me about the States. We arrived in Copenhagen at 11.30, exactly 25½ hours after leaving London and John Massey (a dancer from London who is working with us) and the director Paul Waldorff, met me. We started rehearsing at one and carried on all afternoon.

In the evening the whole company went out to Skodsborg and that is the nicest thing of all. Skodsborg is a little way out of Copenhagen on the coast and we are all staying there together in a big house by the sea. Our host and hostess, Kel and Doris, are very nice. The beach is at the bottom of the garden and we can swim before breakfast in the mornings and walk along it in the moonlight in the evenings and see the lights of Sweden in the distance.

The theatre is in Klampenborg not far from Skodsborg and we open on 20 May and play every night (except 5 June) until 21 August. By then I ought to have saved a bit of money. At the moment we are rehearsing every day and all day 10–6.30 and we all go to a restaurant for lunch and supper. The food, together with board and lodging, is only 15/- a day, which is excellent value and saves the fag of cooking and it also means that we get three good square meals a day.

Sometimes we take a horse and cart from the theatre to the restaurant through a park where we've seen many reindeer and antelopes. The weather on the whole has been wonderful and once we open I look forward to doing some classes in Copenhagen with Bartholin.[1]

The crowd in the theatre here are considerably nicer than they were in Sweden, which makes a difference too – except for Gaubier. He gives me the pip and always wears a hairnet. Among the girls and boys we have people from France, Spain, South America, Germany, Poland,

---

1.   Birger Bartholin (1900–1991), a Danish ballet teacher and choreographer.

Finland, Sweden, the United States, England and Denmark. Quite a collection don't you think?

Tonight I'm going to go out with Phil, the boy who drove back over the continent with us a couple of months ago. It'll be nice seeing him again as he was kind. Just before I left London I got a letter from Runer Jacobssen about my luggage. He said he'd sent it by plane to London airport but had called me S. M. Ottie instead of S. Molteno but he'd contacted them and I'd hear from them in a couple of days, which I did. Andrew, a boy I know in England, promised to drive me there on the Saturday before I left, which was the only day he had the car and I was grateful to have the help. Unfortunately, fate was against us because as we were driving along, just before we got to the airport, an old woman walked straight into the middle of the dual carriageway with three lanes of fast-moving traffic in it and was hit by three cars, including us, and unfortunately was killed. There was absolutely nothing we or anyone else could have done to avoid her and well what else can I say except that a life was lost, which might not have been lost, through my flipping luggage.

Andrew says that I may be required to go back to London for a few days for the inquest, but I hope not. I hate those sorts of things and anyway Gaubier says I can't. Oh Marg, it's so wonderful to be able to see the world like this. You know I've been to Las Palmas, England, Sweden, Denmark, Norway, Germany, Holland and Belgium already. I haven't heard from you for such a long time. I hope you are alright, as I worry quite a lot about you with all that's going on in South Africa. Did I tell you that I saw Verwoerd being shot on television? In fact, there is nothing else on TV and in the papers in either Denmark or England but South African politics.

The latest scandal is that Mr Gaubier has split up with his boyfriend Jörma and has now taken up with Mr Waldorff. Jörma is clearly very upset about it.

Thursday 14 May 1960

I was so thrilled to get a letter from each of you both on the same day and thank you so much for the addresses. I haven't looked up any of them yet, but will do so after 20 May when we should have some more free time. So far, we've been working flat out all day and every day, including weekends, because Gaubier is making a comeback to Denmark after 11 years and is determined that it should be a success. I must say we have an infinitely better group of dancers this time and they're much nicer people too. In fact, I'm very happy in spite of the endless rehearsals and Gaubier's tantrums, accompanied by the continual appearances of ghastly Mr Waldorff.

Two of the boys are married and have small babies of which they are very proud, but all the rest are homosexuals and John from England and Åne from the Stockholm Opera are my special queer friends and they confront me with all their boyfriend troubles. They are so nice though, especially John whom I know from Anna's and we have a lot of fun together.

We are rehearsing at the moment but I have half an hour's break while they are working on something that I'm not in. It's swelteringly hot and also a public holiday in Denmark. When we went out for lunch today we saw crowds of Danes in sunglasses going down to the beach to get tans. Gosh, we are all absolutely exhausted, but have to go flat out as if we shirk we've got to pay a ten-crown fine.

On Tuesday night six of us went into Copenhagen to listen to Marlene Dietrich[2] singing. She was fabulous and her personality comes over the footlights in waves. If it hadn't been her we would have all been asleep in five minutes as the show was from 12 to 1.30 at night and on top of it we'd been rehearsing from 10 a.m. to 7.00 p.m. (that is all day).

Kel, the owner of the house in which we are staying has a whole lot of hairdresser boyfriends who do my hair for me and one of them, Hans, has a prize as the second best in Denmark. He gave me the new Vienna do for Marlene Dietrich and I went along like a peacock with a stiff neck. Since then I've washed it, so it's like a mop until next time.

I've met some of my old friends from the Stadsteater in Malmö who are now working in *My Fair Lady* in Copenhagen and we are looking forward to a proper reunion, as soon as we have some free time!

2.   Marlene Dietrich (1901–1992), German actress and singer.

Gaubier has got himself an assistant ballet mistress from the Royal Theatre and she sits out front with a little book in which she writes down all our mistakes and then announces them afterwards.

Marg, I don't know whether or not I'll be able to get your material here but I will buy the magazine and have a jolly good try; otherwise, perhaps I can ask Jo, or even Hallam, to try in England, but I'm afraid I can't do anything until after we open. Clothes here are not a patch on London or Sweden, but what dreamy silver! I'll try and buy you some for the new house. The plain Jansen is my favourite as it has such a wonderful cut. What a pity we're such a big family because a set of knives, forks and spoons for eight would cost rather a lot, but anyway I'll see. The glass too is very, very nice, but is risky to send in the post.

I'm so glad that the coffee pot arrived safely and that you like it. I was a bit nervous in case you didn't. Or perhaps I could send you some nice teaspoons!

Would you like me to come home sometime in September and stay for a few months and return to London round about March? One can now get a return ticket from London to Cape Town for about £77, and if I manage to save about £100 here, I don't see why not. I have £100 sitting in London and perhaps I could get a job in Cape Town for a few months.

Perhaps it's a ridiculous idea though, but the winter in London is so grim and I would so much like to see you all again. What do you think about it? The most important thing is whether you want me to and if you have space for another body from outer space.

I've got so blasé about travelling around the world that it doesn't frighten me in the least now and going to London is like going home for the weekend. I have roots there now and so could never be afraid of starving. Perhaps Ant and I could go over together. It wouldn't cost you anything. I've supported myself for 15 months so I see no reason why I shouldn't go on doing so. Of course, if an exceptionally good job comes along I'll take it. How's my little Frankie now? I suppose he's not so little anymore and does Martin still hate his schoolteacher? I'm still waiting for a picture of Vicky and Anthony. I have one of Anna, Frankie and Martin, but not of Vicky and Ant.

I seem to have run out of news, but thought I'd better write in any case. At the moment, every day is more or less the same. Get up in the morning – rolls and coffee overlooking the sea all together in the big dining room. Catch the bus from Skodsborg to Klampenborg at 9.17. Walk round the shops, go to Bakken and rehearse until one. Change, take a horse and cart to Ryttergården for lunch of smorgasbord, return at 2, rehearse till 6.30 or 7, supper at Ryttergården, catch 9.40 bus, go home, have a glass of wine and a chat, go to bed.

31 May 1960

Thank you so much for you letter and I must say that the thought of you coming over to Europe next year thrills me no end.

I've been doing some classes in Copenhagen with Bartholin, and I like them very much. Life in the theatre is the same as ever – for the last week or so we've been hanging on a string over this Chilean tragedy as one of the girls Isabella has her family there. We scanned the papers daily and followed the earthquakes as they went further and further south and through her hometown. We'd almost given up hope of their survival when yesterday a telegram arrived to say they'd been saved, so we all heaved a sigh of relief and life goes on as before.

Tomorrow morning the theatre doctor is taking me to the hospital for an X-ray because I've had a cough for three months and have lost 15 lbs; but I feel all right so I don't think I have TB, but it's better to make sure anyway. Yesterday I went to the dentist but I had no holes – thank goodness. I've had my hair cut short – short, short and I look like a convict but it feels dishy.

Torben Grandt has had an illegitimate child and his wife is in Rome. I haven't seen him but heard through a friend of his at the ballet class. I think he's going to get a divorce as he wants to keep the child and his wife doesn't have any.

Rudolpho, a dancer from Argentina, has just brought his wife and three-month old son from Stockholm. The baby is the sweetest, most intelligent child on earth and as you can imagine, when it's around I'm in my seventh heaven. Gaubier has gone to Gothenburg for a while. Sunday the 5th is our free day and, among other things, I'm going to see Hamlet's castle at Helsingør. I find the theatre trying and miss Jo and her inspiring London friends. I'd very much like to come home for our winter (your summer) as the thought of a winter in London without work petrifies me, but I doubt that my finances will run to it. Our work here finishes a month after the London auditions for the next season, but there's no point in worrying now.

There's one person in the company with substance – Roberto from Spain. He reads philosophy in French, but doesn't speak English or Swedish and, as my French is evil, it's impossible to have a conversation with him. The weather has gone cold again and I haven't saved any money yet. My word, but Denmark is expensive – every time I go to class its 10/- down the drain.

7 June 1960 (to Anthony at Medical School in Cape Town)

I feel bad about not writing to you when you've been so wonderful about writing to me – I adore hearing from you and when are you coming overseas? Don't go to Uppsala – I'm sure you won't like Swedes (they're grim). Cambridge is much nicer I'm sure! Anyway, hurry up because I miss you and if you're good I'll show you around London.

I still love Denmark, and living by the sea – the summer has come and we spend most of our time in our bikinis on the beach. I do classes in Copenhagen with Bartholin (a very good and well-known teacher).

On the 5th we had the whole day free and five of us went sightseeing. We first went to Kronborg Castle in Helsingør, which is where Shakespeare set *Hamlet*. Afterwards we had a picnic lunch in the woods and then went to see Fredensborg Palace where the king has his summer residence. The king was home so we couldn't go inside, but we walked in the grounds, which, with the green trees and grass and rhododendrons in full bloom, were beautiful. Later we went to the old church in Roskilde dating from 906 where all the Danish kings are buried. There is a pillar there against which Peter the Great of Russia used to measure his height.

At Kronborg Castle I met two South Africans who had left Johannesburg two weeks ago and they gave me all the news about Verwoerd.

Kronborg Castle.

22 July 1960

I've just sat down to take a breath in my shambolic room with the radio blasting and an hour to spare before lunch. I've been lying on the beach reading Dostoyevsky's *The Idiot*, but a big black cloud drifted over obliterating the sun and, hence, my source of warmth, so I was forced to return to the house and the seclusion and privacy of my matchbox room.

For the last couple of weeks I've had visitors – Niña, Jo and Pippy Eriksen.[3] Niña wrote a little letter to say she was coming for her holidays. I was thrilled to bits and got up at the crack of dawn to go and meet her at the station. We arrived back, had breakfast and just as we were sitting down in my room getting to know each other again, Terry announced that someone had come to see me, and who should it be but Jo, standing there barefooted, blonde hair hanging over her radiant face and a ruddy great canvas bag slung over her shoulder. 'I've come

3. Daughter of Sven and Pam Eriksen from Elgin. Pam came and stayed with the Moltenos at Rowan House while Sven was dying in Groote Schuur Hospital.

to stay,' she announced emphatically; and like as how we're from the same stock and get on so well I was just thrilled to bits.

The three of us tore down to the beach – had a dip and then sat down on the beach and talked and talked and talked as we sifted sand between our fingers and toes. She'd hitchhiked here and so had many tales, and extremely amusing ones at that, to tell.

Later we were called up to lunch and Niña and Jo were a little shaken by what rather extraordinary people I live with. It made me realize what one can get used to and just accept as normal. There they sat around the huge dining room table speaking French, Spanish, Swedish, Danish, German and English all at once. Paul was swigging back gin and trying very hard to put on some false gaiety – Doris at one end of the table was in floods of tears over a recent catastrophe and, at the other end, Brigitte and Dick were splitting their sides with mirth. Roberto was busy talking about 'la vie' to Niña and Jo, and I was translator at that time for that particular conversation. Some were drinking schnapps, others beer, but the most of us milk. Coffee was served and the atmosphere was suddenly thickened by rising smoke; a few got up and straggled noiselessly off while others sat around to finish their discussions so that whoever won the argument could feel satisfied and the others defeated. Niña left to put her clothes away and Jo and I laid out the cards and had a game of patience.

Both Niña and Jo were immediately accepted into the circle and had a super holiday. While I was working Jo, Niña and Ollé, a friend of Ärne's who is also here on holiday, used to go for walks, see films and usually when I got home at about 1.00 a.m. I would find them engrossed in conversation in Ollé's room and consuming innumerable cups of tea. I would join in and sometimes the sun had begun to rise on the horizon and the birds to sing before we went downstairs to bed. Jo and I shared my bed and Niña slept on a camp bed on the floor – the place of honour.

One morning after class the three of us went to an exhibition and Jo and I bought materials and each made ourselves a frock, of which we are extremely proud. The materials are Danish hand painted and only available in Copenhagen.

I made an absolutely straight frock with a high straight-across neck and belt around the waist. I gave what was over to Pippy as she had bought some of the same material and might need it. Jo also made a sloppy shirt for Mike, which she is going to send to him when she gets back to Copenhagen in two weeks' time.

We sewed our things by hand and I got mine finished just in time for a big party to celebrate our hundredth performance. Niña had to go back before the party but I did a little wangling and managed to get Jo along too. The party was held in the poshest restaurant in Copenhagen called the Ambassadeur and Jo and I had the time of our lives and the dinner of our lives also. Before we went into this exotic room we were each given a red cocktail and, as a result, before we even started we were a bit tipsy. Thank goodness Jo and I were put at a table together in a corner, so we could have as much fun as we liked. After the dinner and a few speeches the band struck up and we began to dance until about four o'clock in the morning. Afterwards, we took a taxi home and, once we were there, went out like lights.

One evening when I came home Jo wasn't in my room so I went up to Olle's where I found her and Pippy too. Pippy had come to take her away to Finland with her. They stayed here two days and this morning they were off on the road stacked with rucksacks and a colossal sausage, which was to feed them on the way. I am sorry they've gone now – it's left a sort of awful empty feeling. I feel different from the others here, but perhaps it's a good thing though because now I'll throw myself into classes and start to work really hard and I'll read lots of books too. I always read a lot when I'm working – otherwise I get terribly irritated sitting in the dressing room doing nothing and always having to speak in a foreign language.

Our contract has been extended until 3 October for a tour of Denmark with 25/- extra a day. I think I will probably take it unless I can get work with Elsa Marianne von Rosen. I don't think I will have enough money for a return fare home in September. Between the two contracts we will get 18 days paid holiday. Yes, I did get my luggage back. Andrew sent it to me from London and it was all in one piece.

We are playing to packed houses every night and more than 200,000 people have already attended our performances. I'm so tired though and can't seem to catch up on my sleep and the days seem to be spinning round like a whirlwind. If only we could have one day off – but that's out of the question – Denmark unfortunately hasn't got a Dutch Reformed Church, so no one here seems to take the Sabbath very seriously.

Copenhagen is now full of tourists and the narrow pavements are teeming with Americans laden with souvenirs, ghastly little boys with crew cuts and pampering parents who stuff them with *weiner-bröd* to keep them quiet. Around every place of interest one sees a row of Happy Tour buses, thousands of people with cameras around their necks, all merry and bright trying terribly hard to enjoy themselves. Thank goodness out at Skodsborg we're away from all that and have some quiet and fresh air at our disposal.

The house sounds very nice indeed. It must be such a relief to be out of the flat and to have some elbow room again. I got a card from Jeff Patterson the other day and he's coming to Copenhagen on the 29th, so is Brian Cornelly, an ex UCT medical student and now practising in London. What I'll do with them I don't know, but they can no doubt amuse each other.

4 August 1960

I was astonished and sorry to hear about Nancy Cartwright's illness[4] and also about your spot of bad luck and difficult period,[5] and I sincerely hope that it will pass very soon. I only wish I could do something to help you, but if I sent you money it would be such a measly pittance as Danish exchange is very bad that I think it would be better if I saved up and then, when I get myself settled into something more permanent and you are still in need, perhaps I could help you then.

At the moment I'm living in agonizing suspension and hope as Elsa Marianne von Rosen has expressed a desire to have me in her company

4. Nancy Cartwright, who was Selina's godmother and mother of Justin Cartwright (a well-known novelist in the UK), had been diagnosed with breast cancer. However, she made a good recovery and lived into her nineties.
5. Selina can't recall the nature of their difficulties, but presume that they were financial, for this was the time when Margie was building Lane House and letting out Rowan House to the Godfrey family.

Scandinavian Ballet, but it is very difficult as the company is sponsored by the government and permits only Scandinavians to dance in it. She will see what she can do and at the moment I'm waiting on tenterhooks for a reply. My work permit expires very soon and my chances I'm afraid are slim – it frustrates me very much that I may lose a wonderful chance only because of my nationality. Anyway, if that doesn't come off I will definitely go with Gaubier until 3 October in Denmark. Our season here has been prolonged until 28 August and from then until the tour I will stay in Denmark and be paid about 25/- a day. It will be a wonderful chance to do classes flat out as I find Bartholin a teacher from whom one can learn very much. At the moment I am doing classes three times a week, as with two performances practically every day and not one day free I find I can barely stand on my two legs.

We've had a wonderful bout of weather here recently, which helps no end to keep one's spirits up. The other night it was so beautiful and warm that Roberto and I decided to walk all the way home from the theatre to Skodsborg. We walked barefoot along the coast and it took us two and a half hours. We could see the lights twinkling in Sweden, hear the waves beating against the shore and, although it was as warm as toast, lightning was flashing through the sky. We picked roses from the hedges on the way and there wasn't a soul in sight. Sometimes Roberto can be so nice and he was that night, but at other times he makes me so angry that I fume with rage and then at the most crucial moment my French fails me and as a result he naturally comes out on top. We had an almighty row at lunchtime today and he's simmering in his room while I sit here writing to my dear parents so far away and feeling terribly lonely and sorry for myself.

John is in bed with jaundice and only gets up for the show every evening and Árne is in bed with a fever. Dick has just recovered from the mange and I've still got a shocking cough. My X-rays were OK so I haven't got any foul disease, but I think it's because we never have a long enough spell of good weather, never have any rest and vegetables only once a month, so it doesn't surprise me that I can't throw it off. Yesterday I was at class and afterwards my American composer friend, Paul, and I went to visit Domy from Israel, who is confined to bed because of an unfortunate accident to his knee. We spoke the whole afternoon about all sorts of things and were finally driven away to a Chinese bar by hunger. Domy gave me a book about troublesome teenagers and one that I'd already read to Paul.

I've got through so many books since I've been here as I find them a wonderful escape from the monotony of everyday life. The other dancers in the theatre see me as a 'witch' or 'idiot' because I play cards, read palms and thousands of books; they clearly think I'm abnormal because I don't enjoy spending all my money on alcohol and being in the company of the most boring people on earth. Perhaps I have gone a bit barmy. I feel that I'm growing further and further away from most people and prefer to hold onto just a few for friends.

Jeff passed through Copenhagen for a couple of days at the beginning of the week and I spent an afternoon with him on the beach, and felt a distinct lack of contact. The only thing we had in common was that we were both from South Africa. He thinks I've grown much too serious and mix too much with ultra-sensitive people. OK ships ahoy – hoist out the yachts and let's have a jolly time. I'm sorry but I don't find it jolly – not for a lifetime anyway.

Copenhagen is still full of tourists; the future is still unsettled; Jo is still in Finland; the people still drink, shout and fight like a lot of barbarians; everyone rides a bicycle and the traffic gives me a heart attack because everything misses everything else by a fraction of an inch; Ballet Theatre was here but we couldn't see it; Greco's company is also here and we can't see that; the symphony concerts too are out of our reach. We had a lovely pudding last night and I really must go and do some ironing as I have nothing to wear otherwise. I love you all very much and can't wait to hear from you again.

Sunday night, 28 August 1960

Here I sit all curled up in a dilapidated chair in a funny little flat way up at the top of an old, old house in Taarbaek.[6] Isabella[7] is lying on a bed with her nose buried in *Le Petit Prince*, which Lillian gave to me

---

6. On the east coast of Denmark , north of Copenhagen.
7. Isabella was a dancer from Chile. Selina no longer remembers her surname.

on the last night. The table is littered with debris and the rain is pouring down, beating against the little half-moon window and it subsides only to let the house be shaken by thunder and lightning – and yet there is a wonderful stillness, although rather empty and lonely. It always hurts a little when things finish and you know that soon everything – all the memories, times together, up times, down times, tears, work, laughter and fun are just memories that disappear in time and that really we are all so alone basically, and those fears, complexes and insecurities have to be held down as each one of us is about to take a big confident step into the darkness and all in a different direction.

We had our last performance – number 175 – glasses of sherry and dainty little *smörgas* were handed round, followed by long unnecessary speeches. I was a little tipsy and depressed and Rudolpho held onto me and fed me and was like a big brother – then we traipsed to the taxi laden with dirty tights, make-up and much luggage and when we got home we talked and talked and talked – and at three o'clock I went to bed and we said goodbye to the ones going to Stockholm, Finland, Italy, Germany and God knows where. Then, at 7 o'clock the next morning somebody was shaking me and when my eyes opened, it was Roberto and I must see him off to Paris. I got up, washed my face, drank lots of coffee, called a taxi, loaded it up, in my best Danish said 'Paris Express' and we were off, eyes heavy from the night before – but we found the train and waited while people were clipping tickets and so forth and I had to speak to Roberto very quietly because, as he so rightly and logically pointed out, given that it was the Paris express, surely some people spoke French, and my accent was so English that they would squirm. It made me smile to think of something like that because I'm so proud that I can speak French at all that I can hardly walk for pride and I want to get up on top of the highest building in Copenhagen and shout '*Je parle français, écoute!*'

Anyway he was gone and I walked away; the streets were empty and I wandered around and finally found my way into a coffee bar, which was just opening up, ordered a coffee, took out a book I'd bought, *Farewell to Arms* by Hemingway, and read and read and read until it was time to go to class – and afterwards to a film rehearsal and then to visit Isabella, who persuaded me to move in with her, which I've done, as it's so cheap, until the tour begins on 13 September.

Last night we went into Copenhagen to meet two dancers from the Pantomime Theatre in Tivoli and afterwards the two boys took us to the Cazz Bar for a beer. It's a homosexual bar, so it wasn't surprising that we met Gaubier there and he said he'd sacked Jurek from the tour on the railway platform when he was on his way to Paris and my heart sank because I like Jurek and it must have been awful for him to hear about it at a time like that.

I was so angry because Elsa Marianne von Rosen hummed and hawed and telephoned and couldn't make up her mind and then when I said – 'answer yes or no tomorrow,' her answer was no and I signed with Gaubier for a 19-day tour – and then two days later she phoned and said, 'please I want to take you now, now, now' and I'm so angry because I've signed another contract and hers is such good work and for longer too. Well, she can go to hell, as what does she expect me to do? Starve while she makes up her mind whether or not to take a bloody foreigner. Well, I'm sorry, but time waits for no man – not even Countess Elsa Marianne von Rosen with her Scandinavian Ballet and all her money. Now she'll have to do without my valuable services. She's made me suffer enough keeping me on a string so long and now she needs me and she can't have me, and I need her and it's too late to have her. Irritating woman – can't people make up their minds at the right time? Oh well, I'll drop the subject because it makes me so angry.

Now I'm having a paid holiday from Gaubier Ballet until 13 September on 25/- a day. Isabella and I are the only two still in Copenhagen, as where are we to go? She lives in Chile and I in South Africa!

The weather is frightening and every now and again Isabella and I sit bolt upright as the lightning and thunder torment us. Just a moment ago something outside was hit as we have just heard a terrific crash and the sound of something falling. Well, I hope we're still here tomorrow morning. Årne Rassett dyed his hair black and it's come out bright blue. Shame, he was so upset and Doris and I were laughing until our sides almost split.

After the tour, which is of Denmark's provinces, I will return to London and try and find work – I'll probably go back on 3 or 4

October. The day of my birthday I'm out of work – perhaps that is good luck! And to London for the third time – what's that about third time lucky? The only thing is that it's a bad time of the year, but I daresay I'll be OK. I will return having saved approximately £150, so that should keep my head above water for a while anyway.

I'm working flat out with Bartholin now and hope to be just startling when I get back – I feel that my dancing is improving a lot, which is what is spurring me on at the moment. You'll be glad to hear that I've met the Bruhns and have spent two pleasant afternoons with them. They have been extremely kind to me and I like them both very much – I may go and stay with them for a couple of days sometime soon. The film will probably be finished by Thursday.

Isabella has lent me Rudolpho's bike – he's gone to Stockholm and she will have to go up for a few days soon to settle some affairs there. I miss you terribly so please write – perhaps you have. Until 3 October send to my old address as I'll always go and look for post and then afterwards c/o Standard Bank of South Africa, 9 Northumberland Avenue, London? as I don't know where I'll be staying, probably with Georgie or Jo.

Chapter 6

London yet Again

10 October 1960

I am terribly sorry that I haven't written home for so long – I really feel bad about it, but so much has been happening lately that time went by quicker than I expected it to.

I think that the last time I wrote was shortly after we finished the season in Copenhagen and I was in the midst of the film. Well, that's all finished and we were blessed with a short holiday for about two weeks. Everyone else went home to their various countries except me and Isabella , so we decided to pay a visit to Stockholm. We hitchhiked there and back attired in blue jeans and beat pullovers. We made the journey in one piece (only just) and spent the first night in Stockholm sleeping on the steps outside a police station and the next day moved into a flat in the old town where we stayed as guests of Oscar Montiel. While I was there I did classes every day with Lia Schubert.[1] We met many fascinating people and spent a most hectic and extremely cheap week there.

As soon as we arrived back in Copenhagen we were flung into rehearsals again for the tour. A couple of days later we were on the

---

1. Lia Schubert, born Vienna 1926, moved to Zagreb in 1930 and then to Paris to escape anti-Semitism. She worked in the resistance movement and lost her mother and brother in the war. She was the only member of her family to survive the holocaust and she nearly didn't when the Gestapo tracked her down to a performance in Marseilles, but her colleagues smuggled her away. She was artistic director of the Ballet Academy in Stockholm for 11 years before going to Israel in 1968.

train to Slagelse – a grim little town, but we only spent one night there. The next day we went on a long trip by bus and ferry to Aarhus.

There Isabella and I stayed in the height of luxury in the Royal Hotel, which had a green bathroom. It was heaven and we were there for four days. After Aarhus we went all the way up to the north of Denmark to a lovely town called Aalborg, where we danced in the most beautiful theatre I've ever seen. In the evenings we usually eat in a night club called the Ambassadeur, as nothing else is open. There, there was a conjurer and the works – we had a wonderful time.

Well, we had to tear ourselves away from Aalborg at the crack of dawn one morning, and went down to Herning, where we all stayed at the Mission Hotel, which was very nice indeed. After Herning came Odense, the birthplace of Hans Christian Andersen, and one day I went to see his house, where all his writings and letters were exhibited. He lived in a quaint little winding street of very low picturesque houses. The road was cobbled and curved and opposite his house was a little pub where I daresay he got drunk many a time. I liked this town best. It was so sweet, so fascinating and so full of atmosphere and, as the prophecy goes, after the good comes the bad, and we were carted off *en masse* to the grimmest of grim places – the one and only Silkeborg. Our hotel rooms were damp and stank, it was bitterly cold and we were dog-tired. Thank heaven it was only for one day. Then Fredericia, not bad, Aabenraa, by this time I was semi-conscious, Nykøbing, in the south and last of all Roskilde, where all the Danish kings are buried, and not far from Copenhagen. We finished on the night of 2 October and after the show we all went to Copenhagen to celebrate my twentieth birthday at the Cosy Bar and to say goodbye for good.

The next day, the 3rd, I booked my ticket and rushed around the place like a mad thing trying to organize my affairs. I bought a ticket for the 7.30 a.m. train on the 4th.

On the night of the third those of us who were left – just Isabella and me – went to see *My Fair Lady* and afterwards went out with some of our friends who were dancing in it. The next morning I missed the train. Isabella left on the Paris Express and I had to wait until six o'clock that evening for the next one. Anyway, I had 15 books – pocket books that I'd read – and so I decided to sell them. I walked along the back streets of Copenhagen for hours in vain and finally in desperation sold the lot for 2/-. Anyway, by the time I was finished I got onto the train and it screeched out of the station. There we were, all bundled together in a second-class carriage amid a sea of cigarette smoke, suit-cases, chatter and people. Anyway, to cut a long story short, I found that I was on the Paris train.

It wasn't even a surprise to me, so I just sat pretty and resigned myself to changing at 6.30 a.m. in Osnabrük and then waiting for the Hamburg–London train to come through. We chuffed down to Gedser where the train slowly eased its way down into the bowels of the ferry. Finally, we were allowed out and like a herd of cattle, we all instinct-ively headed to the dining room, via ladders and steps and lifts and God knows what. It was a German ship and you should have seen the spread. I tucked in like a vulture, it was the first thing I'd eaten that day and I took each mouthful as if it were my last.

A Belgian layabout sat with me and together we washed the food down with good strong beer. He was amusing – I was glad to have made a friend, and so after three hours when we'd had our passports stamped, bought cheap cologne, and were ready to reboard the train, he came back to my compartment – which made nine – and we ate chocolates – my birthday present from Paul – laughed and felt terribly young and don't careish. Shortly before we got to the first stop after the border at Grossenbrode Kai, the ticket inspector came around, looked at my ticket, gasped and said 'wait'. Yes, the London train from God knows where had been joined onto the front. At the next stop, a mere couple of minutes, I was whipped out and found myself tearing along the platform in high-heeled shoes followed by a fat, puffing, complaining official with my luggage. Hell, I was tired and was put into a very nice compartment on my own, but was told to leave it open because people were getting on at Hamburg.

I made a bed for myself and within five seconds was out for the count – only to wake up a few minutes later with a ruddy great German slobbering over me – what cheek – I gave him such a wallop that for a moment I thought I'd knocked him out. It seemed to have no effect on him though and, after walloping him for about an hour and a half, there were no officials on hand, he eventually got off the train and I was left in peace for another hour, when a whole lot of Germans got in; woke me up, made me sit up, turned on all the lights, took out packets of food, stuffed their faces and then started doing communal crossword puzzles. At eight o'clock I went and washed the soot off my face and one of the Germans took me to breakfast on the train – we travelled through Holland and finally came to the Hoek, where we unloaded, walked miles to the boat and got on for a six-hour crossing.

On this boat I met an extraordinary, bumptious little man who was returning to England for the first time in 51 years from Shanghai, where he had run a large physical culture school. He'd taught Fonteyn swimming for three years when she was a child and was now coming to London to give lectures and to teach boxing to Prince Charles.

I got through the customs at Harwich OK. Quite to my disappointment, they never suspect me and a little while later I was on the train to London having my evening meal with a soldier about 7 foot tall but completely vacant. I arrived in London, phoned Jo and took a taxi to the flat she and Amelia share. This was the same place in which Hallam stayed – it belongs to the Marwood-Eltons,[2] and is at 199 Fulham Road, Chelsea, London, SW3. I will stay there for a few days until Leonie[3] gets something and I'll probably move in with her in Earls Court – so please write to the bank; it's better.

I missed a place in Western Theatre Ballet through missing my train as they know me and were trying to find out where I was, only the day before I arrived and when I phoned it was too late. There is nothing whatsoever in the way of work at the moment and so unless a miracle happens, I'm going to have rather a difficult winter and I'm not looking forward to it very much. I could go back to Sweden on 5 December, but think it would be the wrong thing to do, as it's time I moved on a

2. Selina's great uncle Hallam was an Elton, so presumably the Marwood-Eltons were his relatives.
3. Leonie Urdang started up a ballet school in Covent Garden, which her daughter Solange has been running since her sudden death in 2001.

step and, unless Elsa Marianne von Rosen wants me for another of her tours, I won't go back because if I do I will miss all the good auditions while I'm there. I will use this time to keep my eyes open and when my money runs out I suppose I'll work in a coffee bar or something like that.

I went to a party at Sydney Street on Saturday and saw many old friends again, which cheered me up a lot. I feel a bit depressed though as prospects aren't good and it's raining cats and dogs. I also have too much time on my hands. Leonie told me on the phone that you'd sent me a costume – I haven't got it yet but will probably get it tomorrow. It sounds sweet. Oh, Margie, you're so kind, thank you very, very much. I'm afraid I never got the oranges that Peter said he'd sent. I don't think they could have arrived as I spoke to Skodsborg on the phone and got Peter's letter. Please thank him very much for it.

I'm a bit worried as my money hasn't come through from Denmark, but I daresay it will in a couple of days, but they sure are taking their time.

25 October 1960 (from 39 Cloncurry Street, Fulham, London SW6)

Well, I've just paused to take a breather while I'm sorting out my new room. I've moved into a flat of dancers in Fulham – most of them are away on tours but there are two here at the moment with me – one in Rambert and another, like myself, unemployed. I've come to London at the very worst time of year, having missed auditions for Festival Ballet, Massine's company and Western Theatre Ballet by a few weeks. There is nothing at all, either in a company or on TV, until after Christmas – so it's my duty to stick around and do class, work like mad and just hope I'll get something then. I have my eye on Festival, and a boyfriend there, so at least I have something to work towards.

Anna is marvellous to me and if I can't afford classes I know she'll let me come for nothing and she's told Julian Braunsweg,[4] director of Festival Ballet, that I'd be a good person to have when a vacancy arises. G.B. Wilson has put in a good word for me too.

4. Julian Braunsweg was born in Poland in 1897 and died in London in 1978. He wrote a book called *Ballet Scandals: The Life of an Impresario and the Story of Festival Ballet* (Allen and Unwin, 1973).

Last Sunday Jo and I had lunch with Iona Bowring[5] – I liked them very much. I went to a party last night with William [Perry] and got tiddly on one glass of wine as I hadn't eaten supper – I felt terribly, terribly happy and enjoyed myself immensely. Today G.B. Wilson took me out to lunch and I got a gorgeous steak. I went to visit the Tate Gallery the other day with William and saw some of Salvador Dali's paintings – they shake you rigid with their peculiarity and morbid character, but I must say they stick in one's mind.

It's raining nearly every day and the weather is grim. I went round and chatted to Tony and Jane about old times in Sweden and we had a good laugh – I must contact them again soon. Cornell is on at all the West End cinemas advertising cigarettes – I believe he's on his way back to South Africa.

5. Iona Bowring (1922–2013), daughter of Margaret Molteno and Lenox Murray, who left Tulbagh to settle at Painswick in the UK in 1923. She was the granddaughter of Percy Molteno and Bessie Currie and spent much of her life breeding Arab horses. Her late husband John Bowring, whom she married in 1956, was a major general in the British Army and they had four children.

Chapter 7

Paris Looms

10 November 1960 (from Paris)

It has so happened that just over a week ago – as I was sweating my guts out in Anna's class, wishing for work, wishing Bill wasn't going away, wishing that all the girls hadn't temporarily left the flat, imagining the dreary trudge home at night with my 2/- supper and shopping falling out of my bag, rain falling and no free hand for the umbrella, grey fog and 1/- metres – my friend G.B. Wilson,[1] a ballet critic wafted into the class and asked me out to lunch – and I never say 'no' to a free steak. G.B. was going to Paris by car and said he would appreciate my company if I could spare the time and, since he was going anyway, he would be happy to cover my expenses. It was too good an offer to resist.

He called for me in his car at the crack of dawn last Thursday morning and, in the pouring rain, drove down to Lydd where we took the plane (car and all) over the channel to Le Toquet, and from there drove down to Paris – via Poix where we bought rolls, wine and cheese for a picnic lunch and then we drove on to Beauvais where we saw the old cathedral, famous for its tapestries.

We arrived in Paris at about 5 and I got a room at the Hotel Oxford and Cambridge, in the poshest part of town. It of course included

---

1. G.B. Wilson (1908–1984) was also the keeper of the Science Museum in London and remained a friend until the end of his life. He was an ardent ballet fan and entered the world of ballet through befriending Beryl Grey.

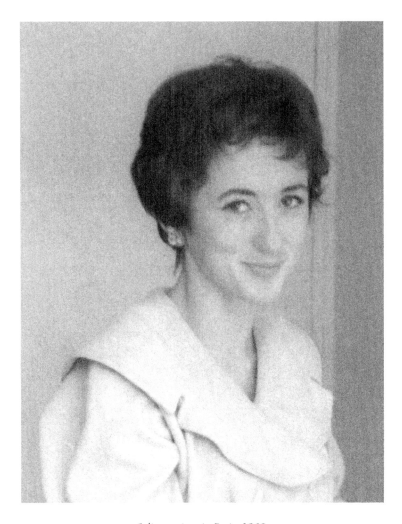

Selina arrives in Paris, 1960.

breakfast in bed consisting of hot croissants and café au lait. You just can't get any more continental than that.

The first night we just had dinner and then had a look around the town. Then came *Friday*. G.B. and I watched a Massine rehearsal in the morning and in the afternoon we went and saw the Marquis de

Cuevas company rehearse *Sleeping Beauty* – it was most interesting and exciting watching them rehearse and sitting there in the Théâtre de Champs Elysée. Afterwards I went to watch Goubé (the man who was so flattering to me soon after I first came to London) give a double-work class. I was too late to do it myself but I will sometime. There was a dancer from the Paris Opera there called Jean-Paul[2] and after the lesson he took me to a café for coffee and a talk – dancers from different lands always have a fantastic amount to discuss!

After that I met G.B. at the hotel and he took me along to the Champs Elysée to see *Sleeping P.* We couldn't get seats so we went backstage as G.B. knows everyone and there I met Daphne Dale[3] who was with us in South Africa for *Petrushka*. I was introduced to Golovine[4] who dances the lead and later to the designer Larrain[5] who gave me and G.B. a place in his private box.

The performance was spectacular with the most beautiful costumes and sets I've ever seen. Golovine partnered Liane Daydé[6] that night but Hightower usually dances the lead role.[7]

2. Jean-Paul Comelin (b.1936) left the Paris Opera to join Festival Ballet where he became a lead dancer. He has worked all over the world, including the United States, and has become a notable choreographer.
3. Daphne Dale (1931–1982) had danced for the UCT Ballet Company. When she was in Cuevas she was married to Nicolas Polajenko, though Selina recalls that the marriage did not last after the company was disbanded and he went first to Geneva and then on to the USA.
4. According to Selina Serge Golovine, who died in Paris after a bypass operation in 1998 at the age of 73, was the best male dancer in the company and a definite rival to Nureyev. Also in the company were his sister Solange Golovina, who predeceased him but was not that good a dancer, his brother George Goviloff (1932–2014), who was a soloist and one-time fiancé of Marilyn Jones, and a younger brother Jean who joined the company sometime after Selina did. While with Cuevas he was married to a Belgian called Liliane van de Velde, but that marriage did not last.
5. Raymundo Larrain (1930–1988) designed the costumes and was more or less running the show during the Marquis's decline.
6. Liane Daydé was born in Paris in 1932. She was with the Paris Opera until 1960 when she joined Cuevas. She was lively, petite and very childish.
7. Rosella Hightower (1920–2008) a Native American ballerina who achieved fame in the USA and Europe. After Cuevas disbanded following the Marquis's death in 1961, she opened a ballet school in Cannes.

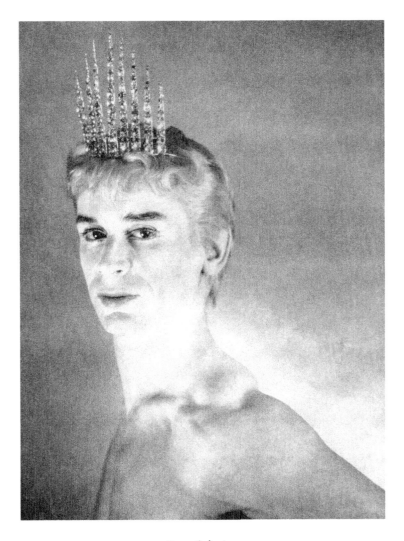

Serge Golovine.

After the performance we walked round Paris a bit and saw the usual things – Arc de Triomphe, Le Tour Eiffel, the Seine, Champs Elysée all glittering with lights, and generally breathed the clean air (which was a change from London) and I liked Paris.

Selina seeing the sights of Paris.

On *Saturday* morning I did my first class with the renowned Gsovsky. His class was so difficult I thought I would die. He's long and wafty, with grey hair; when he gets angry his face goes red, the blood vessels stick out on his neck and he screams so suddenly that everyone jumps sky high – otherwise he is quiet, affectionate and has a subtle, albeit twisted sense of humour. For example, we were doing a pointe-work step from the corner with hops on pointe, balances and pirou-ettes all jumbled together and I was bashing away at it when suddenly he stopped me and started a mock sneezing session. I looked at him bewildered and he answered my look by saying, 'Oui! Tu es comme le temps' – pointing out of the window at the rain – 'tes pieds'. Well, how he figures out a comparison between my feet and the drizzle and sneez-ing in such a short time just beats me![8]

Jean Babillée[9] watched part of the class and remarked that I had a good jump, which pleased me very much.

After the class G.B. and I drove out to look at the Palace at Versailles and I must say that I was quite impressed by Louis XIV's enthusiasm.

That evening I met Jean Pierre[10] at the Studio Wacker[11] and we went out and dined together. Afterwards he had to dance in a stupid opera called Le Roi Davide, which I sat through – but it was nice to see the Paris Opera with its gold ornate decorations and cold distant atmos-phere. It's supposed to be the great pride of the French people but personally I think it's hideous. Anyway, after that I met Jean Pierre again and we mucked around Paris a bit.

The next day, Sunday, G.B. and I went along to the Massine Com-pany to fetch two dancers, Christian and Anna Vaughan and the four of us drove out to Chartres. We had a picnic lunch of French bread, camembert cheese, pâté and red wine in the car in the gardens of Versailles and then headed on to Chartres, to, of course, see the

---

8. Victor Gsovsky (1902–1974) was a Russian ballet dancer, teacher, ballet master and choreographer. He left Russia in 1925 and went to Germany. In 1937 he became ballet master of the Markova–Dolin company and started teaching in Paris. In 1945 he became ballet master of the Paris Opera. His pupils include Yvette Chauviré, Nina Vyroubova (who was in Cuevas), Colette Marchand, Violette Verdy and Vera Zorina.

9. Jean Babillée (3 February 1923–30 January 2014) a French dancer, actor and choreographer.

10. Jean Pierre Alban went on to join the London Festival Ballet.

11. The Paris studio at 69 Rue de Douai where Preobrajenska, Rousanne, Victor Gsovsky, and others taught for many years and which served as an unofficial networking centre for the international dance community until it was demolished in 1974.

cathedral. It was so fascinating. The stained glass windows had to be seen to be believed. The ones I liked best were not so much the brilliantly coloured ones, which were very impressive, but the designs in grey and white, which sounds odd for stained glass but the forms were so perfect and the colours so subtle that I couldn't believe my eyes. In the cathedral they have these water cures and so they were many cripples there offering their thanks by burning candles.

We also saw a service in the crypt where they were anointing these people – we were drawn there by the voices of the choir boys; and on our way out a little French nun rushed out to G.B. and in French said, 'Monsieur, you are big – please change the bulb and there was old G.B. perched up on a chair in the crypt of Chartres changing a bulb. It was most amusing to see.

We dropped Anna and Christian and then G.B. and I dined. Afterwards he took me around the Quartier Latin and on to the Île de Cité where we saw Notre Dame, which looked gorgeous as the moon was situated just above it and reflected the loveliest light onto the stone.

The Quartier Latin was fascinating – just packed with atmosphere. There were tramps sleeping on the streets, Arabs worrying you in the cafés, thin narrow little streets, students, prostitutes making kissing noises, gangsters flattering you as you walk by, higgledy-piggledy hotels and, well, LIFE.

On *Monday* I went to Gsovsky again at the Studio Wacker. Now I must tell you about this place as it really is fascinating. It is situated next to a piano shop in the Rue de Douai, just off the Place Clichy. It is a big building full of ballet studios where all the celebrated teachers teach. On the first floor there is a restaurant where the dancers can eat and gather and in this restaurant I have been introduced to many famous people, including Michel Rènaud,[12] Sonia Arova,[13] Wladimir Skouratoff and many others. After the class on Monday Jean-Paul, a

---

12. Michel Rènaud (1927–1993) associated with Brigitte Bardot and Liane Daydé.
13. Sonia Arova (born Sofia, Bulgaria 1927, died from pancreatic cancer aged 74 in 2001). She worked in Britain and the United States and danced with Nureyev.

friend of his from the Opera called Serge, and I made food and ate together in Jean-Paul's apartment.

In the evening we all went to a class with Peretti,[14] whom I liked very much and I have worked with him and Gsovsky every day since. André Prokovsky,[15] whom I knew from London and who is now a soloist with de Cuevas, was at the class too and afterwards we all went and had a little 'vin rouge' – they drink it like milk here. Afterwards I met G.B. and we went along to Mr Goubé and his wife Yvonne's apartment for drinks.

On *Tuesday* when I came into Wacker to work with Gsovsky I met Jörma in the canteen. Jörma was in the Gaubier Ballet in both Sweden and Denmark and had come to Paris to do some classes. After class, Jean-Paul, Serge and I went to Serge's place to rest before Peretti's class. The boys arranged for me to get an audition with Jean Gaylis for television. That evening Serge took me to see *Psychose*, the most horrifying film imaginable.

On *Wednesday* after class I went along to République in the metro to the Théâtre de la Porte St Martin for a television audition and he accepted me to work for 16 days for 500 new francs, and to start rehearsals on Saturday. After the audition I did another class with Peretti and that night G.B. took me to the Paris Opera to see Chauviré[16] dance *Giselle*. This was followed by a Gene Kelly[17] ballet, and personally I preferred this modern jazz ballet danced by Claude Bessy,[18] to the rather tatty *Giselle*; the décor looked as if it hadn't been changed since Grisi first danced it in the Romantic period.

Thursday was much the same as usual – two classes – lunch with Jean-Paul – film in the evening. I was so tired that I can barely remember what I did. Everything had come to a pitch and I had to simmer down a bit before I started up again.

14. Serge Peretti (1910–1997) Italian dancer and teacher. Spent many years with the Paris Opera.
15. André Prokovsky (1939–2009).
16. Yvette Chauviré (1917–2016) was one of France's greatest ballerinas and she too danced with Nureyev.
17. Gene Kelly (1912–1996) was an American dancer, actor, singer and film director.
18. Claude Bessy (b.1932) French ballerina who worked for the Paris Opera ballet and was director of the Paris Opera ballet school.

On *Friday* morning G.B. and I changed hotels as our rooms had been reserved before for someone else. Now I have a nice little room with a private shower just near the Studio Wacker. Before class on Friday at 1.00 I went with G.B. to watch a Massine[19] rehearsal again. After class Jean-Paul and I lunched together and in the evening G.B. had arranged for me to do a class with the de Cuevas company. I was rather annoyed as those sorts of things embarrass me, but I couldn't get out of it, so just had to clench my teeth and put up with the two miserable hours ahead. I went along to the class and [Daniel] Seillier, the ballet master, put me at the barre in front of a girl who kept kicking me – that's how the girls are in France – thank heaven for the boys. I did a bad class as I was tired and embarrassed.

But anyway, after the class Seillier told me to meet him at 9.30 p.m. on the first floor of the theatre – *première étage* – I got dressed and went to a café across the road where Yvonne Goubé gave me and G.B. a fantastic dinner. By the time 9.30 came I was very lightheaded from *vin rosé*, but I managed to find my way to the *première étage*. As I came in Seillier was running up the stairs and he just told me to wait. Dancers were rushing around in divine costumes; the music was pulsing forth from the stage, only to be interrupted by sudden outbursts of applause. I found a very uncomfortable perch on the corner of a skip piled up with lights. My eyelids grew heavy, my legs began to ache, and I was just about to consider lying on the floor when Seillier reappeared with the Baroness (big chief). He stood a few feet away from me and spoke to her in a low voice and in very fast French that I didn't understand.

She then whisked herself away and Seillier approached me. He stood there and tried to speak English, but he couldn't get one word out, so I said 'speak French; perhaps I can understand' and what I did understand was that he would take me, begin tomorrow, come at 7.00 and do the class, watch from the wings to learn a part. My mouth fell open – Marquis de Cuevas company – one of the world's greatest and like that in such a casual fashion. 'You mean you want ME in the company?' 'Yes, yes, yes, tomorrow.'

19. Léonide Massine (1896–1979), worked with Diaghilev Ballet as a dancer and choreographer. Although he had an affair with Diaghilev he was not gay and went on to have four wives and four children.

Oh, Margie, I hope I understood right, I can't believe it – those sorts of things don't happen to me! What about the TV? I must cancel it. I must stay in Paris. It can't be true. I'll have to wait and see.

I ran back to Yvonne and G.B. Sally Pearce was there too. 'Is it true!' Yvonne says 'yes', 'that's how they are in Paris.' More wine, dazed, whirlwind, G.B. drove me around Paris. I couldn't see anything. I only want to know IF it can really be true!

Today is *Saturday* and terribly late at night. It's all fixed up. I'm a member of the International Ballet of the Marquis de Cuevas performing *La Belle au Bois Dormant* at the Théâtre de Champs Elysée. I was taken on from today and this evening I had to watch from the wings to try and pick up a part. G.B. is going early tomorrow morning and now I'm here in Paris on my own. I must find a room. I must get settled in. My new address is c/o Marquis de Cuevas Ballet Company, Théâtre de Champs Elysée, Avenue Montaigne, Paris 6, France.

Funny this life is. I feel all muddled and lonely and superficial and unsettled and it makes me angry because I have only a right to feel in heavenly ecstasy as from now I will earn 200 new francs a week – about £14 – not bad eh! The TV man will just have to understand, won't he?

Gosh, how I miss you and long to be able to see you and the others again. If things run smoothly I'll probably be in Paris until the end of February and then the company will either go to Cannes or to the States. I don't know anyway because I can't think so far ahead.

27 November 1960 (from Théâtre de Champs Elysée, Avenue Montaigne)

I was so pleased to get your letter – more pleased than you could ever imagine. The house looks marvellous and Anna – well, such glamour. My word, I didn't even recognize her. It made me miss you all so much and want to come home again; and yet what use would that be? It would only stop things when they're just starting. Dancers here aren't like they are in South Africa. It's just a hard, cold rat-race, which consists of a lot of animals earning little and spending it all on classes – sweaty woollen tights with ladders darned six times over, cheap cologne, meals eaten off bits of paper in a dingy hotel room – baths! – well I haven't seen one since I left London, just basins and a hideous

looking bidet that lies at the end of your bed like a tomb, hideous
curtains not washed since Louis built Versailles, washing draped over
the waste paper basket, a few sentimental photos and ornaments,
home shoe repairs. That's my room.

I tidied Serge's room for him once. I like his better than mine because
he can play music in it. He has an old, somewhat broken down gramophone and a pile of scratched and wonderful, in fact quite beautiful,
records; his bed fills up practically the whole room apart from the space
for a sink and a tiny table, for his gramophone, records, ash trays, books,
socks, bread and so forth; he has his washing line strung across the foot
of his bed from a one-foot-square window on one side to the door on
the other. This is where he hangs his dripping togs up to dry. To get
into the room, you have to climb flights of stairs and then fumble your
way through long dark passages, down a couple of stone steps and there
you are under the roof of one of Pigalle's houses and in the home of
Serge where you can hear wonderful music and will always be made to
feel welcome. Serge has a car and keeps bottles of something under his
bed to pour into it each morning. It's a wonderful car, a great big thing,
bright blue in the places where it hasn't been bashed. When I opened
its door for the first time I thought we'd been hit by a bomb. You open
it quite easily for the first four inches and then you have to pull with
all your might because somehow it sticks. Suddenly, before you know
what's hit you there's an almighty crash and 'alors' the door opens and
you presumably are on the pavement. Jean-Paul on the other hand has
an apartment, but then it has no furniture.

29 November 1960

Sorry, I lost my pen so couldn't continue the last letter, but I'll try to
finish this one this evening. It's Tuesday and our day off. I did a class
with Michel Reznikoff[20] between two and four o'clock and now I'm

20. Michel Reznikoff and Rosella Hightower, both at the time with the Grand
    Ballet de Monte Carlo married in Egypt on 29 January 1949, though the
    marriage did not last and was well over by the time Selina met Michel. He
    was a lot of fun and once he got her to pretend she was his girlfriend to
    fool the husband of his German lover, who was visiting her at the time.

looking forward to an early night as usually I don't get to bed until about 2.00 a.m.

My life in Paris is very humdrum and my position in the company, as far as I can see, precarious. When Mr Seillier[21] engaged me, a Mexican girl called Anita Cardus[22] was going to leave to make a film, but unfortunately since then she received a letter saying that the film had been cancelled and now she is staying; that is to say I'm a spare part and as yet have not danced on stage. Nevertheless, it doesn't appear as if they're throwing me out as they have known this for a long time and haven't said anything to me. I get my pay every week; I attend classes and rehearsals and watch the performances from the wings.

At the moment the company is only doing *The Sleeping Beauty*, which is a roaring success, packed houses every night – in fact it's quite a production and they have box-office stars – Hightower, Golovine, Melikova,[23] Vyroubova,[24] Polajenko, Prokovsky and Liane Daydé. The décor by Larrain is exquisite and in fact it is quite a production. Naturally, it's not very interesting to do *La Belle au Bois Dormant* for months on end, but the Marquis de Cuevas, who sponsors the company, is now very, very ill – in fact he is dying of leukaemia and when

When Selina knew him he was a teacher in Paris, but was afterwards associated with the Harkness Ballet in Cannes.

21. Daniel Seillier (1926–2012). After graduating from the Paris Opera Ballet School, Daniel Seillier launched his professional career in 1942, going on to join the Grand Ballet du Marquis de Cuevas ballet company in 1951. Ten years later, he founded the National Ballet of Portugal. Then in 1963, Madame Ludmilla Chiriaeff, founder of Les Grands Ballets Canadiens de Montréal and L'École supérieure, invited Mr Seillier to Canada as a ballet master. In 1965, he left to teach at the National Ballet School of Canada, returning to Montréal in 1980. For close to 20 years, he trained the dancers of L'École supérieure. Daniel Seillier was awarded the Order of Canada in 1993. In 2008, at the age of 82, he retired from teaching.

22. Anita, whose mother always travelled with her, later joined the Stuttgart Ballet along with Marcia Haydée. According to Selina, she was a lovely dancer and very beautiful.

23. Genia Melikova (1924–2004) was a star with the company who afterwards became a distinguished teacher in the United States.

24. Nina Vyroubova (1921–2007) was born in Crimea and was with the Paris Opera before joining Cuevas where he partnered Nureyev in the *Sleeping Beauty*.

he dies there will be no more money as it appears that his wife, the Marquise, would rather have it for herself. The company is now surviving on the fortune rolling in from the box office, so therefore it should be able to keep going for a while after the Marquis dies, but unfortunately they aren't able to mount new ballets. Finally, the company will probably have to be disbanded, unless of course the Marquise turns generous, which as far as I can gather is unlikely.

Anyway, that is the position at the moment. You never know, things can always change. In the meantime, they may even find a cure for leukaemia. At the moment I'm quite happy as things are, as I'm devoting most of my time and energy to improving my dancing. Every day I do a class from 2 to 4 with Michel Reznikoff.

I work with him because he doesn't give a class only, but really teaches. You find with most of the teachers in Europe that you go to class, change, stand at the barre like a row of sardines and do all the exercises one after the other, pay your money, change and go home. But Michel is different – the first day he watches a new pupil intently and then sums up what is wrong. With me he said that my worst fault was lack of control in the back, which of course I've known all my life, but then he tells you exactly how to put it right and I've been working like mad on that – already it is much better and as a result so are my pirouettes, balances, and beats. Within two weeks he reckons that that should be right and then I'll have to start working at my arms. I really feel that I can learn very much from him at the moment. Perhaps later I can go back to Gsovsky for style, but at the moment I feel I've hit the best teacher in Paris.

Renée Jeanmaire,[25] Roland Petit[26] and Ethéry Pagava[27] work with him every day and say that he is by far the best, but my word it's hard work – two hours non-stop and a barre alone for one hour. The only people I know in Paris are those I meet at classes and de Cuevas, but that doesn't worry me as I don't have time to feel lonely. When I'm in

25. Renée Jeanmaire (1924–2020) also known as Zizi Jeanmaire was married to Roland Petit and became a well-known dancer, singer, film star and actress.
26. Roland Petit (1924– 2011) was a French choreographer and dancer.
27. Ethéry Pagava (b.1932) was a dancer, teacher and artistic director.

London I just can't stand being on my own all the time and so always used to go out, visit people, meet people, see things. And then when Bill appeared on the scene I spent most of my time with him and even then we used to get to parties, galleries, cinemas and have super times together, but here in Paris it's different. It's so quick, superficial and insecure that I feel I want to escape. I don't feel I can trust a soul.

I come home in the bus from the theatre at night at about 12.30 and wherever you walk the streets are full of prostitutes – men follow you everywhere trying to pick you up. For the first week you think it's funny and laugh, but now I hate it and want to hit every stupid face that approaches me – they follow you into cafés, trains, buses, everywhere – pestering, pleading and whimpering. How I loathe it.

I am staying in Ternes now, quite near the Champs Elysée and it's a bit better there than in Place Clichy and Pigalle where I was before, but even still I feel afraid. I keep hearing awful screams when I'm in bed at night and that's something I never heard in London.

As far as the language is concerned – it doesn't bother me much because I know enough from Copenhagen to get around; but sometimes when people are having a conversation or discussion I get a bit lost as I still translate in my mind, but I hope that will pass within a couple of weeks. I think I must get a book and study on my own a bit.

Paris is terribly expensive – 1/6 for a little cup of coffee; 10/- for a class; 12/- a night for a sordid room in the cheapest hotel, about 9d for a ride on the metro, and to go to a cheap restaurant and to have meat and vegetables it costs you at least ten shillings. I try to eat as much as possible in my room but I can't cook here, so really one can only just live on £14 a week, which is what we are paid. So really I'm very lucky to be with de Cuevas, as otherwise I couldn't possibly stay in Paris at all. I'd better be going to bed now as this is my one and only free night in the week. Until next time, enjoy your lovely summer weather. We're in mid-winter, but it's considerably warmer here than in London.

1 December 1960

Nothing much has changed since I last wrote except that Serge has got mumps, poor beast. We haven't been paid so I'm without money, but luckily Michel let me do the classes and pay later and he also gave me

some food. People here have been very kind and always tell me to let
them know when I'm broke rather than not eat, which is comforting.
We are getting paid tomorrow though, I hope. The only trouble is that
I took an advance of NF 100, which I'll have to pay back and so for a
week I'll be on half salary, but I daresay I'll manage somehow; just cut
down on meals out. With practice, one should be able to live on quite
a little, but it takes time to learn how.

Jeanmaire and Petit were in class today and I worked like the back
of a tram, but it was better in Seillier's class with the company. It makes
me infuriated when I want to improve so much and then find myself
doing worse than the day before. Bill wrote and told me how much he
was hating touring the provinces with Festival.

Rosella Hightower danced for the last time tonight before taking a
break and handing her part to Vyroubova. I love Rosella's dancing; it
is so austere and executed with such a fantastic technique.

Zizi Jeanmaire is fabulous, alluring, divine, and reckons that Michel
is the best teacher outside Russia. She says there is no good school in
London at all, so I reckon I'm very lucky to have the opportunity to
study in Paris.

Tomorrow there is no performance so I reckon I'll go and see Serge
and cheer him up with a bottle of wine. I hope you can drink wine
when you have mumps. If not, I will.

Did I tell you that Olga Adabache, one of the soloists in the company, was once in a harem and was the favourite wife because she
could do an arabesque. Now she says, 'what a pity he died.' She's the
campest thing this side of the Equator.[28] There is a Dutch girl in the
company called Marian Sarstadt who worked with Richard Glasstone[29]
in Holland. By the way, if you see him do remember me to him – that
is if he still remembers who I am.

Gaubier has been scouting around Paris and London looking for
dancers for Sweden. Thank God I don't have to go back to that dump

---

28. Olga Adabache (b.3 May 1918) in Petrograd, Russia.
29. Richard Glasstone MBE had come from the Congo to the ballet school at
    UCT. He had a distinguished career in the Royal Ballet School and
    elsewhere. Selina went to his wedding to Heather Magoon in the early
    1960s. He also wrote a well-judged biography of Dulcie Howes.

Rosella Hightower.

International Ballet of the Marquis de Cuevas

Direction Artistique: LARRAIN

SERGE GOLOVINE

GENIA MELIKOVA NICHOLAS POLAJENKO
JOAN CADZOW GEORGES GOVILOFF
BEATRIZ CONSUELO ELEONORE VESCO
OLGA ADABACHE

et en représentation

YVETTE CHAUVIRE
RUDOLF NOUREEV
GERT REINHOLM

Premières Danseuses

Daphne DALE Liliane VAN DE VELDE
Marilyn JONES Margo MIKLOSY

Premiers Danseurs de Caractère

Solange GOLOVINA Don SPOTTSWOOD

Solistes

Calliope VENIERIS - Josette GATINEAU - Claudine KAMOUN
Armando NAVARRO - Imre VARADY - Garth WELCH - Jimmy URBAIN

Corps de Ballet

Théréza d'Aquino, Christiane Bérut, Ana Cardus, Jacqueline de Min, Christiane Dibarbora
Patricia Dowling, Katia Dubois, Ana-Maria Gorriz, Monique Janotta, Selena Molteno, Marian Sarstadt, Mady Simmons
Puck Scherpenisse, Ghislaine Thesmar, Francesca Zumbo
Floris Alexander, Yves Chassin, Philippe Dahlmann, Claude Darnet, Peter Hubi, Roberto Ossorio
George Salavisa, Walter Scherer, Don Snyder, Jean-Marie Sosso, Karl Welander

NICHOLAS BERIOSOFF JEAN DOUSSARD
Maître de Ballet Chef d'Orchestre

Peggy VAN PRAAGH Claude POTHIER
Professeur de Danse Pianiste Concertiste

Représentant Général: «Productions Claude Giraud» 252 Rue du Faubourg St. Honoré. Paris, Carnot 29.31 - 06.30

Members of the company, with Selina's name misspelled.

Serge Golovine.

of a country – it's nice to feel that you have gone one wrung further up the ladder (step-ladder). I'd better retire now so that I can be in good form to tackle Michel's class tomorrow – it takes some tackling. Write soon – everyone is clamouring for South African stamps.

14 December 1960

I was thrilled to get Peter's letter mentioning Anthony's success in his exams. Please congratulate him for me. I feel so pleased for and proud of him. Life in Paris is progressing favourably and I am now working on stage with the company, which cheers me up no end. I started off by taking a girl's place as a nereid for Lido's[30] photograph call and also for the photo call I did a page. Seillier told me to keep the page part, which I did for the last three performances and then, at today's rehearsal, miracles happened and now I'm dancing in the 'Prologue' and also have been given a nereid, which is more than quite a few girls in the company do. I'm so happy about it – even although it means I'm getting quite a few more dirty looks than normal.

The rehearsal today went on for hours and in such an atmosphere that I can't describe. I was just a bundle of nerves as I was thrown into two parts without even five minutes' notice. In fact he just said in French, which is always trying as I'm never quite sure that I've understood right – 'the English girl – the last one to join the company, take Mady's [Simmons] part. I was given a shove. Mady did it once through and straight away I had to know it. Thank God it went all right. The second time he just caught my eye and pointed and I made a bee line for the place – fortunately it was the place I'd learnt from the wings and so I knew it.

Yesterday they dismissed a girl from Rio, a soloist,[31] for three weeks for not turning up at a rehearsal, which we had the other morning before a matinée and evening performance. She didn't come because she had diarrhoea and thought that a whole day and night's work would be too much; and at the same time they dismissed a boy from Cuba for good because he was rude to the ballet master in front of the others. They also threw a Greek girl called Calliope [Venieris] out of her part, also a solo, for no apparent reason at all.

In this company they're so many people clamouring to pounce that for the slightest little thing you can lose your parts or be thrown out.

30. Serge Lido (1906–1984) was probably the most renowned ballet photographer of the twentieth century.
31. This must have been Marcia Haydée (b.1937) who went on to become the main star of John Cranko's Stuttgart Ballet.

It's really rather frightening when you come to think of it! You can only get on by having eyes everywhere, a mind and memory like lightning and a mouth that never opens.

Mr Seillier detests people who aren't French and so one has to make a definite effort to pretend you love French people and want nothing more than to learn their language.

So far I've been lucky though as Mr Seillier seems to quite like me – or at least he has not yet shown any signs to the contrary, but it was he who engaged me so I suppose he feels he has to try and see the good side of his decision. Baroness de Fredericksz, the biggest chief of all, seems to like me too, so I just hope I won't do or say anything rash or silly, which could spoil a good start. A new boy joined the company today.

Who should come to the theatre looking for me today, but my Polish friend from the Gaubier ballet Yurek Rytel. He'd been on tour in Germany with the Théâtre de l'Art ballet company and has returned to Paris for a short period. I was so happy to see him again and together we went off and had supper at a Polish restaurant near Place Clichy.

I also saw Roberto the other day – the boy with whom I always quarrelled in Copenhagen – and he says that since I last saw him he has been married and divorced. It doesn't surprise me though, as he's a narcissist and couldn't possibly ever be happily married.

Paris is so cold now that I could scream, especially as all my winter woollies are in London still, but nevertheless from time to time I get a little parcel with a couple of things in it that G.B. fishes out of my case and sends over with friends. G.B. very kindly went round to my flat, packed up all my things and is keeping them for me. Mr Tweedie brought over my alarm clock (the one Anna gave me, and for which I am eternally grateful), a jersey, blue jeans and flat shoes.

André Prokovsky brought over, but has not yet given me, my slacks and warm woollen pants. Jean-Paul is in London now and is also going to bring back a couple of articles so eventually I will have all, probably by summer time.

I don't miss London quite as much as I did a couple of weeks ago, but I have to admit that London has done something to me and, even against Paris, I still think it is the most fabulous city in the world. You can't dig into Paris like you can into London, but perhaps I should get to know it better before I judge. I'm learning French quickly and am beginning to think in it now. If one speaks several languages it appears as if you're well educated even if you're not! Must go to sleep now or it'll be *me* who misses rehearsal.

23 December 1960 (to father, Peter)

I am writing this in a terrible hurry as I have just been to the police to apply for a visa to stay in France and because I am under 21 years of age I cannot do so without your permission. In the meantime, I have been given a document that allows me to stay here until 6 January and if I am caught without it after that, I am obliged to await your permission 'in jail'. So please, I wonder if you would write a letter saying that you give permission for your daughter, Selina Molteno, to remain in France and to work for the Marquis de Cuevas Ballet Company. The letter must be signed by you and by the police if possible. You don't address the letter to anyone in particular; you just enclose it in an envelope to me and I will give it to the man in the company who arranges our affairs. Please, Peter do it straight away and send it in the very next post as I would hate to lose my job here just because of a silly piece of paper. Well, that's enough about that.

Leonie Urdang has come to stay with me for a while as she is spending a short holiday in Paris. It's a great relief as it relieves me of some of the rent.

I'm now dancing quite a lot in the company, which is a great joy as I hung around for ages before I was given anything to do. My chance came when a girl was thrown out for not attending a rehearsal – unfortunately that's how they are in this company, which according to Leonie who saw it last night, is the best that she has ever seen.

I want to thank you and Margie and the whole family for the cheque you sent me for Xmas. I was terribly touched and absolutely thrilled to receive it. I will keep it in a bank until I know whether or not the company will keep me on for their next season and if they do I will use it for something really worthwhile that I can always keep and remember you all by. Thank you from the bottom of my heart.

Here we will work on Xmas Eve, all Xmas Day and Boxing Day, so we can't have a Xmas at all, but I don't mind really, as I am so terribly,

terribly happy to have this job, and live in such perpetual fear of losing it that sentiments like Xmas don't even enter the equation.

After a spell of such cold weather that I thought my ears would drop off and I couldn't feel my feet for days, it has warmed up a bit and life is a little more bearable. Thank heavens I have central heating in my room and so my washing dries overnight and I don't need to have wet, dripping clothes hanging around for days on end – as is always the case in London.

I got a letter from Magda van Essen and will contact her as soon as I have a free moment. It will be difficult though as she works in the mornings and afternoons and I work in the afternoons and nights, but still I'll manage it somehow as she sounds very nice.

I must rush now. I hope you are all enjoying a very happy Xmas and New Year, basking in the sun down south. Please give my love to everyone, including Kulu, Apa and Granny. I will write and thank Kulu for her gift soon. I'm sorry but from me you'll have to have a delayed Xmas as lately my budget hasn't allowed me to send presents, but I will as soon as possible.

2 January 1961

I'm sorry but this is going to be a pathetic little, short, letter as I'm tired and depressed and at the moment nothing is going right.

I haven't been able to do classes for the past week and still can't now as I've had an operation on my foot and it still hurts too much to start working flat out, which in itself is enough to make one depressed – also Marcia [Haydée] has come back to the company and so I have had to give up my best part to her – not directly as she is a soloist, but with all the replacements going down one step it has affected me quite badly. Anyway, there is a chance I will be able to dance it at some performances when Daphne Dale does the Lilac Fairy and Marcia takes her part. There are rumours that 25 people are going to be dismissed from the company when it goes to Cannes and if that is true I will definitely not be kept on and the thought of being without work and without money again doesn't thrill me one bit.

Mr Seillier, our ballet master, has left the company and his place will be taken by Beriosoff, Beriosova's father.

I'm not the only girl who is at this moment living in perpetual fear, in fact most of the girls in our dressing room are more or less in the same boat and feel disappointed that we may have to leave without ever having had the chance to prove ourselves either capable or not.

Anyway – what the hell, even if I were a fabulous dancer I'd still be a bloody foreigner and *me* – that is incapable of buttering up people with influence. Leonie Urdang is staying with me at the moment, seeing Paris, doing classes and sharing my rent. It's nice to have her here, I must say.

After the performance on New Year's Eve I went out with Serge, a dancer in the Opéra. First of all we went to a night club and then on to a party and I had a super time. We drove along the Champs Elysée and everyone was going mad – in fact I've never seen or experienced such an atmosphere *en masse*. Hooters were blurting out political points of view of either '*Algérie française*' or '*Algérie algerienne*' – poop, poop, poop, poooooop, pooooooop, or poop, poop, poop, poop, poop, poop, poop. All this was the result of a speech that General de Gaulle had just given earlier on in the evening.

God – I hope that Peter got the express letter I sent to him asking for a letter of consent for me to stay in France because I have to have it by 6 January for my *carte de séjour* and if it doesn't arrive in time I'm not only put out by the company but by the police too – and that means out of the country. I only wish the company would let us know where we stand soon as I would so appreciate a good night's sleep.

Later

I got Peter's letter when I went to the theatre this evening and it is fine – please thank him very much from me.

This evening just before the performance started we were all called on stage as Madame de Fredericksz wanted to speak to us and we trailed down, trembling and expecting the worst, but it turned out that she was just introducing us to our new ballet master. Beriosoff seems charming enough but we'll have to wait and see what sort of ballet master he turns out to be.

Paris is wet and cold but I feel happier here in spite of it and find I'm coming out easier on my money. I can't think why, besides Leonie's

THÉATRE DES CHAMPS-ÉLYSÉES

DIRECTEUR : F. VALOUSSIÉRE

ADMINISTRATEUR GÉNÉRAL :
JACQUES STEPHANT

DIRECTEUR ARTISTIQUE :
JEAN ROBIN

SECRÉTAIRE GÉNÉRAL:
CHARLES VANNES

INTERNATIONAL BALLET
OF THE
MARQUIS DE CUEVAS

DIRECTION GENERALE : MARQUISE DE CUEVAS

DIRECTION ARTISTIQUE : LARRAIN

PRÉSENTE

La Belle au Bois Dormant

D'APRÈS LE CONTE DE CHARLES PERRAULT

MUSIQUE DE TCHAIKOVSKY

CHORÉGRAPHIE D'APRÈS MARIUS PETIPA

MISE EN SCÈNE DE ROBERT HELPMANN

DÉCORS ET COSTUMES DE LARRAIN

SAISON 1961

La Belle au Bois Dormant programme for 1961 season.

help with the rent, because my doctor's bill came to more than a week's classes and Leonie uses all my soap, Rinso, and writing paper.

I really want to thank you so much for the money you sent me. I'm so happy for it and if the company keeps me – well then I'll let you know what I spend it on and if the company doesn't keep me well then it'll help keep me going until I find another job. I don't worry too much though as I still have £100 odd in the bank in London, which I try my hardest not to touch – but it's nice to know that it's there anyway.

I'm sorry I haven't been able to send you any Xmas presents yet, but I'm sure you can understand my position at the moment, but will certainly do so when things are a little more certain.

I went to a party after the shows on Xmas and New Year's Eve, but besides that nothing, as we didn't stop working at all over that period.

17 January 1961

I can't remember whether or not I've told you how marvellous the cake was. Thank you so much – you really are a fabulous mother.

I've enclosed a cutting about Cuevas; perhaps it will give you a better idea as to what it's all about. The photo of me was taken in the wings the day after I joined the company. The *Offstage* write-up is corny, but still –

I haven't been told yet whether or not I can stay on after the Paris season, which ends on 19 February, but I think it's quite likely that I will as I have been given a place in the can-can in *Gaité Parisienne*. Skirts ahoy and legs up. I'm thrilled to bits about it and so I really hope that means they will keep me on, but I don't like to say for sure until I've been told officially.

I'm working very hard at the moment with classes, rehearsals and performances and lately have had a chance to do quite a bit of dancing while a girl was off with an injured foot. For three weeks after Xmas I was in agony with a poisoned, festering big toe. I spent a fortune on a doctor who hacked away at it and stuck ramrods into my cuticle and then I suddenly got the idea to have a penicillin injection, so I walked into a chemist shop, got it, paid two francs and my foot was absolutely healed up in three days. I'm sure the doctor knew that would work, but was only sucking money from me – the beast! It makes me boil when I realize I wasted 60 new francs (13 francs to the pound) when it only cost me two to cure.

Every out-of-work dancer prays for a stroke of luck which will get her a job (especially at this time of the year). And they do happen – witness the story of **Selina Molteno**, a South African and a pupil of **Dulcie Howes**. She had been dancing in Copenhagen and arrived back in London just too late for the auditions for Festival Ballet and for pantomimes – and with only money enough saved for a few weeks in London (then – coffee bars!). She went to Anna Northcote's class and there ran into **G.B.L. Wilson** who was impressed by her dancing and suggested that she tried her luck in Paris. He happened to be going there, with his car, the following day and offered to take her too. After a week at the Paris classes he took her to see **Daniel Seillier**, the taciturn and efficient ballet master of the Marquis de Cuevas Ballet, and asked him to give her an audition. This Seillier did and said that she could start work the very next day. It all seemed like a fairy tale and Selina could hardly believe that it had happened – and we hope that it may give fresh hope to other dancers at a time when things are bad for them.

Undated clipping from Offstage section of *Dancing Times*.

A girl has been thrown out of the company because she got ill too frequently and several boys too as the company is overcrowded. They are still going to put some more girls out as the management can't afford to keep so many people and as a result I feel very frightened, in fact so anxious that when a list was pasted up on the board I rushed to see if it was what I've been expecting to hear for weeks, that I missed my entrance on stage and have had some money taken off next week's pay as a punishment. Two other girls did the same thing, so I hope Madame de Fredericksz won't dismiss me on account of that. I think we should hear within a couple of days anyway. The anticipation is driving me crazy.

At the moment I am doing classes with Peretti, as with all the rehearsals now I can only manage two hours of class a day. With Michel it makes three and I find I get too tired.

A rumour went around the company that I could read palms – I
read it up about a year ago when I was in London the second time –
and I have been in non-stop demand ever since. Last night after taking
a shower I was called to Golovine's dressing room and asked to read
his hand. He is the best male dancer in the company – in fact he is
such a fantastic dancer that sometimes I can't believe my eyes when I
watch him. I was quite astounded by myself as everything I told him
about his character and his past was true. I don't believe you can say
that on 14 March you will slip on a banana peel, but I do think you
can tell something about a person's health, especially from their finger-
nails, which suggest what physical weaknesses they are likely to have
internally as well as their level of nervous resistance. You can also tell
many things from the shape, texture and proportions of the hands and
fingers. Developments in different places mean different things. Serge
Golovine has the most developed imagination I have seen on anyone's
hand and a self-made success through confidence and work. On my
hand I have the material for success much more marked than he has,
but I have too little nervous energy ever to fulfil myself in that way.

Don't worry – I'm not going out of my mind – I only read it up out
of curiosity and a lack of anything better to do at the time. Please write
soon. I feel afraid and nervous at the moment and would find a letter
from home a great comfort.

17 January 1961 (to Annabel from Montpellier)

What a surprise to hear from you – I can't tell you how much pleasure
it gave me and I was walking on air for days afterwards. It must be
lovely in Cape Town now with the warm weather and holidays on the
go. The winter in Europe is drawing to a close, but the only difference
I can see between winter and summer here is that in winter I wear my
fur coat and in summer my leather one. I only shed it when there's a
heat wave (very rare) or when we go to Israel or thereabouts.

At the moment we're touring France, which is pretty killing as we
keep on changing towns and packing, unpacking and lugging heavy
cases around is more tiring than the actual work.

At the moment we are back in Montpellier for a few days of
rehearsals before going to Nimes. The only thing about France though

that makes me mad is that we only get about half our usual pay and so we have to make do such a lot. We have our little gas stoves that we cart around with us and, believe it or not, I'm becoming quite a proficient cook.

I've given up trying to figure out what we're going to do and where we're going to go in the near future as the company seems to change its mind continually, but it doesn't matter really because every evening they put up a notice on the next day's rehearsals and so forth, so I just live according to that, whether it means catching a train or sleeping in.

I'm rooming with an Australian girl called Marilyn Jones[32] and we have a lot of fun. Sometimes we invite members of the company around and they bring their food, stoves, wine and sometimes even a gramophone, and we have a party until the hotel proprietor orders them out and then we repeat the whole process in the next town.

Between Xmas and New Year we were in Copenhagen and there our way of life changed completely. We stayed on the eleventh floor of a luxury hotel. Doors opened automatically, there was music in the lift, a radio in the bedroom, each room had a private bathroom and a hall with cupboards, a telephone, a breakfast menu a mile long and beds that turned into sofas during the day; thick, edge-to-edge carpeting everywhere and every single convenience you could possibly wish for. I lived like a queen, took massages and dolled myself up to kill. Now things have changed, but it's always nice to have memories; even the hard times we can laugh at afterwards.

Have the three parcels I sent from Venice arrived yet? If not, they should any time as I sent them about a month ago. I hope you like your present and have something to wear it with.

It must be lovely having Margie[33] back – when is Peter coming home again? And is he coming to visit me on his way back? Did Martin and Frankie learn any Spanish? I must say, I was impressed by the way Martin picked up French. He could say more after being in Paris for two weeks than Marilyn can after more than six months!

32. Marilyn Jones (b.1940) was later described as the greatest classical dancer that Australia ever produced, and, to top it all, she is a lovely person too.
33. Margie had been in Chile where Peter had a consultancy with the Food and Agricultural Organization.

I must say that Anthony's cottage sounds fun – I can see you all lending a hand somewhere and getting it decorated. I'd love to come home again for a holiday but at the moment it doesn't look very hopeful financially or otherwise.

I must end off now as any moment Dick will be coming round to drag me out for a coffee and before then I've got to get dressed, wash myself and my hair, my togs and my clothes. I'm still in bed and it's 1.30 p.m. I must say it's nice and warm though with Granny's rug wrapped around as many times as possible. What I'd do without it I hate to think – freeze I suppose.

I love the jersey you sent. It goes with all my clothes. I have a grey skirt that I wear it with in winter, a white linen skirt for summer and blue jeans for staying a home. It washes wonderfully and is turning into my second skin. I must say I've been tempted to sleep in it, but don't like to as I think it might spoil it.

Incomplete undated letter from Paris a short while before going to Cannes on 20 February 1961

Last week we were given our pay and three days off and so it was at that point that I pulled myself together and went and asked 'Are you or are you not going to keep me on after the Paris season?' 'Of course we are; I thought you knew, otherwise I would have told you long ago.' I caught the next plane to London, had a ball and was back in time for the matinée on Sunday. I went to London for quite a few reasons – to see William, my boyfriend in Festival, to get some clothes I had left there, to swap my radio for a portable and also the sales were on, so I got myself two pairs of chic Italian shoes, leather silk-lined gloves to match, a Chinese kimono for the theatre, and some tights and pointe shoes. It really was a terrific two days and did my morale the world of good. Now that I'm back I've been able to throw myself into my work as there seems to be so much ahead.

On 20 February we go to Cannes and stay there until 6 April and during that time for eight days William will be in Monte Carlo with Festival, so that's another ball coming up as the two towns are only half an hour away from each other. After Cannes we leave France and our pay doubles to £30 a week in dollars.

On 7 April we start in Barcelona and remain there until the end of the month – 30 April.

From 3 to 13 May we'll be in Lisbon and afterwards return to Paris for two months (June and July) for another season at the Théâtre de Champs Elysée. I'm not quite sure what happens after that, but I think it's more of Europe and then New York. At the moment we are rehearsing for this as we change the programme for the tour and the company really has a lovely repertoire of ballets.

I've more or less mastered the French tongue now, but I'll have to get cracking sometime on Spanish as practically everyone in the company speaks it and what a wonderful opportunity I have to learn. We have such a mixture of nationalities here it's almost unbelievable. We have dancers from Brazil, Mexico, the States, Canada, England, France, Belgium, Germany, Switzerland, Holland, Austria, Yugoslavia, Poland, Russia, Algeria, East Africa, Spain, Portugal, two Hungarian refugees, Greece – only to mention some of them offhand.

It's bitterly cold here now and so I'm eagerly looking forward to seeing some sun in the south of France soon.

26 February 1961 (from Casino Municipal, Cannes)

How can I thank you enough for that beautiful green costume? It fits me perfectly and I think that the style and colour are really lovely. I got it in Paris the day before we left for Cannes and it is proving most useful here, for at the moment the weather is bitterly cold.

Marilyn and I have rented an apartment together for the season and I must say that it's a pleasure to live in more than one room. The apartment is quite close to the theatre and although it is old there is continuous hot water and all the necessary facilities; and it's such a joy to whip up meals in a real kitchen and to take a bath every day, even although it's only a half size bath tub. Marilyn has just been made a star and so was able to cope with the rent. I'll have to pay her back in dribs and drabs.

The weather is so disappointing. It's raining nearly every day and both pairs of my shoes seem to have acquired the habit of drawing the water into them. Anyway, when we get to Italy I'll buy some new ones – a three-year supply if possible.

Larrain told me that I was to dance the Queen of the Wilis next Sunday, but there have obviously been some hard feelings about it somewhere along the line, as yesterday the cast list went up and I noticed that they had omitted my name. I don't think it could be anything on my part though, as Larrain had never seen me rehearse it. In fact, although I asked every day for a rehearsal, no one would give it to me; nevertheless, I'm disappointed to realize how difficult it is to achieve anything without engaging in intrigue. I'll work on it as best I can anyway – and maybe I'll get a chance later on. If I ask any questions about it I only get a dishonest beat-around-the-bush reply. I dare say life will feel more cheerful when the sun begins to shine, as then I won't mind so much what happens.

I hope and pray with every fibre of my being that I'll be able to see you and Peter soon. According to rumour, we will leave Cannes a week earlier (21 March) for a season in Vienna, but I think that our Italy dates still hold as before. I'm afraid I don't seem able to acquire any firm information from any source whatsoever.

On Wednesday we will be dancing in Nice and on Thursday in Toulon and so that means a couple of grim bus tours ahead, but fortunately we return to Cannes the same night and so at least that will save us the trouble of finding a hotel.

I'm so glad you liked the glasses and that the kids liked their presents. Did the coffee set ever arrive for Anthony? I'm in the throes of making myself a cotton frock, but I have an awful feeling that it's going to look like a shop assistant's uniform.

Friday 3 March 1961

Today is Friday, the sun is shining and Americans are pouring in. Last night was the premier of *La Belle au Bois Dormant* in Cannes and it was, as far as I could gather from the applause and shouting, a great success. This morning at 10 o'clock there was a class for the girls and then afterwards a rehearsal of *Noir et Blanc* – a Lifar ballet. It is a fabulous ballet with all the stars in it and pure, clean technique. I wasn't in the ballet, just an understudy but today, just before the rehearsal I heard that I had to dance it tonight in Nice, where we will give one performance of *Sebastian*, *Le Spectre de la Rose*, *Diagrams* and

Raymundo Larrain.

Noir et Blanc. I have had to learn and rehearse the whole ballet in about one hour and it is extremely difficult as the girl whose part I'm taking is now dancing a leading role and so therefore had to do all the difficult bits and pieces in the ballet, including a diagonal of double pirouettes *en dehors.* I'm petrified as I haven't had time to make the most of it – but still I do it tonight and hope for the best.

In Cannes we usually start working early in the mornings at 10 or sometimes 9 o'clock. Thank heaven I stay with Greta because if it wasn't for her I'd never get there on time, as not once since I've been here have I heard the alarm go off and it's just next to my ear. We leave the apartment with our eyes glued up and feeling like hell, but then after a ten minute run along the Croisette by the side of the sea we've usually woken up sufficiently to do class.

Our class and rehearsal room is lovely. It is right up at the top of the theatre with big windows opening onto a roof that overlooks the sea. Sometimes the girls and boys climb onto the roof to sun themselves when they are not needed during a rehearsal.

I feel so well in Cannes. I eat like a horse and have bags of energy – such a contrast to depraved, sordid Paris, or at least it is in the winter.

Monday 13 March

The last ten days have gone much as usual – classes, rehearsals and performances. Last Monday I went with a group of dancers to Monte Carlo to do a class and look around. I bought a camera and took some pictures. Last Monday was the nicest day I've had for years. We left Cannes early in the morning – tore along the Croisette to get the train and recuperated during the hour and a half journey to Monte Carlo. The Côte d'Azur is so beautiful – it really bowls you over. Finally, we arrive in the Principality of Monaco and a few minutes later the train is pulling into Monte Carlo station, which is on a ledge overlooking the most exquisite bay you could imagine. It's like a fairy tale.

To get to the class you climb numerous flights of steps up the mountain on which the city is situated. The weather was marvellous and our spirits unusually high. Marike, the teacher, gave an excellent class, after which we ate lunch in the quaintest little restaurant further up the mountain. After lunch we took a horse and buggy all over the town, including to Prince Rainier's palace, which in itself is not terribly exciting but from where there is the most fantastic view of the bay.

18 March 1961

The other day we were free and so we hit on a great idea – spend two days in Genoa. It was my idea and Theresa d'Aquino and George Salavisa wanted to come too. We were dead tired at 7 o'clock in the morning but it didn't matter because we were going to Italy – we were getting away from Cannes, Cuevas and every face we see every grizzly day. We would buy some clothes, some shoes and most important of all – a bag for my togs – my tatty one is a laughing stock and I was sick of wearing Rose's and Brigitte's old summer dresses. I'm getting old and I must do it elegantly.

I bought my return ticket – we found places by the window and early in the morning we were wizzing through France, along the beautiful Côte d'Azur. The weather was wonderful – the sea terribly blue and the train full of Italians. Monaco, Monte Carlo, Menton – almost in Italy. This was where my ancestors had lived, where the weather was always fine, the people always happy and the clothes so elegant and so cheap, and I was meeting Bill at the other end.

We're in Italia – Ventimiglia next stop – we craned our necks out of the window and saw little houses perched on the mountainside with tired olive trees bending over them. Advertisements had changed their language and we pulled up into the station. In three hours' time we would be in Genoa. A beautiful man in a black uniform approaches and with a colossal smile said – 'let me stamp your passports!'

First George – 'Ah! Portugal – then Theresa, Brazil, Ah! From Rio and then babble, babble, babble in Italian and Spanish and Portuguese all mixed together, and then 'et Signorita – Française, n'est ce pas? Ah! Non! Sud Africaine!' – a blank face. 'One moment please,' and he disappears and returns with a large book – he ticks something in it and two policemen come and take me off the train – sorry, no go.

I must wait two hours for the train to Menton to get me out of the country; I had to spend those two hours in a waiting room, alone with a policeman and pictures of the Virgin Mary all over the walls. I continued knitting Carlos's tights and, to make it worse, found it necessary to poke the policeman every now and again with the knitting needle, as I was in no mood at all to have some foreign stranger breathing down my neck and whining – 'please'.

Anyway, I finally arrived in Menton and went straight to the Italian consulate in an attempt to get a visa, but of course it was shut – I gathered that it only opened for about two hours every three years and so I had a meal and went back to Cannes instead, knitting furiously and feeling most annoyed. Yesterday evening we danced *La Belle au*

Bois Dormant in Nice. I spent the day in Nice and Monte Carlo. I had to get away because I was in a bad mood.

The day before we went to Toulon and gave a performance there of *Dessin Pour Six*, *Narcisse*, *Soirée Musicale* and *Noir et Blanc*. The performances went very well and it was such a pleasure not to be dancing *La Belle au Bois Dormant*.

Mr Beriosoff (Papa to all dancers) gave me a lift out in his car and so I arrived ages before the bus and got the best place in the dressing room. The drive is lovely and so like South Africa that I could have screamed – it really is strange to see all the same trees and vegetation again, after spending two years in practically the North Pole.

Tuesday 21 March 1961

Still no letter from you and it still breaks my heart. Cannes is just the same as usual – still the walk along the Croisette in the mornings for class – rehearsals and performances. Three performances have been cancelled in Nice, owing to transport difficulties with all the exotic and very bulky costumes and thus we're down to rehearsal money, but that doesn't really worry me as I'd rather have less money than traipse off to Nice every couple of days.

This afternoon we rehearsed *Gaîté Parisienne* in which I dance the can-can, which I adore, but it is rather killing with all its cartwheels and so forth. Yesterday we were free and I meant to spend it seeing the world, but instead Greta [Gardemeyer] sat in bed until lunchtime knitting and then made a day of cleaning and washing. Most of the others visited the islands off the coast of Cannes but I wasn't really in the mood, so instead of doing that and going to a party in the evening we went to bed early and slept nine hours for the first time in months.

Here I feel happy in my work but not in myself as the company is so full of intrigue and scandals that I am afraid to speak, in case I say something wrong. Everyone is watching everyone else like hawks for an opportunity to criticize and thus pull their own self-esteem up a ratchet. It doesn't worry me unduly, but I think it's a pity as the company would lose nothing by creating a pleasanter atmosphere.

1 April 1961 (to Georgina who was in London)

I got your letter this morning and am terribly upset to hear about Kulu's death, as it was the first I'd heard of it. I haven't had a letter from anyone at home since before Xmas and now this has come like a black cloud from the sky. Why must it be Kulu – the one we loved the most and why must it happen when we're so far away and can do nothing to help Apa, Margie and everyone at home? Oh Georgie I want to see you so much. I think we will have 15 days free towards the end of May. Will you still be in London, because if so you're the one I want to come to, and if you're going home, can't you drop off on the way for a couple of days to see me wherever I am? Now we're in Cannes at the Casino Municipal, but on Wednesday we leave for Barcelona; then we're in Lisbon for three weeks and then in Porto for a couple of days. I think it's after that that we may be having a holiday before starting a two month season in Paris. After that nothing is settled. The company may disband owing to the death of the Marquis, or we may go to the States. As yet, nobody knows.

For the last couple of months I've been feeling terribly depressed, which I have no real reason to do because I'm in one of the best companies in Europe, but it's that very thing that has made me feel so lonely, for it's virtually impossible to strike up any sort of rapport with most of the other dancers – the world's greatest bitches are all assembled here.

How do I write to Margie? This must be why she hasn't written to me as it's not easy to find the words for things like this. Write soon Georgie. I need you very much.

4 April 1961

I'm so drunk. I've just been to the brasserie for lunch, but had no appetite so drank too much wine, so what I write will probably be a lot of nonsense, but anyway you'll understand why.

Before going to eat I passed in at the theatre and got Anthony's letter. It made me so happy to hear from home again, but I was terribly upset to hear about Kulu. Anyway, that's life and in spite of everything no one can take the memory of her and what a wonderful person she was, and all that she taught us, away from us. It's ours forever, and I feel happy I knew her so well. I know that this must be hard for you Margie, but my heart is with you all the time.

Today is our last day in Cannes and tomorrow morning at 9.35 we leave by train for Barcelona. It's a long journey – 13 hours and we will stay there at the Teatro del Liceo until the 30 April. From there we go to Lisbon to the Teatro Nacional de S. Carlos, Lisbon, Portugal, until 13 May – then to Porto for two days. Then it's our holiday perhaps for two weeks before we start rehearsing again for our season at the Théâtre de Champs Elysée in Paris for two months. After that, I think comes Deauville and then nobody knows. I so wish we could re-establish the contact we had before and write to each other more frequently. Most of the dancers in the company are hard, horrid, scheming bitches and I find it impossible to build any lasting friendships with them. Up until now I've been sinking lower and lower and losing every scrap of confidence I ever had in myself, and that is exactly what they want me to do most. But now I won't let it happen anymore. I will work for myself and make my life on my own. They're a horrid bunch and I'm not wasting any more of myself on them. If I'm friendly I'm a tart; if I'm unfriendly I'm a snob. They can think what they like and do what they like and so will I. I find better friends in books than among them. I was planning to go to Monte Carlo this morning but overslept, so instead will pack and write letters.

It's hard in this company. The work is hard, but what is harder is to keep up one's morale, especially as I feel so different from the others who think it's more important to look like a Dior model than to dance well. I'm writing this between packing, cleaning and washing, but thank heavens my little lot is nearly over – till Barcelona.

25 April 1961 (to Peter from Teatro del Liceo, Barcelona)

I was so happy to get your card this evening just before the perfor-mance, as I was beginning to despair about the negligence of my parents. Just before we left Paris for Cannes I wanted to phone home but didn't know your number at Lane House and wasn't able to trace it down in Paris. We then left for Cannes where we stayed for six weeks, performing there and occasionally in Toulon and Nice.

During our last week there I received a letter from Georgie saying how sorry she was that Kulu had died – this came as a terrible shock as I hadn't a clue that she had even been ill and Georgie, assuming that

I knew, naturally gave no details whatsoever. I of course immediately wrote to Margie and have been doing so ever since, but still get absolutely no word from her.

Then, the day before we left Cannes for Barcelona, I got a letter from Anthony. He said that Kulu went into hospital after an attack of pains and died quickly about six weeks later; he said that Apa has moved to Lane House and they're renting Foxwold. He mentioned that you'd gone to Chile, but gave no reason why or any address. Whether or not you knew this I don't know, but I suppose that is why Margie hasn't written. I'm sure all the burden is on her shoulders and it must have been a terrible shock to her and the family as I know how much she and we all loved Makulu; and now on top of it she must cope with Aps, as naturally he must be in a pretty terrible state.

I don't think that the postmen actually steal the letters, as everyone in our company except me receives them very regularly from all over the world (even Kenya), but invariably the stamps are removed and replaced by local ones, and anyway Margie always sends air-letter cards, which don't have a stamp on anyway.

We leave Barcelona on Sunday for Lisbon where we will be for 13 days – after that we have a ten-day holiday before starting a two-month season in Paris. During the holidays I will probably go to London to see Georgie. I've lost track of Josephine.

We expected to have a longer holiday and I intended flying home, but to borrow money and then be bankrupt is not really worth my while for just one week, especially as you won't be there either.

This company is excellent and I like the work very much, but I don't know how long I'll be able to stand its poisonous atmosphere as dishonesty, intrigues, jealousies and scandals abound and the dancers form little groups in which they scheme and plot how to get on. Practically all the younger ones other than me and an Austrian girl from Saltzburg have someone to support them, and the only really friendly ones are the stars and some of the boys. I daresay that it's the process of losing one's innocence and learning who one can and cannot trust. I was spoilt at home; you're all so decent and, idiot as I was, I thought the whole world would be the same.

GRAN TEATRO DEL LICEO

EMPRESA: JUAN A. PAMIAS BARCELONA
TEMPORADA DE PRIMAVERA 1961

Ballet

Internacional del

Marqués de Cuevas

Ballet programme cover for Barcelona performances.

In Spain we don't have to scrimp and scrape, starve and eat cheese rinds like in Paris as we get 4400 pesetas a week, about 75 dollars; my hotel is only about 370 a week and food is very cheap too. It's a pity the exchange rate is so bad, so it's more advisable to spend it on things

I need. I might as well stock up on some clothes as the prices in Paris are much too high for us to afford anything beyond one meal a day.

I suppose you know about the political situation in Paris at the moment. Everyone seems petrified of a civil war, but French people make a drama about a hole in their stocking, so I'll believe it when I see it. Please write to me soon, Peter. You know what it's like not to hear from home for one month – just imagine what it's like after four months, and on top of it you're a man and a lot tougher than I am. Honestly, I can't stand it any longer and if Margie won't write to me, please won't you?

6 May 1961 (from Teatro National S. Carlos, Lisbon, Portugal)

I got your letter this morning and am thrilled to hear you are coming to Paris. I have to be back there two days before, so leave your accommodation to me. I'll do the best I can, probably by getting two double rooms in a cheap hotel, but the Champs Elysée is much too expensive, but perhaps we can go to my old hotel, which is near the Arc de Triomphe and within walking distance from the theatre, even although it takes ½ to ¾ of an hour, but a pleasant walk anyway, or perhaps in Place Clichy where the hotels are really very cheap indeed.

Anyway, leave it to me as I'm much more likely to do it cheaply than the airline people. Now about where to come. I will be at the AEROGARE LES INVALIDES at 9.15 p.m. on 30 May. As far as I know all the plane passengers are brought by bus from the aerodrome to that air-station and it's a good place to meet as it's near the centre of Paris. If your bus doesn't go to that station I'm sure you can very easily get one that does as when I arrived back from London the buses were going there all the time. I just can't wait to see you again and I don't think that we're likely to be working very hard at the time as it's just *La Belle* we're doing then. From Les Invalides we can take a taxi to the hotel and natter as we don't open until the next night. If you need to contact me again before then, the only way is to write to the Théâtre de Champs Elysée, Avenue Montaigne, Paris, as I don't know where I'll be spending my holiday; and anyway I'll be back at work on 28 May, so I'll have any word at least two days before. If you send a letter you'd better write 'Attendre l'Arrivé' on the envelope, so they don't send it off to Cannes or some such place. I got your letter in Barcelona, but no others. Lisbon is divine, but I'll tell you all about it when I see you. Just think, we can count the days!

So now I'll sign off and wish you, Frankie and Martin a very, very happy voyage. Please thank Apa for his very nice letter and a big hug and kiss to all who must stay behind.

30 May 1961 (Letter from Margie to Peter)

We have just left Brazzaville and Martin and Frankie are battling nicely for the window seat.

By the grace of God we got to the airport yesterday, not that we didn't have to wait for half an hour there, but I was so tired I almost gave up trying to organise my getaway. I had to move Betty in at the weekend and Jean wished two guests on me too, not that I wasn't too glad to help but what a time! With the added anxiety of strike and riots too I've lost pounds in weight. The strike was a bit of a washout, but the press played it down a lot of course and a very clever move by the government saying the 'leaders' had called off the strike at the last minute which they had not so three-quarters of the non-Europeans were not sure what to do and didn't! Elisabethville airport was heavily guarded – I'm not quite sure who from!

They looked very seedy and the whole place very rundown, though one can't really judge from an airport. We have three babies dangling from the roof in bassinets – one pitch black and too sweet for words; also a Chinese couple – it's terrible to see how lonely and automatically isolated they are – we have too an African girl going from Baragwanath to study nursing in London.

I can't remember if I gave you the dope about our arrival in Chile – it is LH500 flight number arriving in Santiago 4.45 p.m. 15 June (leaving Paris 11.05 p.m. 14 June).

If you can let me know in Paris if you have heard this gladsome news I'd be glad – If you can't meet me don't worry I'll take a taxi to your headquarters office and hope to find instructions from you there.

Friday 2 June 1961

I'm sitting in the Théâtre de Champs Elysée watching a rehearsal of *Sleeping Beauty* with orchestra. Nina was at le Bourget airport to meet us and swept us through the customs etc. in a flash, nobody bothered to look at or ask about our luggage, so delightfully casual they are here and friendly, the porter at le Bourget picked up Frankie and kissed him on both cheeks! Sally is looking thin but very pretty. We are staying in two small rooms on the fifth floor of the Hotel des Deux Avenues, Rue Poncelet – we have coffee and croissants served in our room but go out for all other meals. I took the boys on a boat trip up the Seine, beautiful but bitterly cold – it has been raining ever since the day after we arrived. If only I could park the children somewhere for some hours at a time. They get so fractious being hauled on and off buses, waiting at the theatre or in cafés. If it is fine tomorrow we will take them up the Eiffel Tower. Selina has the day free up to 6 p.m. Tonight all the big wigs are invited to the performance – Aga Khan, Duke and Duchess of Windsor, Maurice Chevalier etc.

Sunday 4 June 1961

It cleared up yesterday and we all 'did' the Eiffel Tower – lunching at the restaurant half way up – miraculous food but it set us back about £5!! Since the war in Algeria everything has sky rocketed in price. This afternoon we are going to Selina's matinée – and tomorrow if it kills me I must find the S.A. embassy and find out what happened if anything at home on the 31st at the birth of our Republic!!

Will be seeing you soon.

All my love, Margaret x

Tuesday 20 June 1961

Thank you so much for your letter and the 15 NF – I was thrilled with both, especially the former, but the latter was most agreeable considering that our pay packet the other day contained only 39 NF – but still, they say that rich people are never really happy!

Margie I can't tell you how wonderful it was having you here and you must never ever think that it was a sacrifice on my part because nothing in the whole world could have brought me more happiness than those two weeks with you did.

I miss you like mad but the aftermath of your visit hasn't yet worn off. I feel much happier, more balanced and altogether a different person. A lot of gossip had been going on about Larrain's new ballet with four girls and four boys – it's come to light, and what should I see on the board but four names of soloist girls and four boys and then, RESERVE POUR LES FILLES – MOLTENO.

I nearly had a fit but perhaps as you say I'm not quite as inferior as I make myself out to be. Today is our free day and so this morning Patricia and I went to a swimming pool and had the most fabulous morning there. The weather now is perfect and I'm feeling in my element flouncing around in my new summer frocks.

Greta and I have a very nice room with two beds, two big windows and a huge veranda for our washing – we look out onto the street and are most comfortable. I bought a packet of maizena but Greta hates it and so instead I have it for breakfast or in the evening when I come home. Whether it's the maizena or not I don't know but I really feel well, full of bounce and energy and enthusiasm – I think it's a combination of the maizena, the weather, your visit, and my new chance.

Nureyev,[34] the Russian prodigy at the moment, has a little drama attached to his life. The company was at the airport leaving for London when suddenly two Russians came up to him and said – 'Sorry Sir but you're not going to London. Here are your tickets and there's your plane to Moscow – you've been mixing too much with the French dancers and so you must go home.' He turned tail and ran and the French police protected him and, under French law, he was a free man

---

34. As noted by Wikipedia, 'Rudolf Khametovich Nureyev (1938–1993) was a Soviet-born dancer of ballet and modern dance, one of the most celebrated of the 20th century.' His defection to the Cuevas company at the height of the cold war as the Kirov ballet company was leaving the airport in Paris to go to London attracted international interest. Selina became close to him and acted as his translator (at the time he could speak English but not French.

and no one could touch him. The papers got wildly excited – 'scandal, NUREYEV – the greatest Russian dancer', 'NUREYEV the world's greatest,' says another, and Lifar says 'NUREYEV and Golovine, the two incomparables,' and then a few days later they announced 'NUREYEV to join BALLET MARQUIS DE CUEVAS for their PARIS SEASON', and so he starts on the 23rd and will dance both the Prince and the Blue Bird. London is furious. The season there had been booked out for months and the headlines are 'CUEVAS STOLEN NUREYEV'. That's who they had been waiting for and now WE have him on a plate.

Must fly now – I miss you like mad and please give my special love to Martie, Frankie and Peter. I hope you had a pleasant journey and a happy birthday.[35] Greta sends her love to you too and to the two boys.

26 June 1961 (to Anthony and Annabel)

I really apologize for the horrid delay but I just couldn't get down to writing a whole letter; I've made several attempts but we have been so terribly, terribly busy and to squeeze in a moment to finish a letter seems never to arrive, but I hope to goodness I succeed this time.

It was wonderful seeing Margie, Martin and Frankie again. I went down to the airport to meet them and to give them a surprise and saw them coming through the various gates. I waved madly but felt rather a fool as all I got back was a good look and then a turn of the head. They didn't even recognize their darling daughter and sister and then Martin precariously walked up to me as if to say 'You aren't perchance the girl that promised to reserve a hotel for me?'

We had the most marvellous two weeks imaginable living together in two hotel rooms, each with one, only just adequately sized bed and Martin was most efficient as he used to go out and make little purchases for us in French. We would tell him what to say and he always came back with the right thing. Frankie was desperate to get a pair of skis in Paris so he could get straight onto the snow from the plane and not waste time buying them in Chile.

35. Margie's 49th birthday had been on 17 June.

We finish our season in a few days' time and then go to Vichy, Geneva, Deauville, La Baule and Biarritz, return to Paris and from then on I don't know what happens. Some English-speaking girls have joined the company but they've fired my best friend Greta; it's a cruel game, it really is. I stay now in Place Clichy and we're working terribly hard at the moment. Things have turned better for me and I've been given much more to dance.

It's Sunday today and in half an hour's time I'm going out with some friends to see a film on the Champs Elysée.

The weather is cold and glum. We had two fabulous weeks of sunshine and warmth at the end of June, but obviously it appears that, that is our lot for the year.

I'm looking forward to going to Geneva as I don't know Switzerland at all and I believe it is a very beautiful city.

Please give my love to Apa, Vicky and Betty. I'm sorry I haven't written to Apa yet, but tell him that he's the next one on my list. I wonder when I'll get a chance to come and visit you all – it would be lovely. Margie showed me a plan of the new house and it looks super. When you write use the Faubourg St Honoré address as the company hasn't given us any addresses for the tour yet. I must fly now.

29 June 1961

Thank you for your letter – what a journey – I'm glad you got there safely anyway! It's so hot – one can only loll around and flop down in whatever café is in sight to recover from the last five steps to get to it. I'm reading a book based on the life of Gauguin so feel all grotesque – as if I'd find a lot of pleasure in having a huge great foot that got into everyone's way.

The Grand Ballet of the Marquis de Cuevas still exists in all its pomp and glory, with little brown envelopes containing a small advance trickling in every once in a while. The powerful ones exert their power, the weak crawl around quivering in fright but the sun hasn't ceased to shine and no Algerians have blown up Clichy yet.

A friend from Denmark – a Swede – appeared on the scene the other night and took me out to eat a sole meunière followed by a steak. For coffee we went to Pigalle, but coffee was off the menu so we had tea and watched a parade of drag queens pass by. I saw Lindsey yesterday and liked her enormously. Peter Goodship – Amelia's current beau – came to Paris and looked me up. We finished off a kilo of lychees on the *Bateau Mouches* and saw *Exodus* in the evening – a most powerful film about the struggle of the Jews during the war.

We gave two open-air performances at the Chateau de Sceaux[36] in the most beautiful setting I've ever seen – *Noir et Blanc* and *Gaîté Parisienne*. It was lovely out there. Nureyev, the Russian escapee had thirty curtain calls and so the propaganda hasn't died down and the romance of it all is far too heady for the French people to ignore. I must go to class now so will continue when I come home.

3 July

It's still as hot as hell and the other night communists threw stink bombs and coins onto the stage when Nureyev was dancing and shouted 'Go Back to Russia'. There was so much screaming that you couldn't hear one note of the Blue Bird pas de deux, which he was dancing.

I've started to work in the mornings again and this time with Madame Nora.[37] The company has taken in a whole lot of new girls and boys – I think that Larrain has a whole lot of reorganizing up his sleeve.

4 September 1961 (from Biarritz, France)

Here I sit in my hotel room in Biarritz missing you like hell and gazing with adoration at that beautiful piece of material I received a couple of days ago. Thank you Margie, it's lovely and I will make an out-of-this-world frock with it. I haven't quite made up my mind what but will

---

36. The Château de Sceaux is a grand country house in Sceaux, Hauts-de-Seine, not far from Paris, France. Located in a park laid out by André Le Nôtre, it houses the Musée de l'Île-de-France, a museum of local history. From Wikipedia entry.

37. Russian born Madame Nora Kiss (1908–1993), alias Eléonore Eugénie Adamiantz, taught ballet at the Studio Wacker, 69 Rue de Douai, Paris, which was very close to where Selina lived in the Rue Lécluse at Place Clichy, along with other notable ballet teachers such as Olga Preobrajenska and Victor Gsovsky.

find a pattern in London, as I am going there next week for ten days' holiday.

Geneva was lovely; the weather was fine and the open air theatre pleasant. I'm dancing quite a lot on this tour and that makes me happy. The Swiss people are grim, thick headed and irritating. The journey from Geneva to Paris was swelteringly hot, exceedingly uncomfortable and rather a bore and so we were all rather relieved to arrive at the Gare d'Austerlitz knowing that at least we had a good night's sleep ahead of us. Early the next morning we were off to Deauville where I shared a room with Marilyn Jones. There we danced at the Casino on the most horrible little stage. The weather was disappointing and the town is stuffed with awfully horsey snobs. It is also very expensive – three times the price of Paris, so I am still up to my neck in debt.

We left Deauville for three days to dance in an open-air theatre in La Baule. There, hotel rooms were unavailable and so instead most of the company, including me, stayed in St Nazaire and took a trip into La Baule every day for rehearsals and performances. La Baule is a very attractive seaside resort and we were all rather sorry to have to return to Deauville. Anyway, we had one surprise there. Peggy van Praagh[38] had joined the company as guest teacher and we are all thrilled with her classes.

The last day in Deauville we had a class at 10 a.m. after an evening in the casino where we were served with a good sized dinner amid much pomp and glory.

Anyway, after class we rehearsed and between times rammed things into our bags and after the performance that night we took a bus to Paris – arriving there at 7 a.m. to catch a train to Biarritz at 8 a.m. The bus journey was murder – a terribly uncomfortable second-class bus with rock hard seats and no room even to put your knees, let alone your luggage.

We arrived in Paris feeling dreadful – tired and bad tempered to find that porters were nowhere to be seen. All we could do was gulp down a cup of coffee, buckle up courage and carry our own bags along

38. Peggy van Praagh had come back into Selina's life. See note for entry of 13 March 1959.

Peggy van Praagh.

miles of platform until we finally found our allotted compartments, where again we sat until evening with no dining car and no source of nourishment; the last straw was when we had to change trains in La Négresse (Biarritz) and, in the process of doing that, I put my knee out of joint. There was at least one consolation and that was that I'd reserved a room, but when I got there I found that the hotel had given my room to Peggy van Praagh as she hadn't made a reservation and naturally was to have preference. The hotel said they couldn't give me one until the next night. I was furious and promptly sat down on a sofa in utter exhaustion and wished you'd taken me to South America; but fortunately Ana-Maria offered to share her bed with me for the night and now I am safely installed in a room on my own. I had my knee put back in joint and now conditions are much better. The stage is big and until yesterday the weather perfect. The theatre overlooks the beach and for once I have a pretty room.

In a few days' time we have holidays and I'm off to London. After that we're going to Israel, Rome, Copenhagen, Stockholm, Vienna and, perhaps, even Japan.

9 September 1961 (from London)

I've arrived in London for a ten-day break after three days without sleep, but nevertheless am feeling in top form. We gave our last performance in San Sebastian on the night of the 6th – it's a pretty little town with a great statue of Christ on top of a hill, so when it gets dark all you see is this illuminated figure hanging in the sky and I must say it looked very impressive.

André [Prokovsky] has left the company now and so on the last night he invited us all to drink lots and lots of *sangria*. After that we took the bus back to Biarritz where we dined, packed and at the crack of dawn caught the train from La Négresse (Biarritz) to Paris.

The journey was crowded and rather uncomfortable, but we nevertheless had a nice group in our compartment and so amused ourselves until 5.30 when we arrived in Paris at the Gare d'Austerlitz.

Marilyn and I took a room together but couldn't for the life of us get to sleep, so when morning came we quickly got up – booked out of the hotel and tried to get to London. Marilyn was in a hurry to get there that day, so we couldn't go together as I couldn't afford anything but a 'Skyway Tour'.

Anyway, I fixed her up and saw her off as she couldn't cope herself due to the language and then managed to fix myself up with a ticket for 5.30 a.m. the next morning – I'd be in London by 11 a.m. I spent the rest of the day rushing around doing various things. In the evening I saw *La Verité*,[39] a good but horrifying film and then spent the rest of the night in the waiting room at the Gare de Lyon – the only place available in which to sit, and chatted until 5 a.m. to an American society girl and a student from Luxembourg. Finally, I bade them farewell and, feeling rather tatty, smelly and tired, mounted the bus at République. We got to Beauvais to catch the plane, but had to wait five hours because of fog.

I finally arrived in London. G.B. [Wilson] is in Edinburgh until the 10th, the bank was already closed and so I couldn't find out where Jo [Josephine Molteno] was (I don't even know if she's in England) – in fact I feel she may be in Greece. Leonie [Urdang] too I could only find out through a bank. Fortnum & Mason where Georgie works was closed and so I just took a taxi to her flat only to find that she'd left it in the spring.

I couldn't bear the thought of imposing myself on Angela Rowe and company. I didn't know where to go so I took a bus to South Kensington station and stood there paging through my address book and

39. *La Verité* (1960) starring Brigitte Bardot.

finally phoned up Stella Firth to try and find out where Georgie resided – she didn't know but very kindly has invited me to spend tonight with her; therefore this paper as I left my luggage in the *consigne*. She gave me Rhoda's number and Rhoda gave me Georgie's number plus an invitation to the country, but Georgie's not at home. Stella has now gone out, but I'm very comfortable and looking forward to the holiday.

On my last day in Paris I went to Guiraud out of curiosity and found your heavenly letter. Thank you Margie – it's kept me going ever since.

I'm not quite sure where we'll be in December and January, but I think Italy as I heard that we'd be having Xmas in Milan – we go to Rome too. After the holiday we go back to Paris on the 22nd and rehearse for about a week before parting for Israel – I think my twenty-first will be on the boat to Israel. We shall do three towns in Israel, including Jerusalem, and then comes Germany, Scandinavia and Italy. As soon as I find out exact dates I'll let you know as I'd absolutely *adore* to see you all again. I really must go to sleep now; otherwise, it will be my fourth night up.

18 September 1961 (from grandfather Apa now staying at Lane House, Tennant Road, Kenilworth, Cape Town)

Dearest Selina,

I do feel so lost without my dearest May who died in hospital at Wynberg in March last. Anthony who finishes his course in medicine in December is certain to pass well and your family in general have all been very good, but I haven't yet been able to let Foxwold.[40] Samuel[41] is in charge there and looking after the place. All the Foxwold stuff, furniture, books and my effects are here. Rowan House is well let to Bennie Godfrey, a rich master builder, friendly neighbour. Shall be glad to hear how you are getting on and when you may be paying the Lane House a visit.

---

40. Foxwold was the name of Selina's grandparents' smallholding on the top of a hill in Koelenhof, near Stellenbosch.
41. Samuel and Ellen, with their two children Eliot and Emily, had lived in a cottage in the grounds at Foxwold for many years and were employed to do the cooking and general housekeeping.

28 September 1961 (from Paris)

We are now back at the Théâtre de Champs Elysée for a rehearsal period until 9 October. We're doing classes with Peggy van Praagh every morning and rehearsals every afternoon. We've only just been given our dates for the tour and so I'll let you know all that I know so that you can make your plans accordingly. On 9 October we leave Paris for Israel by plane. From 10 to 12 October we perform at the Tel Aviv Main Auditorium. On 13 October we leave Tel Aviv. On 14 October we're at the Theatre Edison in Jerusalem. We are not sure yet about the 15 and 16 October, but on 17 and 18 October, we are at the Armon Theatre in Haifa, 19 October in Nathania, 20 October is a free day, and on the 21st we are back in Jerusalem, the 22nd and 23rd in Haifa, with the chance of a prolongation until the 25th. From 26 October until 1 November we are on a boat trip from Haifa to Hamburg.

I must fly now to class, so I apologize for this skimpy letter, but I wanted to get the dates off to you as soon as possible.

Wednesday 11 October 1961 (from Tel Aviv, Israel)

Well here we are in Tel Aviv on the east side of the Mediterranean Sea – the sun is beating down and I'm completely overcome by a drowsiness that is almost impossible to shake off and that I dare say is due to the sudden change in climate and altitude.

Well, I'll start in Paris from my birthday. Your letter and the cheque arrived on the very day and have done more for my good luck and happiness than you can imagine. Thank you very, very much – it really was a lovely surprise. We were just going to start class when one of the dancers appeared with this letter – I worked well and Nureyev praised my work and afterwards Peggy van Praagh called me aside and told me that I'd made a lot of progress and that Larrain was very pleased and wanted to give me a push – but that I still had a lot of work to do on my arms. That night we were given free tickets to go to the opening of the Hungarian Ballet and so we all dressed up and afterwards had a dinner to celebrate my birthday.

The next night the Viscomtess de Ribes had invited us all to a cocktail party, so I cashed the cheque and bought a dress with the money; put up my hair, and, to my utter surprise, Larrain rushed up to me,

Puckie Scherpenisse and Selina.

kissed me on both cheeks and started introducing me to a whole lot of Paris celebrities, including the novelist Françoise Sagan; the next day Madame de Fredericksz said, 'Oh, Selina you looked lovely last night!' and Mr Larrain immediately assigned me a solo, or at least a pas de trois, in *Somnambule*, which I am to do tomorrow – so you see Margie, you gave me a very lovely twenty-first birthday present – thanks.

The flight from Paris to Israel was out of this world. We took the Caravelle jet from Orly and stopped off for half an hour in Rome. The weather was perfect and so not a sight was missed – the Lake of Geneva, the Swiss Alps (snow-capped), the coast of Italy, Rome, Athens and the Greek islands. The most spectacular sight of all was coming down into Israel by night and seeing the lights of Tel Aviv from the Mediterranean Sea.

Here I have a room with Marilyn [Jones] and Puckie (a Dutch girl) and last night we gave our first performance since San Sebastian, gathering from the applause I think it was a great success. We did *Noir et Blanc*, *Somnambule*, a pas de trois with Serge [Golovine], Beatriz[42] [Consuelo] and Margot[43] [Miklosy], and the third act of *La Belle [au Bois Dormant]*; afterwards the audience rose in a body and rushed up towards the stage for the curtain calls.

42. Beatriz Consuelo (1931–2013) was a Brazilian born principal who joined the company in 1953 and became a star in 1959. After the company disbanded she joined the Opera in Geneva, where she spent the rest of her life. Selina remembers her most for the tiny little dog she took with her everywhere and even smuggled onto aeroplanes. She dated George Goviloff and Claude Darnet, but those relationships did not last. She had a son called Frédéric Gafner in 1969, who also became a dancer. His father Claude Gafner had been a dancer, but became a photographer after an accident.

43. Margot Miklosy had escaped from the revolution in Hungary. After Cuevas disbanded she became a big star with the London Festival Ballet.

It's so hot here and I have a streaming cold and feel terribly tired, but I'm sure we'll get used to it in a couple of days. The company is not sending any mail to Israel, so I hope they'll be a fat letter waiting for me when we return to Paris afterwards on our way to Hamburg.

My love to you all and I sincerely hope that our little rendezvous in Italy still holds. You have our dates, so it's up to you.

We are in Paris now for two days after Israel and before Hamburg and I was so disappointed that there was no letter waiting for me from you, but perhaps you didn't get the letter I sent from Israel as it had such a beautiful stamp on it. Anyway, I hope you did and it's not really *such* a long time since I last heard from you. However, I would love to know when and where I'll see you again so I can make plans and daydream about it.

30 October 1961 (from Paris)

Israel was fascinating. We saw so much of so many interesting and historical things. One day we went to Nazareth and saw the dugout cave in which Joseph and Mary lived, and the carpenter's shop where Joseph lived before he married. In those days – it seems – they lived like cavemen. From there we went to the Sea of Galilee and Tiberias and when I see you again I'll tell you all about it. I saw practically everything of interest in Israel except the Dead Sea and King Solomon's mines, which I'm sorry about but we didn't have the time.

Every day was perfect and to commemorate it all I invested in a few exquisite pieces of jewellery – two necklaces and a set of earrings – (1) small blue stones on a dark background; (2) blue stones set inside a silver band, rather Scandinavian; and (3) dangling coral earrings set in old silverwork. We returned from Israel by boat, which we took from Haifa, a gorgeous city built on the side of a hill and overlooking the Mediterranean.

The trip back took five days and the ship was pretty primitive and filthy – there were cockroaches everywhere, in our beds, on the floors and even crawling over the bread, but it didn't really matter as it was such an interesting trip. We stopped at Cyprus for two hours but weren't allowed to go ashore and then we passed Crete and all the places around there, but most interesting of all was going through the

Straits of Messina between Sicily and Italy and seeing the volcano (I've forgotten its name) [Mount Etna] actually sending off an eruption.

There's been one change of programme for the tour and instead of going to either Rome or Munich as is marked, we will be going to Bologna in the north of Italy instead of either of them.

I did the *Acrobats* in Tel Aviv and it went more or less OK. Larrain never saw it though as he stayed in Paris, so I hope he gives us another chance to do it in the future.

It looks as if next year's season in Paris will run for one year – but that's just a rumour, so I don't know how true it is.

Let me know if there's anything you'd like me to get for you or for the family in Germany as it's very cheap and good for things like radios. I'd like to get Anthony something special for an engagement present, but I don't exactly know what – can you suggest something. I know that it's Italy for the girls though.

Beginning of letter missing but probably around 12 December 1961

In Hamburg the craziest thing happened. Someone pressed the fire alarm and all the *Belle au Bois* sets were drenched in water. In fact, the whole theatre was. What a display of hysterics followed and the papers were full of accusations of sabotage and all the rest the next day. Hamburg was cold and wet, but fortunately we stayed opposite the theatre, so the dreadful weather didn't inconvenience us more than was necessary. The travelling we've been doing recently has been killing and I seem to be in a perpetual state of jumping down everyone's throat. How much longer I'll be able to stand this racket, I just don't know. Our Copenhagen contract has been cancelled as they won't pay for two planes to transport us there from Italy, so it looks very much as if we'll be having Xmas in Paris again. Peggy van Praagh is leaving the company in March to return to Australia, which really will be a terrible tragedy for us.

I got a very nice letter from Apa yesterday and he seems full of beans, and is anticipating your return home. When am I going to see you again? I'd so much like to speak to you as I feel it's time I did something about my life. I have to think hard because life in a ballet company is making me more and more nervous, and I don't see the point as sincerely I don't care two hoots whether I get on or not. I like the life all right, but hate having no home and no opportunity to meet people outside this narrow warped circle. I don't mind making sacrifices for something worthwhile, but all it does is make us more odd, narrow minded, nervous and antisocial than ever before.

I know I'm only 21, but years go by quickly and I can't see (if I continue like this) I'll ever be able to have a home and family of my own, which to me is more important than a career. Being a ballet dancer, in many ways, is very much like being a nun and I just can't say that I'm cut out for it.

21 December 1961 (from Paris)

Well now it's Xmas time again for the third year running and I can't even start to say how much I miss you all, but then it's not necessary to explain because I'm sure you understand perfectly.

On Xmas day I shall be flying with the company to Copenhagen from Paris, where we are now rehearsing after completing our tour of Italy.

I sent you all a Xmas parcel from Venice with presents collected from all over Italy, except for Anna's which I got in Israel. I'm sorry they'll be so late but I couldn't get them off earlier, but anyway when they come I hope you'll like them and that they'll arrive in one piece.

Mr Larrain seems very pleased with my work and has told various people that he has many things in mind for me later on, including the Queen of the Wilis, but doesn't think I'm quite ready for it yet, but nevertheless I'm working very hard and Peggy van Praagh told me that I'm making a lot of progress.

Italy was lovely – we started in Bologna and from there went to Turin, Genoa, Trieste and finished up in Venice.

I liked Genoa and Venice the most – Genoa because it wasn't so cold and Venice because it was so beautiful. No buses, no cars, no bicycles – just gondolas and our frozen feet, but I couldn't believe that such atmosphere and beauty still existed on this earth. St Mark's Square is something I'll never forget for the rest of my life. It really is sad to think that in about 50 years this whole city will sink and be submerged by water and that scientists who can build atom bombs can't seem to find a way of preserving such a beautiful city.

We had a lovely snowfall while we were there, and it was so nice to walk all wrapped up along these secluded streets (straight out of the past) while the snowflakes got all tangled up in your eyelashes.

The first day after we arrived in Venice we were free for the whole day and the whole night and so Imray,[44] Margot, Marilyn and I hired a car and at the crack of dawn we caught a boat to the west where they have roads and cars and drove, for the day, to Verona. Verona – the beautiful old city of Romeo and Juliet is still alive today, Juliet's balcony, tomb and the church where they married is still there too and we saw it all – the square where Dante used to roam, which now has his statue in the middle, the Piazza des Herbes where the chariot races used to be run is just round the corner from Juliet's house and the church of St Zeno is the most beautiful building I have ever seen in my whole life. Passing through Milan we stopped for a few hours and I saw La Scala and the cathedral, but the church of St Zeno in spite of its modesty moved me more than the cathedral in Milan, which is the greatest and most impressive in the world. Such perfect form and proportions – I didn't realize were possible; and we just stood in the square of St Zeno watching the sun set behind the church until it was so dark that we couldn't look anymore; and so then we saw the insides of things, among them being a church dating back to AD 400, which had been recovered in one piece from underneath an earthquake.

And now that we're back in Paris it seems to me that it's quite ugly. Never mind though – I can't spend my whole life looking at the church of St Zeno. You'll be glad to hear I'm sleeping and living in my long woollen pants. I've never known such cold, damp weather as Europe is experiencing now.

I'm so glad to hear that Jo [Josephine Molteno] is getting married to Mike [Macrae] in January – he's such a wholesome, human person and I'm sure they'll have a lot to give each other. I've sent Anthony a nice wedding present which will be just perfect for his little cottage.[45] Happy Xmas to you all.

---

44. Imray Varady was Margot Margot Miklosy's husband and they had fled from Hungary together. They later both joined Festival Ballet, where Margot's career took off in a rather spectacular manner.
45. They never acknowledged the coffee set, for it had broken in the post. Perhaps Selina's packing had not been up to scratch.

* * *

On *Monday 25 December 1961* the chartered plane that was to take the company from Paris to Copenhagen on Xmas morning caught alight shortly after take-off. With a burning wing the plane returned to Orly airport to make a crash landing on the runway. After landing, the fire was quickly extinguished by spraying the plane with foam and the members of the company had to spend a dreary Xmas day eating an unappetizing Xmas dinner and waiting for another chartered plane to arrive from the Middle East to take them to Copenhagen that evening – the experience severely dampened Selina's appetite for air travel.

* * *

16 January 1962 (from Montpellier)

Thank you so much for your letter and the 12 dollars enclosed – I was thrilled to hear from you as I was beginning to get quite desperate.

At the moment we are touring La France – thrilling – and we've already done Lyons, Grenoble and Montpellier and I'm afraid that I'm completely lost as far as where we're going next as the company keeps changing its mind, so I just get onto the train when we're told to and get off when everyone else does.

A group of us has what we call our family and always travel in a compartment together and enjoy ourselves thoroughly. The members are Marian [Sarstadt] from Holland, Puckie [Scherpenisse] (also from Holland, Armando[46] [Navarro] from Buenos Aires, Dick from California, Garth [Welch][47] from Australia, Patricia [Dowling] from Oklahoma

---

46. Armando Navarro (1930–2013) began his career at the Theatro Colon in Buenos Aires. He came to Europe in 1956 where he joined Cuevas and there met Marian Sarstadt, whom he married. When the company disbanded they settled in the Netherlands where Armando became artistic director of Scapino Ballet.

47. Garth Welch (b.1936) Australian dancer and choreographer. After the Cuevas company disbanded in 1962, he returned to Australia with Peggy van Praagh to join the Australian Ballet. He and Marilyn Jones married and had two sons, both of whom became dancers. The eldest, Stanton, is now

Selina with Marian Sarstadt, *c.*1967.

and me. Marilyn [Jones] always travels first class because she's a first dancer. We've got ourselves wonderfully arranged and all we have to do when we arrive is (i) Garth gets out and Armando passes the cases through the window to him on the platform; (ii) Patricia gets the porter and his wheel barrow; (iii) I arrange the taxis and (iv) Puckie gets the luggage from the train to the taxis. We've got it so taped now that our cases even have their own special places in the train and the whole performance takes only a few minutes and then we can relax and watch our French comrades shouting and screaming while they lose their luggage and get stuck in the passage.

From Grenoble to Montpellier we had it hard though as we changed trains three times and it was raining buckets all day – we got absolutely soaked and my fur coat is quite clean now. To celebrate the occasion we sang 'Oh What a Beautiful Morning' – Garth sang the solos and we all joined in for the chorus. We all have one thing in common and that is that we're anti-French.

We were free today and I enjoyed myself doing practically nothing of any interest, but what I did was such fun and all because of Anna's letter, which I got this morning – a letter from Granny[48] too and a card from a student I met once who wishes me a happy Xmas. Then

director of the Houston Ballet in the USA. They divorced and have two grandchildren from their second son.

48. This is Selina's paternal grandmother, Lucy Lindley Mitchell Molteno who came to South Africa from South Carolina in the late nineteenth century and there married her grandfather John Charles Molteno.

Marilyn and I (she'd also got mail) went and had a tart and a coffee to celebrate and then we went to the Monoprix to buy shampoo. They have such nice things in the Monoprix here so we looked at them for about an hour. Of course I couldn't buy much because you know how poor we are in France, but I did get some new suspenders to hold up my old suspender belt, some cotton and a refill for my Ratio Bleuet [gas stove].

Then, as we were going home, we bumped into Dick and he begged me to go and have a pastry with him, so I did, and he had also got a letter and thus over the pastry we discussed every aspect of the life histories of the people who had so kindly written to us.

Afterwards I went home and mended all my clothes (quite a job) and then Dick called for me and took me out to dinner in a cheap restaurant – now I'm home again and writing to you. I enjoyed today so much. It's so nice to have an *ordinary* day; it reminds me of Saturday afternoons at home in winter when we used to sit in the sewing room and watch you sewing.

Spottswood has been sacked; Mr Larrain really is turning into a maniac and Floris [Alexander (1943–2006)] broke his foot during *Noir et Blanc* the other day in Lyons; Peggy van Praagh has left to have an operation on her hip; she'll join us in Cannes to recuperate – maybe – and we have a new teacher called Maria Fay.[49] There is talk of Volkova[50] joining our company in June; I do hope so. She watched us doing a class in Copenhagen. Papa [Beriosoff] is being nice to me at the moment and in Grenoble told me about Buddhism in great detail, which was kind of him because, after all, I was ignorant on the subject. I'm knitting a pair of tights for Ghislaine[51] [Thesmar] because she can't knit. She's very nice and has lived in South Africa for a while – her

49. Maria Fay (1928–2019) was a Hungarian-born teacher of marked distinction. She turned chubby legs into long lissom ones through her strong emphasis on 'pulling up'. She also worked in London as well and inspired many, including Leonie Urdang.
50. Vera Volkova (1905–1975) was an influential Russian ballet dancer and teacher.
51. Ghislaine Thesmar (b.1943 in Beijing). After the company disbanded she married Pierre Lacotte and worked for the Paris Opera. She had a successful career in ballet.

father is a French ambassador and she seems very cultured and pleasant. Work is agreeable at the moment as we don't only do *La Belle*. I'm so sick of that wretched ballet now and whenever I see one of those puce costumes I want to throw it out of the window.

6 March 1962 (to Annabel from the Casino Municipal, Cannes)

Thank you so very, very much for the lovely green costume. I adore it, it fits perfectly and you couldn't possibly have thought of anything more useful. Thank you very much.

I got a letter from Peter today and he is coming to Cannes on the 21 March and I'm just hoping and praying that it's the 23rd that we leave for Vienna and not the 21st, as I would hate to miss him. He is terribly distressed as he hasn't heard a word from Margie and says that because of that he can't make any plans. It's difficult too because this company never seems to know our exact dates either!

Anyway, if you can press Margie to write to Peter c/o UNTAB, Casilla de Correo 2257, Buenos Aires – where he'll be until 17 March I'm sure that he'll be much happier.

18 May 1962 (from Van Spinkestraat 106, Amsterdam)

I'm sorry I didn't write sooner but somehow we've been dashing around so hectically that I've hardly had time to sleep – let alone write letters. First of all thank you so much for the package you left for me in Paris. The iron of course is absolutely ideal for me, the books a gift from heaven and the other bits and pieces exceedingly useful. It really was a wonderful surprise – thank you very, very much. I hope you had a pleasant trip home and the family must be in their seventh heaven having you back again. The only really sure dates we have so far are on 23 May we return to Paris for rehearsals; on 28 May to 3 June we're in Brussels; and from 5 to 13 June in Amsterdam. I know that there is also Vichy and Athens to follow, but can't say exactly when.

I've had a fascinating holiday here and have met many interesting people in the Amsterdam art 'milieu' – I even bumped into Peter Cazalet once. At an art exhibition I met a contemporary artist called Flip van der Bergh who told me that he sent some pictures to South Africa but had all his nudes returned!

I was surprised at how unlike the Dutch people are to the Afrikaners at home and apparently the Dutch Reformed Church hardly exists at all. It's wonderful to have a holiday and get completely away from the environment of the company and now I really am looking forward to seeing them all again as after a rest they're completely different people, and somehow easier to get along with. I am glad you enjoyed your trip to Yugoslavia – I only wish I could have been with you – it was a pity our holiday came just after you left – in fact it's a flaming shame.

Puckie has started doing classes again in Amsterdam, but I'm not going to as I think that one works much better by having a complete rest, so I'll probably start again on the 24th with the whole company.

7 June 1962 (from Amsterdam)

I received your letter yesterday; thank you very much. We are back in Amsterdam now, having since the holidays spent one week in Brussels. From here we leave on the 13th for Vichy and on the 27th fly for a three-day season in Athens. After Athens we return for 15 days to Paris where the company will give its ADIEU CUEVAS performances.

The Marquise[52] has said that she's tired of being generous and from the end of this month will withdraw all the aid we have. Her lawyers too don't like all these American dollars being spent in Europe, and so here I am on the premises watching the company die and crumble before my eyes and, unless a miracle happens, we are all out of work as from 15 July. They informed us one month before and so the Marquise is not obliged to give us a penny – they plonk us in Paris and that is it – it's a shame as we are having fantastic successes at the moment, but regardless of the success it is impossible to run a company of this size and calibre on a profit as the expenses are so large and unless another millionaire decides to sponsor us we are on the rocks.

52. The Marquise was the widow of the Marquis de Cuevas, Margaret Rockefeller, whose money had in effect been financing the company. Later she married Raymundo Larrain who, being so very much younger than her, gave her a wheelchair and false teeth for a wedding present. Raymundo somehow managed to get hold of her money, though died of Aids at a relatively young age.

Selina in the Netherlands, 1962.

Cuevas is the last of the international privately-owned companies in existence and therefore, unless I can become a British citizen and work for Festival, the last company I'm entitled to join, I'm in an impossible position. Anyway, the thought of joining Festival Ballet doesn't particularly attract me and I doubt if I'm entitled to British nationality given the short time I've spent in England.

Madame de Fredericksz told me that the company went through endless battles to keep me on as even the French government, which is so free and easy, didn't like the idea of employing a South African.[53]

53. South Africa left the Commonwealth in 1961 and, because of the apartheid regime, was now beginning to become a pariah. These were interesting times. Evidence of the Algerian War of Independence was obvious in Paris, with lots of Algerian refugees on the streets and feelings about the outcome running high. Claudine Kamoun was Algerian, so the company was sensitized to the anti-colonial struggle through her concerns. The cold war was also at its height, which was partly why Nureyev's defection from the Soviet Union was such a landmark event, for it was a political as well as a personal statement. Rudolf Nureyev made it clear to Selina that he was making a personal career decision and probably did not care too much about the politics.

Selina, Robin and Marian Sarstadt in London, 1967.

What do I do without a bean? Just sit on the waves and see where they take me? I need a quiet, lonely spot in the sun to sit and think, but you pay dearly for quiet lonely spots and I just seem to be trapped. My first thought of course was to come home, but that also raises complications – how silly of me to think of seeking refuge in the past and it's so hard when you can't look into the future.

21 June 1962 (from Vichy)

Thank you so much for your sweet letter. I can't tell you how relieved it made me feel and the thought of coming home sounds fine, but the problem of finding another contract to come back to presents quite a few difficulties, as it is too late in the season to sign contracts for September. After Athens we return for 15 days to Paris where the company will give its last performances. Holiday time is now starting in Europe and therefore it won't be possible to work until September next year – auditions for that start from March onwards. I have written to John Cranko, but even before that I knew the chances were slim as people there had already enquired on my behalf. Anyway, I'll wait for his reply before striking it off my wish list. In any case I think I'll come home even if I don't have anything definite to come back to.

It only makes it a little harder and more expensive when I happen to come back. I only wish that I myself at least knew what I wanted, but I don't.

Here in Vichy we are camping to save money – bloody uncomfortable, cold and invariably wet – so I hope it is worthwhile. It's awful to see the company crumbling, for there is no hope for them at all at the moment, but on the other hand one never knows what a change might bring. It is not a question of contracts as we had already signed a marvellous one in South America – it is just that the company has to be owned by someone, as it's impossible for any company, especially one this size, even if every house is full, to run at a profit.

Rèna Sanikou has invited me to stay with her family in Greece and I'm happy about that. We fly from Vichy on the 26th and arrive there at 6.30 on the same evening by an Olympic Airways chartered flight.

I feel so sorry for poor Mr Larrain. He's taking it as if he's having to give up his own children and, although he's not by any manner of means going to starve, I feel sorrier for him than for any of us. Personally, I couldn't care less if I dance again or not. In fact, I really don't know in my heart of hearts what I really want to do, so perhaps coming home will be the best solution of all. We have two Danish stars from the Royal Theatre, Copenhagen with us now – Henning Kronstam[54] and Niels Kehlet.[55] The latter is camping with us here.

The Marquise has decided that instead of a Paris season we will finish on 30 June in Greece and will then each get one month's salary (the French one, which is half the touring one) in severance pay.

On arrival in Paris on 1 July I will stay a few days and then go to London to G.B.'s house to book my passage and collect my things together. My address in Greece is c/o the company, Theatre Antique, Athens. In Paris you know it and in London it is c/o G.B. Wilson, 54 Mortlake Road, Kew Gardens, Surrey, England.

---

54. Henning Kronstam (1934–1995) renowned Danish dancer, ballet master and company director.
55. Niels Kehlet (b.1938) became a soloist with the Danish Ballet Company in 1961. He and Selina kept in touch for a few years after the company disbanded and she has a feeling that he married a violinist, though is unsure about that.

Margie, thank you very much for your offer to help me financially; it is very kind of you and I accept it with pleasure. One should be able to fix all that up through the bank in London. I enquired in Amsterdam about Union Castle bookings and they apparently have plenty of free places, so I don't think much trouble should stem from there.

* * *

G.B. Wilson had been a very important influence during Selina's sojourn in Europe and he maintained contact with her until his death in August 1984. It therefore seems appropriate to include his obituary in *The Times* by Ivor Guest who wrote as follows.

OBITUARY G.B. WILSON: Ballet writer and photographer

The world of ballet has lost one of its best loved figures in the death of Mr G.B. Wilson on August 20.

For those who knew him, it will be hard to believe that he will be seen no more at performances and functions at which dancers gathered together, for he missed so few of them and, until the last few months when his illness began to be apparent, he seemed to have been spared the changes that come with the onset of age.

He was a man of several parts. By profession he was a scientist, ending his career as a Deputy Keeper at the Science Museum, but ballet was his all-absorbing and undying passion. His ballet-going days extended back to Ashton's *Tragedy of Fashion* and Diaghilev, but it was not until the wartime years that, encouraged particularly by his friendship with Arnold Haskell, his involvement with dancers began.

With his ubiquitous camera he photographed dancers at work and play for nearly half a century, amassing a collection of photographs of unique historical value. His *Dictionary of Ballet*, first published in 1957, was for many years the standard work of its kind, revealing a profound and encyclopaedic knowledge of the dancer's world. It was also in 1957 that he began to contribute his monthly page, 'Off Stage', to the *Dancing Times*, a compilation of chatty jottings in which a wise sensitivity and his love and concern for dancers shine through every time.

To several generations of dancers he was a father figure, both friend and mentor, and after his retirement he performed an invaluable service to boys and girls graduating from the Royal Ballet School by finding places for them in ballet companies all over Europe. He had many contacts there which he cultivated in his regular forays across the Channel in his inseparable old Rover.

He was a man whose contribution was so personal that no successor will carry on his work, and for that the ballet world which he enriched will be poorer.

Chapter 8

Back Home
to Cape Town

6 July 1962 (from Kew Gardens, London)

Here I sit in the coffee bar of the Gare du Nord with one hour to spare before my train goes to London.

Yes, you'll be delighted to hear, I'm all fixed up; and will be arriving in Cape Town on the *Cape Town Castle* on 26 July, so see that you're there to meet me with the whole brood, the Combie for the luggage and cream of tomato soup for lunch. I'm so excited as I really am looking forward to coming home again to enjoy a few home comforts and the company of my own stock.

I had one worry and that was how to endure those ghastly bores who try so hard to be merry and bright on these Union Castle ships – but Puckie solved that problem by advising me to wear dark glasses, a large hat and not to speak to anyone. I think it's a marvellous idea – pretend to be a spy and make some poor innocent become frantic. It'll be a challenge to see if I can put on an act for two weeks and now I am really looking forward to the trip.

I'll spend five days in London bashing around and just somma starting my never ending holiday – and my God I need it. I haven't had a holiday for longer than ten days in three and a half years and I really feel I deserve it.

I stayed with Rèna in Greece and it was pretty divine. We had a marvellous time there – lolling around during the day because of the heat and then living at night. We danced in the ancient Greek theatre under the Acropolis and the sky was a blue that I have never in my life seen before.

After the performance we would go and eat in Plaka (the old quarter of the taverns) and what with the accompaniment of the guitar and fantastically spiced food, well it was just heaven and so deliciously warm. On the last night the whole company had dinner out of doors on the banks of the Mediterranean. Between courses we took trips out into the bay in a ferry and when we had to leave Athens the next evening it was a tragedy, but we had a pleasant flight. Everyone was in high spirits and havoc reigned in the plane.

At the moment Paris is cold and slightly dead. The studios are crowded with out of work dancers and now 60 more from Cuevas, all hoping, working and clamouring for a non-existent chance for some work that will pay the rent. It's pathetic that there's so little outlet for so much talent. I'm glad I'm not with them – I really am.

I got the money for the car but my God what a performance it caused.[1] It came to 4800 NF, but under no circumstances could I get it out of France – especially as I had my own savings to cope with as well. One can only buy travellers' cheques to the worth of $130 and there I was stuck with this fortune; and a transfer would take ten days, which would mean missing the boat. I pleaded, argued and tried to reason with the bank, but got nowhere and, to make it worse, I couldn't find a Union Castle office in Paris. Finally, I demanded to see the manager. '*Mais madame!*', they gasped with their hair on end, '*Il ne voit pas les clients.*' – 'I want to see *le directeur de la Banque de France à son bureau là-haut*,' and they muttered some kind of excuse. By this time I was so furious that I couldn't have cared if it was de Gaulle himself and went straight up to his office and marched straight in. Such charm, consideration and eagerness to help would have been difficult to find anywhere. He bought my ticket to Cape Town, my ticket to London with Peter's money from the car – transferred the rest

---

1. Margie had bought a car in France and was now asking Selina to sell it and reimburse the money to her. As she explained, it was not an easy feat, but she did the best she could.

to Barclays Bank Cape Town and arranged for me to get, through various means, my own money into travellers' cheques. The remains of Peter's money is therefore in Cape Town, but although it is his money I had to put it into my name. In order to do it under his name, I had to have more particulars than I had. Anyway we can fix that up when I get there.

I got a return ticket because if I take the trip I get a reduction both ways and if I don't take the trip I get a refund with the reduction for the outgoing trip taken off – so don't be startled when you see the miserable remains of the car. It was the only thing I could do too, as the idea of all that money going out of France was just too much for them to bear. Must catch my train now. See you soon.[2]

15 July 1963 (from Pamela Chrimes's house in Newlands, Cape Town)

Thank you Marg for your letter – it was so super hearing from you and so strange that you bumped into Steffi and Mr and Mrs Petrinovic – I found the latter couple especially charming and would love to meet them sometime again. So much has been going on since you left that I don't quite know where to begin, but anyway I'll try and remember as much as possible.

I enclose a sample of what I am to wear as Rosemary's bridesmaid[3] – I can't say I am enthralled. The dress is not too bad I suppose and maybe if I dyed it black afterwards it may come in useful. The red doesn't suit me at all, but still I'll only wear it once in that colour.

Mrs Lunt [Pamela Chrimes's mother] has been stirring up as much trouble as it is possible to stir up and I spend a lot of time alternately humouring her and Annie [Pamela's maid]. Besides that, everything at Kumasi is fine and we are enjoying staying here very much. Pamela arrives back next Monday.

2. This was the end of Selina's ballet career in Europe. She carried on for a short season in Cape Town to dance the ballerina in *Petrushka* with Richard Glasstone in the title role. In retrospect, she had no regrets that it ended and had clearly played a part in that happening. Now back in South Africa, she was wondering what to do with the rest of her life. Margie and Peter were in Chile, so she was still trying to forge a contact with them. She enrolled at UCT to study French, history, and social anthropology.
3. Rosemary Taylor, with whom Selina stayed when she first came to London, was now getting married.

At the moment I am being tormented by Cynthia's brother David[4] who is down here on holiday from Rhodesia and, after having seen every film in Cape Town, I am having a terrible time trying to shake him off. The other night he proposed to me and I got the giggles because it was so obvious that he had rehearsed his speech; and what made it even worse was that he drove into a donga [ditch] and couldn't get his car out again. He kept talking about life's fulfilment as I was desperately trying to discourage him without being unduly cruel.

Last week I went to Groote Schuur [hospital] for a day because Anthony insisted that I had a lump cut out of my bosom and Tessa wouldn't let him do it. I quite enjoyed all the pomp and ceremony attached to the procedure and it was nice to receive so much undivided attention for a whole day. The lump was benign and so I'm not on my death bed yet.

Practically everyone I know has gone to Johannesburg for the NUSAS Conference and so Cape Town is pretty dead. It will be nice to get back to university again.

Carol[5] wants me to look after Granny for a month while Sannie[6] has her baby – it is so close to the exams though and I am quite loath to do it, but of course I will if she can't get anyone else.

A few weeks ago Philippe Knight[7] took me along to St Monica's

---

4. Cynthia Stekhoven was Julian Stekhoven's first wife – his sister Tessa was married to Selina's brother Anthony – and her brother was presumably visiting Cape Town and trying to distract himself while he was there. Selina, clearly, was supposed to ease the social situation.
5. Carol Williamson was Peter's older sister and the one on whom the responsibility for looking after her mother rested. Selina ended up having a very high regard for her.
6. Sannie was the wife of Carol's son, Denys Williamson. She and Denys converted to Catholicism on their marriage, so consequently had a lot of children – in fact a dozen in all. Denys was a High Court judge and, although rather reactionary politically, had a huge amount of charm.
7. Philippe Knight was the brother of Selina's close friend Brigitte Knight and, although Brigitte was now married and living in Canada, Philippe and she kept up a platonic friendship when she was in Cape Town. It was only years later that Brigitte revealed that Philippe had suffered so badly from depression and had never managed to hold down a proper job. He lived with his mother until her death and is now a recluse.

Home to help him deliver a baby. It was quite a performance, especially as the baby weighed 10lbs 13ozs – a beautiful black baby that looked about four months' old.

Johnny[8] is away in the army at the moment and Vicky was thinking of going up to Johannesburg for the holidays, but she didn't as it seemed too much of an effort to organize it all. She has arranged her passage to South America and apparently Cooks say that one must do it now as the ships are pretty booked. What do you think I should do about it? Shall I leave it or book also as I don't know as yet if FAO will be willing to pay for me.[9]

I've had to go along to Syfrets[10] for a little extra money as I found it impossible to come out in June, as I've had to pay for food for Vicky and myself at Kumasi as well as rent on Vicky's behalf to Anton – but I think that I will be able to manage from now on. We asked Carol if she could help by giving Vicky something while she was not at Lane House, but she had already paid the full rent into your account.

Margie, did you slip that R10 note into my bag? If so, thank you very, very much as it was a great help. Thank you too for the post office cheque – it really will set us up nicely.

Tessa gave a very pleasant dinner for the family for Anna's twenty-first and Vicky and I bought her a really sweet brooch we found at an exhibition in the Argus Gallery. How maddening for you not having a car! I do hope that you get it soon. You know Marg you left your lovely eggshell blue frock behind. What do you want us to do about it and your green coat? Shall we send them or would that be too risky?

Everything at home is fine. We miss you all a lot and hope that the boys are getting on well at their new school.

Please give Martie and Frankie my love and as their birthdays are coming up soon, MANY HAPPY RETURNS as well.

---

8. Johnny Berryman later became Vicky's husband.
9. The FAO was apparently prepared to pay for the trips of consultants' children who were under the age of 21. Selina would love to have gone to Chile, but was never free to do so when she still qualified on age grounds.
10. The Syfrets Trust was looking after Peter's financial affairs while he was in Chile and it was Selina's responsibility to ensure that she provided them with all Peter's financial business as it came through the post.

Annie[11] is looking after us as if we were her own children and we even get breakfast in bed. She does all the shopping and very economically too.

This holiday has been one series of social outings. I'm quite exhausted and look forward to week days and weekends being two separate things.

4 October 1963

I would like to thank you so much for that lovely bunch of red roses and poppies that arrived for me yesterday. They really made my birthday. In spite of being terribly busy yesterday I had such a nice birthday – a sweet Finnish dressing table jar from Tess and Anthony, a length of material from Anna and a really lovely petticoat from Vicky. Mrs Wegerif[12] gave me a tin of Blue Grass talcum powder and Tess and I had tea with her yesterday afternoon to celebrate. Robert[13] was so sweet about my birthday. He couldn't wait until the 3rd to give me my presents, and so my birthday really started on the afternoon of the 2nd. He bought a cake, which the whole family had at Tessas, and then every now and again he kept on giving me another present. Among them was a year's subscription to the English *Vogue* magazine. Maybe he thinks I could do with some sprucing up. Varsity work is difficult and there is so much of it to revise for the exams that I have grave doubts about being able to make the grade. But one exciting thing has happened. I got an A- for my last essay on the First World War. Do

11. Annie was Pamela Chrimes's maid. Pamela Chrimes (1922–1992) had been Selina's ballet teacher since childhood and was later a very close friend of Margie's. She had had a rough deal over the ballet school when Dulcie Howes excluded her from the main position. Lots of hurt and accusations of betrayal ensued, but she was nevertheless a wonderful person who remained close to everyone's hearts for the rest of her life, cut prematurely short at the age of 70.
12. Sylvia Wegerif was Tessa Molteno's mother.
13. Robert Watson, who became an explosives expert from working in the mines and had been in the British army, offered his services to the African Resistance Movement (ARM), a militant anti-apartheid organization. Selina and Robert had a close relationship. When the organization was destroyed by the apartheid regime Selina was imprisoned and interrogated (twice). Robert fled to London but disappeared from her life shortly thereafter.

you realize that that is 70 per cent? And I did it all on my own. Robert only recommended some books that he thought would be helpful to me. Robert is rather useful in that respect because he has a vast library on a large variety of subjects. He is always giving the family things to read and we have to read them for fear of hurting his feelings.

I don't suppose you get to hear about all the political activities going on in this country! Albie Sachs[14] has been arrested again, and there are many reports about political prisoners who have mysteriously died in their cells. One prisoner was found hanged by a belt in his cell. Prisoners are not allowed to wear belts! Medical reports stated that he had died of some kind of gas poisoning. It sounds pretty fishy – it seems as if things are really coming to a head on a big scale.

Today we finished history lectures, next week we finish French lectures and then until the exams we are free to swot. And hell, there certainly is a lot to do. My trouble is that I am so slow. I am able to grasp the subject, but only after hours of slow reading, drawing pictures and long discussions, either with myself or with someone else. There just seems to be too much to get it all into my stupid little head.

Vicky has broken up and yesterday she came to the history lecture. The subject was 'The Rise of Hitler'. She says she didn't like varsity and hopes that it is better in South America. It was probably because she hadn't been to the lectures leading up to it.

Afterward we went and had our TB tests, which are being given free at the moment. We get the results on Monday. Johnny's vaccination took and mine didn't, but I don't know whether it should or not. Johnny says that it shouldn't but a nurse told me that it should, but I am sure that I am fine considering my need for a two-way stretch is becoming more and more urgent. I must fly now; I've got a lecture in ten minutes' time.

Thursday 13 December 1963 (to Annabel and Anton)

Congratulations to both of you. Yes, Anna you passed History II; we didn't expect you to but you did. It is printed up at varsity. A third

14. Albie Sachs (b.1935) was quite a presence in the anti-apartheid struggle and later a prominent judge in post-apartheid South Africa.

class, mind you, but nevertheless you have made the grade. I personally, as one of your stock, am proud of your wonderful achievements. I also checked up on Anton and you too have got through the whole lot. That is all that I really wrote to say, but I suppose that I had better waffle on a bit or otherwise the letter will be embarrassingly short. The only question I can think of asking is, 'Do you like the big hole?',[15] and as you probably won't write, I just have to assume that you do.

Cousin Mildred[16] is staying with us as from today and is sleeping in Margie's bed. As a result, showers are out for the semi-hygienic members of the family. You see, it's not only the room but everything adjoining it as well. Never mind though, she is very nice. She even let me take her for a drive around the Cape Peninsula to see the sights and whenever a near thing happened she always said that it was the other car's fault. That is what I call a loyal relation.

Petrushka[17] is now finished and I got my fat cheque, thank God. Now I feel a bit despondent about the thought of having to do something mundane. I will try and arrange it tomorrow. Everybody is fine. Johnny[18] had an intruder at Longworth, but chased him off with the jaffle iron.

I am making myself a navy blue suit and it looks as if it is going to be hideous, somehow more suitable for Granny than for me. By the way she came to the ballet with Aunt Nan[19] last night and got terribly muddled up. She thought that Petrushka was Coppélia and asked me why I didn't sit in the window like last time I did it. Fortunately, she had forgotten that all I did was sit in a window in Coppélia … it's trying when people can't even tell when you are dancing the main part.

15. This is a reference to a diamond mine in Kimberley, where they were staying at the time with Anton's parents.
16. Mildred Brock (1897–1992) was an American cousin of Selina's paternal grandmother. She stayed with the family in South Africa and was delightful. Later, in the 1970s, Robin, Selina and their children stayed in her son Mitchell's flat in New York.
17. Selina had been arm-twisted into performing the lead female role in the University Ballet School's performance of Petrushka.
18. John Berryman, Vicky's boyfriend and later husband.
19 Aunt Nan was Selina's Granny's sister who lived in the United States.

Frankie has acquired a revolting white mouse with a pink tail. Tessa ran over a dog, but didn't kill it and the weather has been fine but windy.

Selina in Cape Town, 1963.

Index

Printed in Great Britain
by Amazon

77709757R00153